The Life, Times, & Trading Secrets of the World's Greatest Investor

SOROS

The Life, Times, & Trading Secrets of
the World's Greatest Investor

ROBERT SLATER

McGraw-Hill

New York   San Francisco   Washington D.C.   Auckland   Bogotá
Caracas   Lisbon   London   Madrid   Mexico City   Milan   Montreal
New Delhi   San Juan   Singapore   Sydney   Tokyo   Toronto

Library of Congress Cataloging-in-Publication Data

Slater, Robert (Robert I.)
  Soros : the life, times, and trading secrets of the world's
greatest investor / Robert Slater.
      p.   cm.
  Includes index.
  ISBN 0-7863-1247-5
  1. Soros, George.   2. Capitalists and financiers—Biography.
3. Investments.   I. Title.
HG172.S63S58   1996
332.6'092—dc20
  [B]   95–6557

McGraw-Hill
A Division of The McGraw·Hill Companies

This publication is designed to provide accurate and authoritative information in regard to
the subject matter covered. It is sold with the understanding that neither the author or the
publisher is engaged in rendering legal, accounting, or other professional service. If legal
advice or other expert assistance is required, the services of a competent professional
person should be sought.

> *–From a Declaration of Principles jointly adopted by a Committee
> of the American Bar Association and a Committee of Publishers.*

    4 5 6 7 8 9 0 QBP 9 0 9 8
ISBN 0-7863-1247-5
Printed and bound by Quebecor Book Press

Cover Photo: Greg Marinovich/SYGMA.

Credits for Photo Insert: page 1—Reprinted from *Financial World.* Copyright 1994. All rights
reserved; page 2, top—Courtesy of Byron Wien; page 2, bottom—Courtesy of *Business Week*;
page 3, top left—Courtesy of Allan Raphael; page 3, top right—Courtesy of Benny Landa;
page 3, bottom—Simon Apesteguy/GAMMA LIAISON; page 4—Simon Apesteguy/GAMMA
LIAISON; page 5, top—Simon Apesteguy/GAMMA LIAISON; page 5, middle—Simon
Apesteguy/GAMMA LIAISON; page 5, bottom—Jeffrey Markowitz/SYGMA; page 6, top—Greg
Marinovich/SYGMA; page 6, bottom—Daniel Simon/GAMMA LIAISON; page 7, top—Greg
Marinovich/SYGMA; page 7, bottom—Paul Kern/SYGMA; page 8—Abe Frajndlich/SYGMA.

Contents

Preface

This is not an authorized biography. I mention that at the outset because it answers the first question most people ask an author when they hear he or she is writing a book about someone. The idea of doing a profile of George Soros was mine. After writing a book in 1992 on General Electric chairman Jack Welch, also published by Irwin Professional Publishers, I looked around for another important business personality to profile. I hit upon Soros. When I contacted his office to let him know what I planned to do, I was put in touch with David Kronfeld of Kekst & Co., the firm Soros chose to handle his public relations.

We had a pleasant thirty-minute meeting, in which I gathered that no one else had been contemplating or was in the process of doing a book on Soros. I explained to Kronfeld that I hoped to remedy that, and that I would notify him if and when I got a contract. I asked him not to convey anything about the project to Soros and his people at that time; Kronfeld gave me the impression that he would wait for my phone call.

When I got the go-ahead to do the book a month later, I called Kronfeld right away to inform him that indeed I would be doing the book. He replied that "unfortunately, the Soros people had decided not to cooperate with you." He did not give any explanation. Considering that I had not even written to Soros to inform him of my plan, the reaction was not what I expected. Kronfeld then told me that he and Gershon Kekst, head of Kekst & Co., had recommended to the Soros people, whoever they are—they were never identified—that they cooperate with me. He said they had tried to "plead your case" but without success. I thanked him, but pointed out that I had not asked him to plead my case, nor was I asking for cooperation. I would be asking only for interviews with Soros and his associates, which seemed to me in everyone's interest—Soros's and mine. I asked whether I would be able to interview staff workers at Soros's various foundations in Eastern Europe. Kronfeld suggested that I contact Frances Abouzeid, who handled public relations for that aspect of Soros's efforts.

In a telephone conversation, Abouzeid said that Soros had "made a commitment" to someone else who was working on a book about him, and therefore he and his associates "would not have the time" to spend with me. I said I planned to go ahead with the book and hoped Soros would change his mind. Abouzeid did indicate that I would be able to interview people connected to Soros's foundations.

And so I began research on this book, hoping to talk to as many people as possible who had known Soros and worked with him both on the philanthropic and on the investment side of his career. At the outset, I decided to focus on those who worked for the Soros Foundations in Eastern Europe.

In Bucharest, Romania, the Soros staff treated me royally. They picked me up at the airport, drove me to meetings with foundation staff, and permitted me to sit in on private foundation meetings and to interview anyone and everyone, from the directors on down. They provided me with the kind of cooperation that I had sought, and that seemed a good omen. Later in Budapest, Hungary, I set myself more complicated goals than just interviewing foundation staff. I also wanted to track down people who had known Soros from childhood. Finding them was not easy, but eventually I came across several. Their memories were usually fresh, and they seemed to enjoy the chance to reminisce about their schoolmate or childhood friend.

In Budapest I also had a brief introductory meeting with Soros. I had had no idea that he would even be in Budapest when I had planned to be there. But it turned out that he was in town to meet with the executive directors of his foundations in Eastern Europe and the former Soviet Union—and that he would be present at an evening reception for them on March 8, 1994, at the Taverna Hotel. As luck would have it, I was supposed to interview a foundation employee at the hotel, so I seized on the chance to introduce myself to Soros. The first person I met that evening, however, was Frances Abouzeid. In a friendly voice, she said she would try to arrange for me to meet with Soros briefly before the reception. Failing that, she said she would try to set a meeting up when I was in New York the next month. She later returned with word that it was not at all certain

Soros would be coming to the hotel that evening, so I would have to wait until April. I was, to say the least, disappointed.

I chatted with other Soros people—and then Soros walked in. He was walking very briskly, but I darted over to him. Abouzeid accompanied me and made the introduction.

I said I was writing a book about him.

Soros replied that he hadn't known about the project.

Hadn't known about the project? How could he not have known? I was, needless to say, taken back. After all, both David Kronfeld and Frances Abouzeid told me that it had been Soros who had decided not to cooperate with me on my book.

I briefly sketched in my background and said that I wanted very much to meet with him.

He said he could not make any promises.

I persisted. I told him that I had already had some fascinating meetings with acquaintances of his in Budapest who had known him from childhood. I reiterated that it would be important for me to talk with him.

He seemed to thaw a bit, for he said that when I was finished with my research, we would meet. Soros then said to Frances Abouzeid, "He can come to the meeting tonight. It will be off the record."

I was very pleased with this turn of events.

But then Abouzeid intervened: "No, we want it closed."

Soros looked at me apologetically. "I have to follow her judgment." I was astounded that George Soros had bowed to a public relations aide in deciding whether or not someone writing a book about him should attend a reception.

As it turned out, I never met with Soros again. In five countries, however—the United States, England, Hungary, Romania, and Israel—I was able to interview many of his associates, dating back to the earliest days of his investment career. Thanks to those interviews, I believe I have been able to portray George Soros in all of his complexity. Fortunately, Soros has often spoken on the record, in newspaper, magazine, and television interviews. Because of those interviews, I have been able to provide a sense of what Soros believes on the issues affecting his career. And, he has written three books, one about his financial theories (*The Alchemy of Finance*), the other two about his philanthropic endeavors (*Opening the Soviet System* and *Underwriting Democracy*). Here and there in those books, Soros writes about himself personally, helping me to round out his personality.

I have also benefited from a series of fascinating interviews I arranged with financial analysts both on Wall Street and in the City of London. Some of these analysts did not know Soros personally, but they were able to describe the milieu in which he functioned and provide me with insights about how the financial community works and how it has reacted to Soros's phenomenal investment record.

Conducting research on a living public figure for an unauthorized book is never easy. In this case, I felt particularly challenged, conscious as I was that Soros wanted to keep his closest associates, including his public relations aides, from talking with me. In several letters that I wrote to him, I stressed that I saw it as my obligation as an author to provide him with the opportunity to comment on certain episodes and certain statements that people had made about him. This argument failed.

Indeed, on May 31, 1994, I received a letter from Sean C. Warren, general counsel of the Soros Fund, in essence a response to the second of two letters I had written to Soros asking for an interview. Warren wrote that the purpose of his letter was to confirm that Soros would not cooperate with me, since he was cooperating with another author writing a book about him. "As I am sure you can appreciate, Mr. Soros and his affiliates have very limited time which they must allocate carefully. Consequently, Mr. Soros has also requested that persons affiliated with his foundations and other entities not respond to your inquiries." Warren reiterated that "no one will be available to meet with you" and that I should "please cease calling Mr. Soros and the foundations regarding meetings."

He closed the letter with what was essentially a plea: "In your letter you state that you wish to meet with Mr. Soros in an effort to make your book as accurate as possible and out of a sense of 'fairness.' Although no one will meet with you, I am sure that you will nevertheless use your best efforts to fulfill your journalistic responsibility regarding the accuracy and fairness of your book."

I was rather bemused by the plea. On June 20, 1994, I wrote a letter to David Kronfeld, putting to him a series of questions about Soros that I had hoped to discuss in person. I noted that the general counsel had asked me to be fair and accurate while acknowledging that I would have no access to those who were in a position to help me do that. I received no reply from Mr. Kronfeld.

I happily discovered that Soros's reach extended only so far. A good number of his former employees were more than willing to share their views of him with me, almost always on the record. I am deeply grateful for the lengthy interviews they conducted with me. In contrast I felt at times as though I was playing cat and mouse with the Soros people. I would call someone up, ask for an interview, the person would agree, but then would cancel. In one case, a woman agreed to an interview, noting that the Soros people had already contacted her, asking her not to talk to me, but she decided that she was going to do so anyway. On another occasion, a close Soros associate agreed to meet with me. After a lengthy interview extending over a full evening, the person called the next morning to say that she had learned from the Soros people that she wasn't supposed to talk to me. I had to turn our on-the-record interview into one "not for attribution." In cases like these, George Soros's long reach was evident.

Despite these constraints, I can say confidently that this book provides the most in-depth look at George Soros to date.

A word about my editor, Jeffrey Krames. Once again, I have had the great pleasure of working with him on a major book project. In so many ways he has been there with support, advice, and enthusiasm, helping me to shape the project, sharing my excitement with the topic, pointing out ways to strengthen the text. He has helped turn a complicated challenge into a wonderful experience for me, and I am deeply grateful.

I wish to thank Bruce Liebman for handling some important research assignments in New York. Thanks to him, I was able to get my hands on a whole series of valuable articles about Soros with relative ease. My thanks also to Zelda Meislin Metzger and David Nachman for their assistance.

I also wish to thank those with whom I had the chance to talk: Frances Abouzeid, Edgar Astaire, Ferenc Bartha, Cimpoca Narcisa, Leon Cooperman, Beth Davenport, Csilla Dobos, William Dodge, Daniel Doron, Don Elan, Dinu C. Giurescu, Alex Goldfarb, James Grant, Anca Haracim, Charles Hoffman, Miklos Horn, Dale Jacobs, Gheorghe Jumuga, Radu Jugureanu, Anatole Kaletsky, Laszlo Kardos, Stephen Kellen, David Kronfeld, Benny Landa, Arthur Lerner, James Lister-Cheese, Niel MacKinnon, George Magnus, Sandor Magyari,

Dragos Munteanu, Susan Margitta, James Marquez, Evyln Messinger, Robert Miller, Yoram Morad, Raphael Morav, Jiri Musil, Ferenc Nagel, Ronald O'Regan, Gur Ofer, Lois Peltz, Dan Petreanu, Karl Popper, Bogdan Preda, Allan Raphael, Michael Rembaum, James Rogers, Jeffrey Sachs, Nicolai Sanud, Herta Seidman, Barnett Serchuk, Yehuditte Simo, Mark Slater, Alin Teodoresco, Pal Tetenyi, Ana Todorean, Chris Turner, Tibor Vamos, Miklos Vasarhelyi, Lazar Vlasceanu, Byron R. Wien, and the others who asked not to be identified.

Allan Raphael, James Marquez, Byron Wien, Don Elan, and Chris Turner read parts of the text. I am grateful to them for giving their valuable time and for their comments.

A word of thanks to my family: My wife Elli was always there, supporting, suggesting, reading drafts, taking care of our family while I hopped from one country to the next in search of yet one more detail about George Soros. She was most understanding, most helpful, and I thank her for everything. I thank my children—Miriam and her husband Shimi, Adam, and Rachel—for just being there and for adding so much joy to my life.

Each time I write a book about business, and this is now my fourth, I am reminded of how much closer to the subject, in practical terms, are certain members of my family. A number of them not only displayed the requisite enthusiasm but went beyond that by adding important points of clarification and insights, and I wish to thank them for all their help: my brother, Jack Slater; my brother-in-law, Judd Winick; my nephews, Michael Winick, Mark Winick, Jeffrey Slater, Mitchell Slater, Craig Jacobs, and Jerry Bedrin; and my cousin, Melvin Slater. They are the "businessmen" in my family, and they are one of my most important audiences. My most important "audience" is my late father, Joseph G. Slater. However subconsciously, he inspired me to find the whole topic of business endlessly fascinating. I was stubborn at first, wondering what exactly it was about business that turned him on. Later in life, I found out, and I believe he would have been pleasantly surprised and amused to find out that I finally got his message. To him, above all, I give my thanks. I dedicate *Soros* to Joseph G. Slater.

Robert Slater

One

The World's Greatest Investor

September 15, 1992, 5:30 PM

Settled back in his high, leather chair behind an oval desk, George Soros gazed out the large windows to the left, taking in the breathtaking view of Central Park and the rush-hour activity some thirty-three floors below. He was thrilled to be once again part of The Game.

Lately, when he entered the Soros Fund Management office in midtown Manhattan, Soros had begun to feel more like a visitor than the boss. But today he belonged. Today he could climb a mountain. Or break the bank. He was confident that he could still play The Game . . . and play it better than most. Maybe better than everyone.

So what if he spent most of his time in recent years traveling in faraway places? His operation had run smoothly since 1988, when he entrusted it to a much younger man with a glittering financial record, Stanley Druckenmiller. When Soros did show up at the office, he and Druckenmiller ran the place in tandem, even though they sometimes clashed over how to read the financial markets.

Ordinarily these days, though, Soros was more likely to be off in Eastern Europe or the former Soviet Union, helping to shape and nurture the philanthropic foundations he had established in the 1980s to turn those countries into models of democracy. Devoting all his energies for years to probing the financial markets, he had made all the money he would ever need. Now, in the autumn of his life, he sought to escape the office routine as much as possible. Now he preferred to huddle with his foundation staffs in Hungary or Romania, to slog through the muddy streets of Bosnia, to take part in adventure.

But today was no ordinary day. George Soros was about to lay down the biggest bet in financial history. His heart should have been

I

pounding, he should have been pacing the floor, shouting nervously to terrified staff. But that was never his style. Only his mind was racing. He sat, a portrait of calm, asking himself the question he had always asked whenever he was about to jump in and make a splash.

Is this the right thing to do? Am I going to drown?

As he stared at the first flickering white lights of the city, Soros's mind drifted a few thousand miles away. Would he be better off in London? He wasn't entirely sure. Maybe today it didn't matter.

George Soros had always taken great pleasure in staying far from the financial precincts down on Wall Street—had always gotten a special charge knowing that he had figured out how to make a ton of money without having to toil in the shadow of the New York Stock Exchange.

Given the way he played the investment game, given the contrarian style he had successfully adopted in reading the financial markets, he had no reason to graze with the herd downtown. He was content to be in Midtown. Content to take this respite from his usual adventures. His office had a warm, homey feeling, a few paintings on the wall, family pictures on the desk. But just a few feet from Soros's office, the staff sat in front of cold computer screens, peering straight ahead, as if the slightest head movement to the left or right might suggest they had fallen asleep on their watch. On a wall a sign, which appeared to have been composed on a computer, read: I WAS BORN POOR BUT I WILL NOT DIE POOR.

It was George Soros's credo. Now in his 62nd year, wealthy beyond imagination, he knew that he had won the "contest," that he would not die poor. Indeed, he might well die one of the richest men in America. Yet no one dared suggest that it was time to take the sign down. The others in the office needed an incentive, after all. Some were wealthy in their own right, worth millions of dollars. They wouldn't die poor either. Indeed, it was as if those who toiled alongside George Soros had all taken part in the gold rush, and all had struck gold. The Soros Fund Management office did not look like Fort Knox, nor was it as difficult to penetrate. It did, however, have the same intoxicating smell of money.

But as the city slowly sunk into darkness, Soros barely noticed. He was a global trader. An investor who was as interested in the financial markets of Tokyo and London as those of Wall Street, as intensely curious about economic trends in Brussels and Berlin as he was about those in Peoria or Poughkeepsie. Today his mind was not in the office; it was in Western Europe. That was his chief concern at the moment.

He had been following developments in the European economic community for the past few years and had sensed that the fuse was lit for a great financial explosion.

Soros was a master financial theorist, and he liked to test his theories in the laboratory of stocks and bonds and currencies. And what a wonderful laboratory it was. There were no gray areas. None whatsoever. A stock either went up, it went down, or it stayed the same. Any theory about how the stock market operated could be tested on a day-to-day basis.

> "Discern the chaos, and you could become rich."

Many investors believed the financial world to be rational, convinced that stock prices had a built-in logic. Discern that logic, and you could become rich.

Soros would have none of that. He thought the financial world was unstable, chaotic. Soros thought: Discern the chaos, and you could become rich. Trying to fathom the financial markets, as if their movements were part of some gigantic mathematical formula, would never work. For Soros was convinced that mathematics did not govern the financial markets.

Psychology did. More precisely, the herd instinct.

Figure out when and how the herd was going to get behind a certain stock or currency or commodity, and the successful investor could get out in front.

That was the Soros theory in a nutshell.

Today, George Soros was testing his theory out on the entire European financial world. He had been applying it there for the past few years, laying back, waiting for the timing to be right, waiting for the murmur of the rumbling herd.

And when he heard it, he would be ready to pounce, ready to seize the opportunity. When he sensed he was right about a financial situation, he was ready to throw caution to the wind. This time, he was sure he was right.

And this time, he was ready to place the biggest bet anyone had ever made in the investment world.

If he lost, well, he would lose some money. No matter. He had lost money before. Take the October 1987 stock market crash. He had read the market wrong and had to cut his losses. He had been out $300 million.

But more often, he had won money—for his elite group of clients—and he had done it so well for so long that by June 1981 he had already been called "The World's Greatest Money Manager" by *Institutional Investor* magazine.

In only one year since 1969, when he established his flagship Quantum Fund, did Soros have a losing year. That was in 1981. Quite simply, no one had done as well for so long in the financial markets as George Soros. Not Warren E. Buffett, not Peter Lynch. Not anyone.

His record was the best on Wall Street.

In his office late that day, Soros kept thinking about London. It was now 10:30 in the evening there. That was where the action was today. Not in New York City.

A look of satisfaction crossed Soros's face. He thought back to November 9, 1989, that crucial day that the Berlin Wall came tumbling down.

Everyone knew how significant that day was for modern history. Others believed, or at least they hoped, that with the fall of the Berlin Wall, a new unified Germany would rise and prosper.

Soros thought differently. He often did. Being a contrarian was his secret. He sensed that the new Germany would have a hard time trying to finance the unification. He also sensed that Germany would turn inward, worry about its own economic problems, and dismiss as less important the economic problems of the other Western European countries.

An inward-looking Germany would have vast implications for the economies—and the currencies—of the other countries in Europe. So Soros believed.

He watched and waited.

In 1990, he had watched Great Britain take the fateful step of joining forces with the new Western European monetary system, the ERM, or Exchange Rate Mechanism. Soros thought it was a mistake for Britain to participate. The British economy was not strong, and by joining the ERM, the British were essentially linking themselves to the strongest economic power in Western Europe—the new united Germany.

It was a linkage that, for better or for worse, would make Britain ultimately dependent upon the Germans. As the strongest economy in the region, Germany had the power to decide what was good economically for the rest of Western Europe.

That dependence upon Germany, thought Soros, would eventually prove fatal for the British.

For Britain might want to move one way in its monetary policies—and it would not be able to. It would have to link those policies with the dominant German monetary policies.

Just as Soros had predicted, 1992 brought a financial crisis to Western Europe. A number of economies there, including Great Britain's, had sagged. Britain wanted to lower its interest rates.

The Germans, however, were unwilling to reduce their interest rates for their own domestic reasons: They were deeply afraid that inflation would recur in Germany. They remembered with horror the 1920s, when inflation was the poison that brought the German economy to collapse.

If Germany would not drop its rates, the other European countries could not afford to drop theirs. To do so would have put them in jeopardy of weakening their currencies, and once weakened, those currencies would be prey to speculators.

So Britain was increasingly trapped.

Its economy was deteriorating. Since it was overvalued, the pound was under increasing pressure. Britain wanted to improve its economy, but to do so, it needed to reduce the value of the pound, making its exports more attractive.

But Britain was forced, under ERM rules, to keep the pound at 2.95 German marks.

Over the summer of 1992, British political leaders insisted that they would survive the storm—and that there would be no devaluation of the pound. Britain would not leave the ERM. Somehow, they would muddle through.

Nonsense, thought George Soros.

He knew better. He understood how dire was Britain's economic situation. It would not be possible for them to remain in the ERM. They would have to abandon ship.

The crisis began in mid-September.

Rumors started to surface that the Italians would devalue the lire. Traders in New York rushed to sell their lire.

On Sunday, September 13, the Italian lire was devalued—but only by 7 percent, still within the range set by the ERM's rules.

Investors made a good deal of money betting that the European central banks would honor their commitments to keep their currencies within ERM ranges. It seemed like a bad bet to wager on an ERM realignment that went beyond the ERM's rules.

But if the Italians had devalued the lire, which they said they would not do, did that not mean the emperor had no clothes? That all the promises from other governments meant nothing?

Perhaps there would be a second wave . . . perhaps it was time to start selling sterling?

Suddenly, in different parts of the world, investors and corporations all at once lost faith in the willingness of Western European governments to permit the ERM to determine exchange rates. Now they were eagerly trying to get rid of a variety of weaker currencies, including sterling.

As September 15 wore on, George Soros's confidence that Britain would pull the pound out of the ERM was growing.

It had been Stanley Druckenmiller who had thought the time ripe for making a bet against the sterling. He talked to Soros about doing something. Soros gave him the green light but urged his head trader to bet an even larger sum than Druckenmiller had in mind.

And so Druckenmiller, acting for Soros, sold $10 *billion* worth of sterling.

Leaving for his Fifth Avenue apartment, Soros seemed a man of extreme self-confidence. He slept well that night.

The next morning at 7:00, the phone rang at Soros's home. It was Stan Druckenmiller with news. Soros heard the trader say that all had gone well. While George Soros had slept, he racked up a profit of $958 million. When Soros's gains from other positions he took during the ERM crisis were tallied, they totaled close to $2 billion.

The British called September 15—the day they were forced to pull the pound out of the ERM—Black Wednesday.

Soros called it *White* Wednesday.

It was this bet, this single act of placing $10 billion on the fact that Britain would have to devalue the pound, that made George Soros world famous.

It was, and remains, his greatest coup as an investor.

Because of that bet, Soros—"The World's Greatest Investor"—became a legend in the financial world.

After September 1992, myths grew around George Soros.

The central one was that he could move markets: A word from him about a certain commodity like gold, or a currency like the mark, could cause a shift in trading. Prices would rise or fall, all because of what he said.

He seemed infallible, worthy of emulation.

A reporter doing a television documentary on Soros in December 1992, two months after his coup against the pound, was impressed with Soros's seeming ability to move markets: "You invest in gold, and because you invest in gold everybody thinks they should invest in gold, and the price goes up. You write an article that questions the value of the deutsch mark and the deutsch mark goes down. You make an investment in London real estate and overnight it seems that the trend of downward prices is reversed. Should one person have that much influence?"

Seeming to enjoy the compliment, Soros sought to offer some perspective.

"Currently," he began, "the influence I have is exaggerated. In fact I'm pretty sure it is. And it will correct itself because people will realize"—he gave a big smile—"I'm not infallible, and you know, just as I'm currently swept up on a wave of interest, I'll be swept down."

Wrong on both counts.

His influence had not been exaggerated. Nor was the wave of interest in him about to diminish.

In a *Business Week* story, he was asked how it felt to be a guru. He said he was amused.

Amused.

Some people were becoming less than amused.

By 1994, the myths surrounding Soros were so pervasive that Washington was beginning to pay attention. If indeed a George Soros could move markets, and if fortunes could be made or lost by the actions of one man, was he not a danger? Should George Soros not be reined in?

That became one of the main themes surrounding the man who by the mid-1990s had scaled a height in the financial world few others had even attempted.

As the world's greatest investor, he had amassed more money than most people will ever see in one lifetime, or a hundred lifetimes. Yet, that fact only partly accounted for the mystique surrounding him.

George Soros was far more than a man who made a few billion dollars. Far more than the Man Who Broke the Bank of England, as *The Economist* called him. Far more than the Man Who Moves Markets, as he was dubbed by *Business Week*.

Money, as it turns out, at one time had only marginal appeal for Soros.

He did not set out to be a world-class investor, to make huge amounts of money. He had yearned instead to be a man of ideas and had always found it more comfortable to move in the realm of the intellect than that of finance.

Yet, he found he had a gift for earning money—a great deal of money. It seemed to come easily. Perhaps that was why he felt tainted by money. He wanted to do more with his life than simply accumulate wealth.

Not that Soros considered financial speculation immoral or thought it mere gambling. He made no excuses for what he was doing; he simply did not get a kick out of it. Soros yearned to make a contribution to others—a contribution that would be remembered.

He pictured himself as a philosopher rather than a financier. He liked to call himself a failed philosopher, as a kind of reminder of what he had once tried to do in his early years but had abandoned.

His great dream was to add knowledge to the world, knowledge about the way the world worked, about how human beings functioned in that world. As a student, Soros had begun to search for such knowledge. His quest drew him into the world of philosophy, and for a time he wanted to be a professor of philosophy. He studied economics, but he always seemed to be more of a visitor to that world than a permanent resident.

Feeling cheated by the way economics was taught to him, Soros thought economists lacked a practical understanding of the way the world worked. They dreamt big dreams, talked only about ideal situations, and made the mistake of thinking that the world was a very rational place. Even at that early age, George Soros knew very well that the world was far more chaotic than economists would have people believe.

As he began to formulate his own theories—theories of knowledge, theories of history, and in time, theories about finance—

Soros anchored his convictions to his bedrock belief that the world was highly unpredictable, thoroughly irrational—in short, hard to figure out.

He tried to advance those theories in book form but had a difficult time making them understandable and readable. Sometimes even he had a hard time fathoming what he had written. Frustrated that the intellectual world was too difficult to conquer, he set out to find worlds that he could conquer.

The decision was, in one sense, easy. He had to make a living anyway. Why not try to show all those economists that he understood the workings of the world better than they did by making as much money as possible? Soros believed that money would give him a platform from which he could expound his views. Making money, in short, would help him to be a philosopher after all.

The world he entered, the world of high finance, carried the potential for great rewards. The risks, however, were daunting. It was no place for the faint of heart.

Perhaps the timid enjoyed a few good years. But eventually, the strain got to them, the strain of being responsible for other people's money. The price was high, paid in the currency of lost sleep, leisure time, lost friends, a lost home life because all hell was breaking loose in the financial markets. In time, the faint of heart found other work.

Soros, in contrast, was not faint of heart. He seemed to be ice-cool. He displayed no emotion. When an investment paid off, he took satisfaction. When it did not, he did not run to the nearest roof or skyscraper. He was calm, even-tempered; rarely did he laugh hysterically but rarely did he get morose.

He was, he liked to say, a critic; indeed, he eventually joked that he was *the world's highest-paid critic.* The term suggested something of an outsider, someone above the battle. "I am a critic of the processes. I am not an entrepreneur who builds businesses. I am an investor who judges them. My function in the financial markets is that of a critic, and my critical judgments are expressed by my decisions to buy and sell."

Though he had been in the investing business since 1956, first in London, then in New York, his career truly started in 1969. It was then that he launched his own investment fund called the Quantum Fund. He remained active in it—except for a few years in the early eighties—for the next 25 years. In the late eighties, he adopted a lower profile, spending most of his time on his philanthropic activities. He always, however, stayed in touch with the people who were handling his funds.

Quantum was one of the first offshore funds that was freely available to non-American investors. Most other offshore funds were limited by American law to 99 investors and ordinarily required a minimum investment of at least $1 million. It was also a hedge fund, an ultrasecretive investment partnership of wealthy people who were willing to take incredible risks with their money in order to get even richer. Soros's fund sold short, used complex financial instruments, and borrowed large quantities of money—strategies not available to mom-and-pop investors.

When hedge funds began years earlier, a small group of managers adopted a strategy of mixing their stock acquisitions. These funds were hedged in the sense that managers divided their portfolios between long positions on stocks that would profit if the market rose and short positions on stocks that would profit if they fell.

Soros and a number of other hedge-fund kings discarded that strategy and moved beyond the American stock market, betting on broad global shifts not just in stocks but in interest rates, currencies— the overall direction of financial markets. On an average trading day, Soros's funds were buying and selling $750 million of securities.

And the results he achieved were nothing short of astounding. If someone had invested $100,000 in 1969 when Soros established the Quantum Fund, and reinvested all dividends, he or she would have been worth $130 million by the spring of 1994—a compound growth rate of 35 percent. Achieving this kind of return on a much smaller fund, say one of $50 or $100 million, would be considered remarkable; to do so with a multibillion-dollar portfolio has amazed Wall Street.

A share in Soros's Quantum Fund that sold for $41.25 in 1969 was worth $21,543.55 by early 1993; it would have paid out a large amount in cash distributions as well. By June 1994, that share cost $22,600. To qualify as a member of the Quantum Fund, one needed to invest a minimum of $1 million. Soros owned, according to most reports, one-third of the Quantum Funds.

Soros had not obtained his money "the old-fashioned way." The nineteenth-century captains of American industry—entrepreneurs like Rockefeller or Carnegie—had obtained wealth by building things, by producing oil and steel. George Soros neither owned nor ran his own corporation. Nor did he have any other power base. His specialty was nimble moves in the financial markets, using a great deal of capital.

Though small in physical stature, Soros looks rugged, athletic. He has cropped, wavy hair and wears wire-rimmed glasses. Some think he looks like an economics professor or a ski instructor. He speaks English excellently, though a slight trace of a Hungarian accent remains. One writer described him as "an intense, squarely built man with a wrinkled brow, an angular chin, and a thin mouth. His hair is cut *en brosse.* He has a flat, slightly harsh voice. . . ."

Somehow people expect Soros to be a gruff fellow, and they are surprised that he looks no different from most others. "He doesn't look particularly wolflike," wrote *The Guardian.* "His relaxed air and lilting Hungarian accent lend him the style of a European grandee. His forehead is furrowed, suggesting hours spent pondering the state of the world—an impression of scholarship which he is eager to encourage."

To a writer for *The Observer,* Soros seemed to fit right into the European mold. "He is a slightly built, elegant man stamped with the indelible courtliness and restrained irony of Austro-Hungarian café society. In an earlier age one could easily have imagined him sipping his mocha over chess with Trotsky in the old Café Central in Vienna."

The Independent, the British newspaper, summed up Soros's looks this way: "He is no glitzy Gordon Gekko, antihero of that quintessentially eighties movie, *Wall Street.* He looks a decade younger than his years, perhaps as a result of his compulsive tennis playing and lack of interest in the flashy lifestyle that New York offers to the seriously rich. He neither drinks nor smokes, and his taste in food is modest. He comes across like an earnest, rather untidy Middle European professor."

By the late seventies and early eighties, Soros found the pain of investing to be too severe; it was the pain that came from running an investment fund that had grown way beyond what Soros thought was a manageable size.

He was, however, *a survivor.* He had learned that art from his father, and he had practiced it during World War II hiding from the

Nazis in 1944 in Budapest. To survive in the financial markets some-times meant beating a hasty retreat. That's what Soros did in the early eighties. He adopted a low profile. He let others handle the fund.

And he came to a fateful conclusion. He wanted something more from life than success in the investment world. Since he was no hedo-nist, money could bring him only so much. He wanted to turn his money to good use. Since he needed no approval from family or boards of directors, once he decided how to spend money, he could go ahead and spend it.

That kind of freedom, that kind of power, induced him to think at length and carefully about his options. Eventually, he settled on a grand project to encourage open societies, first in Eastern Europe, later in the former Soviet Union.

> "To survive in the financial markets sometimes means beating a hasty retreat."

Soros had left Hun-gary years before be-cause he could not abide political systems that had been ruling his country—first fascism in World War II, then communism in the postwar years. The "closed" so-cieties that had sprouted throughout Eastern Europe and in the Soviet Union offended him, for he was a firm believer in the kind of politi-cal and economic freedom that flourished in America and in Western Europe.

Others—frequently Western governments, sometimes private foundations—had tried to make a dent in these societies. Never, however, had a private individual from the West sought to make such far-reaching changes.

Soros believed he was equal to the challenge. Just as he had taught himself to do with his investments, he would start slowly, monitor his progress carefully, spend his money prudently. His hope—and it was a very long-term hope—was to pry open these closed societies.

Using his own financial resources, he wanted to plant seeds among those people in Eastern Europe and the Soviet Union who would in turn, however gradually, influence their own countries to adopt the Western-style freedoms that Soros cherished. To have an impact without arousing suspicion would be hard, to win the approval of the political authorities for his efforts might be impossible. He wanted, however, to give it a try.

He actually began his aid efforts in South Africa in 1979, but that was a failure. Turning to Eastern Europe, he established a base in Hungary in 1984. Later, he established himself elsewhere in Eastern Europe and in the Soviet Union.

Just getting a toehold in some of these countries was an achievement, given the suspicions and hostilities of their governments. In time, though, Soros Foundations blossomed. By the mid-nineties, he was donating hundreds of millions of dollars to these foundations. In 1992 and 1993, Soros gave away $500 million and made commitments to give away another $500 million. In 1993, he donated more to Russia than many Western governments had, even after he had proclaimed the situation there "cataclysmic."

George Soros, *the world's greatest investor,* had become George Soros, *the world's greatest philanthropist.*

He had become the most important private Western donor between the Danube and the Urals. Praised by many as a saint, damned by cynics as an intruder, Soros had finally found a way to make a difference, to gain some respect, and to do something outside the precincts of Wall Street and the City of London.

The philanthropy aimed at opening up closed societies gave him far more satisfaction than accumulating all that money. It also gave him far more exposure. He liked the publicity—indeed he was eager for it, because he was interested in letting the world know that he was not simply an exceptionally rich man.

Yet Soros was not entirely content, for he sensed that he would be expected to lay bare his secretive world of investing in the process. He wanted publicity, but only good publicity. He wanted to remain a private figure as much as possible, but his profile was too high, his accomplishments too substantial, his reach too vast.

Once Soros understood that it was impossible to escape the searchlights of public scrutiny, he sought to exploit his newfound fame. He had always veered away from revealing his investment positions. Suddenly, he became talkative, making public declarations about what parts of the financial markets he liked. He had never shown any great interest in international affairs. Yet, there he was, offering advice in public on a whole variety of foreign policy issues, from NATO to Bosnia, hoping to attract the attention of the world's leaders. He especially wanted American politicians to take notice. In the short term, Soros's talkative spree backfired on him. He won no new respect. He was accused of an excessive case of hubris.

Now in his mid-sixties, Soros was adamant in asserting that he was a philanthropist first and foremost and that his investment days were well behind him. He continued to try to keep as low a profile as possible with respect to his investments. Yet stardom had been thrust on him because of his 1992 coup against the pound. And he himself seemed to court a certain amount of publicity. He was quite prepared to let the world in on all of his philanthropic activities. He continued to guard his private investment world even as the public sought to discover more and more how this man had become the world's greatest investor.

The story that follows is an attempt to examine the life and career of this remarkable man, both the public and private worlds of George Soros.

Two

I Am God

Little children harbor fantasies about themselves. They want to distinguish themselves from others, or to lay claim to being superior, or to attract much-wanted attention.

The child who is meek, or scrawny, or just plain bashful delights in dreaming that, with the snap of a finger, he can become a Samson, a Stallone, or—minus the thick accent—a Schwarzenegger. The kid who rarely leaves home, denied the chance to travel to faraway places, wishes he could be an air force pilot, or an astronaut.

A psychiatrist, if pressed, can always guess the basis for such fantasies: The child loved his or her mother too much, or too little. The child admired his or her father too obsessively, or not obsessively enough.

Yet, what is one to make of a child who believed he was God?

What is one to make of young George Soros, growing up in upper-middle-class surroundings in 1930s Budapest, an otherwise normal child who had many friends, loved sports, and behaved much like other children his age?

How much easier it would be to explain away such grandiose thoughts as the fleeting daydreams of a small child had George Soros, as an adult, shown some sign that he had outgrown these messianic beliefs.

Yet, as an adult, he offered no sign, no dismissive gesture, no footnote signifying that he no longer clung to such wild convictions, but only the suggestion of how difficult it was for someone to believe himself a deity.

"If truth be known," he wrote in one of his books, "I carried some rather potent *messianic fantasies* with me from childhood, which I felt I had to control, otherwise they might get me into trouble."

One way he controlled those fantasies was to speak about them as little as possible. In one of the rare instances when he did speak about them, he told the British newspaper, *The Independent,* on June 3, 1993: "It is a sort of disease when you consider yourself some kind of god, the creator of everything, but I feel comfortable about it now since I began to live it out."

And in the longest reference to these fantasies, a passage in his 1987 book *The Alchemy of Finance,* Soros disclosed how painful it had been for him as a youngster to carry around such beliefs, a burdensome secret he was disinclined to share with others.

"It will come as no surprise to the reader when I admit that I have always harbored an exaggerated view of my self-importance—to put it bluntly, I fancied myself as *some kind of god* or an economic reformer like Keynes or, even better, a scientist like Einstein. My sense of reality was strong enough to make me realize that these expectations were excessive and I kept them hidden as a guilty secret. This was a source of considerable unhappiness through much of my adult life. As I made my way in the world, reality came close enough to my fantasy to allow me to admit my secret, at least to myself. Needless to say, I feel much happier as a result."

What a startling thought—reality came close enough to his fantasy of thinking himself God.

Did George Soros truly mean that the life he was leading as an adult, a successful financier, and a philanthropist somehow approximated the childhood fantasy of thinking himself divine?

Apparently, he did.

Other than in a few fleeting references, Soros has not elaborated in public on why he believed he was God and what he meant in making such a claim. Perhaps, if pressed, he might have persuaded people that he was just kidding, that he did not believe himself God after all. Here and there, he even joked about his childhood feelings. A journalist once suggested to Soros that he should be appointed pope.

"Why?" he asked. "*I'm the Pope's boss now.*"

What one is left with is a man who, even as an adult, was convinced that he had been endowed with traits unique to him.

George Soros as God.

If it doesn't quite ring true, it at least helps to explain the enormous self-confidence he had as a child and would carry into adulthood.

Because George kept his childhood fantasy a secret, it is not surprising to find that none of his childhood acquaintances remembered him insisting he was divine. They did recall that he enjoyed lording it over the other children. Most of his adult associates believed that when he disclosed that he thought himself God, Soros had been deliberately exaggerating, a way of asserting his own superiority over others. Almost as if they were apologizing for Soros's hyperbole, they sought to explain away his fantasy by arguing that he had not meant what he said.

What George Soros meant, said one, was not that he *was* God, but that he believed he could talk to God! Another thought Soros was merely expressing a sense of omnipotence: Suggesting that he was God had been his tongue-in-cheek way of comparing himself, as others might do, to a Napoleon.

It was as if those who knew George Soros wanted to bring him down to earth, so to speak. It was as if they did not want to have as a friend or colleague someone who actually believed himself to be God. These same people would have dismissed anyone else who muttered such thoughts as certifiably nuts. They couldn't do that with George Soros. He was, after all, someone they held in awe.

Who imbued young George with such ideas?

Perhaps his parents did. They certainly doted over him. Yet Tivadar, the father, and Elizabeth, the mother, doted over their other son, and there is no indication that he felt godly.

George was born in Budapest in 1930. Whenever biographical details appear, whether in press releases put out by Soros-sponsored organizations or in Soros's books, the day and month of his birth are omitted. Only the year is given. The reason is not clear.

He was born with the Hungarian name Dzjchdzhe Shorash. In time, the name became anglicized to George Soros. Although the name is pronounced *Shorosh* in Hungarian, George accommodated his American and British acquaintances by pronouncing his last name Soros.

His only sibling, a brother named Paul, had been born two years earlier.

Whatever his faults, Tivadar Soros served as a forceful role model for his younger son. He was an attorney, who by the time of George's birth had lived through his most formidable—and formative—experience. An Austro-Hungarian prisoner of war during World War I, Tivadar then spent three turbulent years in Russia—from the opening days of the revolution in 1917 to the civil war in 1920. During those civil war years he was on the run in Siberia, hoping to survive. Whatever he had to do to *survive,* he did, no matter how unpleasant.

In recounting those perilous years, Tivadar told the boy that in revolutionary times anything was possible. Though hardly a recipe for survival, these words carried great weight with his son. Gradually, George learned that his father was a clever, even wily man, who, by using his wits, had outsmarted many a person. Young George held him in the highest respect.

Ferenc Nagel, a year younger than George, still lives in Budapest. He is a chemical engineer and works for Tungsram, the well-known Hungarian lighting manufacturer. He met George for the first time in 1936 at Lupa Island, the summer retreat on the Danube River an hour north of Budapest where the Soroses and Nagels had homes. When things went wrong, Nagel recalled, Tivadar had always found a way to cope. "He was never seriously beaten." That, said Nagel with an air of finality, was Tivadar's legacy to his son. So was being pragmatic. George acknowledged as much: "What side of the revolution was he on? Oh, both sides of course. He had to be, to survive." To George what was important was the fact that Tivadar possessed the qualities of a survivor.

Survival became an ennobled value in George Soros's life.

Some of Tivadar's character traits appeared admirable in war, but less so in peacetime. Indeed, by the 1930s Tivadar no longer appeared heroic to the inhabitants of Lupa Island. Dark in appearance—black hair, black eyes—he was handsome, had an athlete's solid build, and loved sports. He also had a reputation for having a roving eye, for spending excessively, and for displaying little enthusiasm for hard work. "My father does not work. He just makes money." So it seemed to young George.

Ferenc Nagel retained a sharply defined image of Tivadar Soros getting ready to go to work one summer in the 1930s.

Tivadar took the 7:00 AM boat daily from Lupa Island to his office in Budapest.

"When he heard that the boat was coming," remembered Nagel, "Tivadar put on his trousers and began shaving. He went out to the boat with the razor blade in his hand, and continued shaving on the way to the boat and during the boat ride. It was all in order to sleep to the last minute. This was very unusual for a lawyer. He was always very, very tricky."

Tricky meant not following convention, not playing by the rules, cutting corners.

If others held Tivadar in disrepute, George seemed more sympathetic to his father's lifestyle than did others who recalled Tivadar's fondness for avoiding hard work. Sure, George Soros admitted later, his father worked very little after he came back from World War I. That was not, however, all bad. Tivadar was around that much more, and George liked that. He enjoyed the chance to talk with his father and to learn things from those conversations. If others found Tivadar less than careful about his spending habits, George was unmoved. To him, it simply did not matter that his father's financial fortunes ebbed, then soared, then ebbed again. However unintentional, Tivadar communicated to his son a message that would stay with him throughout his life: "Part of what I learned was the futility of making money for money's sake. Wealth can be a dead weight."

To someone like Tivadar, who placed physical survival above all else, having too much money had its drawbacks. It tempted others to try to get their hands on the money of the excessively wealthy. Having too much wealth could make a person soft, making survival more difficult. Tivadar communicated these values to his son and they stuck. Later in life, wealthy beyond most people's wildest dreams, George Soros exhibited little excitement over the accumulation of so much money.

The greatest gift Tivadar bestowed on his younger son, however, was simply paying a great deal of attention to him. He talked to him often, passed along a few secrets about life, as he had come to understand them, and generally made the youngster feel important. Beyond instilling in the boy a sense of his own self-worth, Tivadar bolstered the child's self-confidence, assuring him that, just as the father had, the boy would learn how to overcome great odds, how to handle tumultuous situations. And just as Tivadar had, George would learn that frequently it was best to search for unconventional methods to solve problems.

If Tivadar taught the youngster the art of survival, George's mother Elizabeth passed on an appreciation of art and culture to her younger son. He was deeply attached to her. Painting and sculpture, music and literature were all important parts of Elizabeth's life, and she tried to imbue her son with a love of these things as well. George was more inclined toward drawing and painting, less toward music. His later interest in philosophy seems to have stemmed from Elizabeth Soros's own interest in the subject. Although the family spoke Hungarian, George eventually learned German, English, and French.

Yehuditte Simo, a childhood acquaintance who remembers George as "a very pretty little boy," lives today in Budapest. She knew George and his parents from Lupa Island.

Elizabeth's life was "not easy," she recalled. Tivadar's free and easy spending habits, and his indifference toward work, proved continuing sources of tension at home, and try as she might, Elizabeth could not prevent the tension from surfacing from time to time. Small, fragile-looking, and light-haired, Elizabeth was a traditional housewife, looking after her two sons, presiding over a home that seemed more Hungarian than Jewish—for, like many upper-middle-class Hungarian Jews, Tivadar and Elizabeth were distinctly uncomfortable with their religious roots. "I grew up," Soros told acquaintances later in life, "in a Jewish, anti-Semitic home." Because he was blue-eyed and blond-haired—resembling his mother rather than his dark-featured father—George did not look Jewish, and he beamed when other children would tell him, "You don't look Jewish." Nothing made him feel happier than to be told he did not have the appearance of a Jew.

So dismissive of Judaism was Tivadar that he would go to great lengths to pose as a member of the Christian community. During World War II, for example, he urged George to beg for cigarettes from the soldiers. Tivadar would then turn the cigarettes over to Jewish shopkeepers. To Tivadar, the whole point of the exercise was to be able to pass himself off as a kind gentile expressing solidarity with them. It seemed safer that way.

Despite his efforts to distinguish himself from the crowd, George Soros's childhood friends remembered him as less than an extraordinary child. He may have envisioned himself as being divine, but none of his friends thought he possessed any special qualities, even of a nondivine dimension. He was, according to all accounts, no genius, but he was intelligent and often demonstrated initiative. When George was ten years old, he edited a newspaper he called the *Lupa Horsbina,* the *Lupa Trumpet.* He wrote all of the articles and for two summers sold it to families on Lupa for a small charge. Ferenc Nagel recalled him being somewhat aggressive with older people. "When he believed in something, he defended it very strongly. He had a hard and dominating character."

The youngster excelled in sports, especially swimming, sailing, and tennis. Lupa had two tennis courts for forty families, an obvious luxury. He disliked soccer, considering it an upper-middle-class sport, and therefore not for him.

Games intrigued him, all sorts of games. He was especially taken with one called *Capital,* a Hungarian version of *Monopoly.* From the age of seven, he played it frequently with the other children, among whom he was the best. The worst was George Litwin. It was no surprise to George's childhood friends that George Soros became a master of high finance, and Litwin . . . a historian.

Winning at *Capital* all the time proved boring to young George. To liven up the game, he introduced new rules. One was to make the game more complex by adding a stock exchange. When Soros returned to Hungary in the 1960s, the burgeoning financier sought out Ferenc Nagel, who asked him what he did for a living. "You remember as children we played *Capital?"* Soros asked with a smile. "Well, today I do the same."

The children of Budapest had to attend school until the age of fourteen. For poor families, sending their children to school beyond that age was difficult.

Miklas Horn, an economics teacher in Budapest, attended primary school with George. They met for the first time in 1940 when both were ten years old. Later that year they moved on to a state school for the upper middle classes. Horn remained George's schoolmate for the next six years.

In elementary school, George was outgoing. That explained why he and Miklos Horn were not great friends. "George was a very audacious, outgoing fellow while I was solid, quiet. He liked to fight with the other boys. In fact, George learned how to box, how to defend himself."

In George's school, all the grades were divided into two classes, Jews in one class, non-Jews in another. George and Miklas Horn were in the Jewish class. Horn has a vivid memory of the Jewish and non-Jewish youngsters getting into many scraps. While the fisticuffs were not an outgrowth of anti-Semitic feeling, Horn recalled, it was not lost on the boys that the fighting seemed to occur mostly between Jews and non-Jews. Horn observed: "Underneath you could feel the anti-Semitism. The fighting had a sort of political implication as well."

Though young George got into his share of fights, his schoolyard violence was not a response to anti-Semitism. Indeed, Miklas Horn suggested, he was careful not to identify himself too closely with either class, keeping on good terms with both Jews and non-Jews.

Although the adult Soros liked to think of himself as an intellectual, he was a late bloomer, and his schoolmates do not remember him as an outstanding student. Neither do they recall any subject he particularly liked. According to Miklas Horn, "George was not an exceptionally good student. He was somewhere in the middle. But he was somebody who could talk very well."

Pal Tetenyi attended the state school at that time and, like Miklas Horn, remembered George Soros as no more than an "average" student. One incident remained fresh in his mind. It occurred in the spring of 1942 when both he and George were twelve years old.

George and Pal were attending a meeting of the Boy Scouts, at which it was announced that an Esperanto Society was being formed. Those interested in joining the society were to write their names on a piece of paper, which had been placed on a certain bench. As a prank, George grabbed the piece of paper, making it impossible for Tetenyi to sign up. "George was very sarcastic," Pal recalled, "and I was afraid that he would make fun of me. I wanted to get back at him. We began fighting." Locked in heated battle under the bench, the two boys quickly discovered to their great embarrassment that an angry teacher was standing over them. For their fighting, the boys received a written warning.

When World War II began in September 1939, George was nine years old. But his life hardly changed, for the Nazis posed no threat to Hungary at that time. Indeed, life for the residents of Budapest remained routine. Sometime after the Soviet army had invaded Finland in that opening year of the fighting, George read a local newspaper appeal for aid to Finland. Rushing over to the newspaper office to respond to the appeal, he made a distinct impression upon the editors, who thought it unusual that a nine-year-old boy would take the trouble to offer aid to people in a far-off land. The editors ran a story on young George's visit to the newspaper office.

As the war progressed, however, the threat of a German invasion of Hungary loomed larger. George Soros and the rest of the Hungarian Jewish community were not to escape the war. Indeed, in the years that followed, the war was to come home to them in an unforgettable way.

Three

The Cellars of Budapest

L ife for the residents of Budapest in 1943 had an eerie calm. By this time, Allied forces had gained a foothold in southern Italy, and their fighter planes were within reach of Budapest. While the city seemed free from the threat of attack, bitter fighting raged elsewhere in Europe, and the danger loomed that it would spread to Hungary. Coal was in short supply, and schools closed because air raids were feared.

By the spring of 1944, Jewish communities throughout Europe had been largely wiped out by the Nazis. Fears grew that Hungary's one million Jews, the largest Jewish population in Eastern Europe, would be next. Word was spreading of mass exterminations at Auschwitz. The Russians were moving westward. But would they break the Nazi stronghold over Europe in time to save Hungary's Jews?

For the Jewish population of Budapest, *the nightmare seemed imminent.*

March 19, 1944, was a Sunday, and so the Soroses were at Lupa Island. They were too far away to hear or see the frightening events unfolding near Budapest to the south: German tanks were moving along both the Buda and Pest shores of the Danube. The Nazi invasion was on. It was a "peaceful" invasion: No shots were fired, and the only sounds were of the tanks' clanking chains and whining motors. The streets were quickly deserted, as everyone sought the shelter of home until assured that it was safe. The main preoccupation was to grab for a phone.

Along with many others in Budapest, George believed that the Nazi invasion of his country would be short-lived, most likely no more than six weeks. It seemed to make sense. The Nazis were in retreat elsewhere. The war seemed to be winding down.

Six weeks. Not a long time.

But no one really knew. All that one could do was hope for the best and hide. To be on the streets could prove a death sentence.

The Jewish community of Budapest was divided into the dreamers and the realists. The dreamers clung to their illusions. They had believed up to the last moments before March 19 that Hitler's forces would never come. Even as Nazi tanks were rolling down the streets, the dreamers insisted that it would not be so bad for the Jews, that all those reports of Jewish persecution elsewhere in Europe could not possibly be true, that the war, at any rate, would soon end.

The realists also believed that the war would be over soon, but they believed the reports of mass exterminations at Auschwitz and elsewhere, and they wondered whether the fighting would end in time to save them from similar persecution.

The dismaying reports rang true to Tivadar Soros. He had been concerned about the Nazis since their rise to power a decade earlier. Having watched their rampant, senseless violence explode into world war, he worried that the violence would eventually reach Hungary, Budapest, and his family.

Having survived one form of tyranny during World War I, Tivadar vowed that he would help his family make it through another. He had few financial worries because he sold off some real estate early in the war. He radiated supreme self-confidence; his calming presence comforted George, Paul, and Elizabeth. Ferenc Nagel, then a boy of 13, recalled the maudlin guessing game his own father played that spring, trying to predict how many of his family and friends would be wiped out. Half of them at least, was the father's gruesome prediction; then in the next breath, he said knowingly, "Not the Soroses. Not the Soroses."

Tivadar was a survivor. He would look after his family.

Over the next 12 months, 400,000 Jews from Budapest were killed, sad testimony to the prescience of Ferenc Nagel's father. The survivors, including George Soros and his family, endured terrifying days and nights.

When the Nazi authorities gave the Jewish Council of Budapest the task of distributing deportation notices to Jews, the council turned that gruesome task over to small children.

George was one of those children.

At the council's offices he was given small pieces of paper on which people's names were written. Each paper contained orders for a person to report to the rabbinical seminary at nine the next morning and to bring a blanket and food for twenty-four hours.

George sought his father's advice. Showing him the list, he watched his father grimace in pain as he realized that the Nazis were rounding up Hungary's Jewish attorneys!

"Deliver the notices," he instructed his son, "but make sure you tell each person that these are deportation notices."

George obeyed, but he discovered that some of those he told were not about to hide from the Nazis, even if it meant being deported. If the Nazis had decreed that Jewish attorneys were to be deported, that was the law, and the law must be obeyed.

"Tell your father," said one, "that I am a law-abiding citizen, that I have always been a law-abiding citizen and I am not going to start breaking the law now."

Tivadar Soros was a handy father for these horrific times. An automatic death sentence hung over Budapest's Jews—a death sentence that would include young George if the Nazis discovered that he was Jewish. The nightmare of a journey to a concentration camp suddenly took on a gruesome reality.

"This is a lawless occupation," Tivadar told his son. "The normal rules don't apply. You have to forget how you behave in a normal society. This is an abnormal situation."

An abnormal situation meant that it was all right for George to behave in a way that might otherwise seem dishonest or criminal, his father explained. The presence of the Nazi authorities in Budapest justified such behavior.

Tivadar arranged for George to function in this "abnormal" situation. To assure that his son was not taken by the Nazi authorities, Tivadar bribed a Hungarian government official to permit his son to pose as the godson of a non-Jewish official in the Hungarian Agriculture Ministry. Tivadar purchased false identity papers for the boy, papers that were the key to his survival.

For the duration of the war, George Soros became Janos Kis.

Tivadar also offered financial support to the official's Jewish wife to enable her to hide from the Nazis. In later years, George Soros described his father's actions euphemistically as a mere "commercial transaction."

The Hungarian bureaucrat whom Tivadar bribed was responsible for confiscating the belongings of Jewish property owners who had already been taken to Auschwitz.

George accompanied him on his journeys around the country.

For the teenager the risks were enormous. "Had I been caught, I would have been killed," George Soros remarked with a lack of emotion that belied how dangerous his situation really was.

Hiding was essential. One refuge was a cellar, encased in solid stone walls. Its entry was down a set of winding, narrow stone steps. Within the cellar another hiding place, offering even greater concealment, lay beyond a locked door. The family used the second, inner hiding place when someone came to search the house.

In all, George and his family had access to 11 hiding places. Often they spent weeks in the attics or basements of friends, never knowing whether they would suddenly have to vacate the spot. If the 14-year-old George experienced fear at these times, he never admitted it later.

Indeed, for him, the year seemed *one big adventure.*

On one occasion, both Tivadar and George were hiding in the same place, both with false non-Jewish identities. They spoke to one another, but not as father and son, in order not to betray their true identities.

On another occasion, while the Soroses were holed up in a cellar, George, Paul, and Tivadar passed the time by playing games. The stakes were a small amount of candy. When George or Paul won a game, he ate his winnings. Tivadar, perhaps recalling an old survival trick from World War I, refused to eat his.

George found the whole experience of the war during 1944 thrilling, and he described it later as the happiest year of his life. He felt like the film hero Indiana Jones, oblivious to danger, immune to the fears others felt. Having Tivadar around made a big difference: George was terribly proud of his father and, encouraged by Tivadar's self-confidence, thought him a genuine hero.

For all of his apparent faults, Tivadar taught George valuable lessons about the art of survival.

One: *It is all right to take risks.*

Having risked his life daily during the latter part of World War II, Tivadar came to believe that most other risks were worth taking.

Two: *When taking risks, don't bet the ranch.*

Never risk everything. That would be foolish, impractical, and unnecessary.

Hiding from the Nazis, however, George Soros had no choice but to risk everything. When he accepted those false identity papers, he knew that exposure meant death.

Later, in his business career, he would have more latitude.

He would not have to make life-or-death choices. He could take risks without having to worry that failure could cost him everything. He could even enjoy risk taking. As long as he left himself room to recover.

> **"When taking risks, don't bet the ranch."**

"I'm very concerned with the need to survive," he told a television interviewer at the height of his success in 1992, "and not to take risks that could actually destroy me."

The war taught George one other lesson.

We all have preconceived notions, and these perceptions don't necessarily correspond with the way the world actually functions. The lesson George learned was that *a gap exists between perception and reality.*

It was that gap that he would eventually explore as he weaved his theories about human knowledge and, later, about the financial markets.

In the fall of 1945, George Soros was back in school. With the war over, Jews and non-Jews were no longer separated into two classes. George was 15 years old and like the other students who lived through the Nazi trauma, mature beyond his years. That trauma was still evident in many of the students. Pal Tetenyi recalled that "the discipline in the class was terrible. Many of us had small guns which we took to class. It was a good thing to have a gun. It showed we were mature. But it was childish."

The residents of Lupa, including George and his family, visited the island in the spring of 1945, the first time since the end of war. They exchanged wartime stories, recounted how they had managed to survive, and talked of plans for the near future, plans that were linked inextricably with what they thought might happen to postwar Hungary.

Each of them wrestled with one agonizing question:

Should one leave the country?

Having survived the Nazis, the Hungarians did not want to trade one menacing existence for another. If the new government was likely to be Nazi-like in its treatment of the citizenry, it seemed better to leave, and the sooner the better.

Yet, whether the new government would be benign or hostile was not clear. More to the point, no one could say with certainty how large a role the Soviets would play in Hungary's government.

Some of the Soros family's friends were hopeful, eager to believe that all would be well, that the Soviets would prove far more benevolent than the Nazis. Others were suspicious and cynical. They were ready to pack their bags and leave while they could, while it was still possible to obtain a passport.

Among the latter group was George Soros. He felt it was time to leave Hungary and head for the West.

He left on his own in the fall of 1947 at the age of 17. Eager to finish his engineering studies, his brother Paul remained in Hungary another year. George's first stop was Bern, Switzerland, but soon he moved on to London, a place that sounded attractive to the teenager. Thanks to his father, George had enough money for the journey. But once there, he would be largely left to his own resources. His only money had come from an aunt who had already reestablished herself in Florida.

Although England was supposed to provide George Soros with a happier life, he found himself with too little money and companionship to enjoy what the city had to offer. This was one of the most difficult episodes of his life. He was lonely and virtually broke. Still, he tried to find some light in the darkness. Sitting in a London coffeehouse, he thought to himself half-humorously:

"Here I am. I have reached bottom. Isn't that a wonderful feeling? There's only one way to go."

It was, of course, not a wonderful feeling to have "reached bottom," and all that the 18-year-old could do was go from odd job to odd job, hoping that his luck would eventually turn. He took work as a waiter at a restaurant called Quaglino's in London's Mayfair section, a place where aristocrats and film stars dined and danced the night away. Sometimes, when his cash flow was nearly zero, George sustained himself by eating leftover profiteroles. Years later, he remembered envying a cat because it was eating sardines while he was not.

Part-time job followed part-time job.

In the summer of 1948, he did farm work as part of the "Lend a Hand on the Land" program. The man who would in the early 1990s come to epitomize high finance organized a strike so that the farm workers could be paid piecework rather than a day rate. Because of Soros's efforts, he and the other employees earned more. In Suffolk, he harvested apples. He also worked as a house painter, and later boasted to friends that he was not a bad painter at all.

The odd jobs, poverty, and loneliness proved no fun at all, and in the ensuing years, George could not rid himself of those hellish images. "I carried certain fears with me out of this that were—not so good. Fears of reaching—of hitting the bottom again. Having hit it once, I didn't want to hit it again."

Four

Like Freud or Einstein

I n 1949, George Soros enrolled as a student at the London School of Economics. The LSE, as it was widely known, was one of England's great educational institutions, an ideal place to study, whether one wanted a career or an academic life. The school attracted an international student body and was generally regarded as leaning toward socialism, largely because the socialist theoretician Harold Laski taught there. It was an ideal place for someone like George Soros, who wanted practical training in economics and at the same time was eager to study current trends in international politics.

He attended some of Laski's lectures and took a course with John Meade, who in 1977 won the Nobel Prize in economics, "though," Soros confessed later, "I didn't get much out of that course." The school was also home to a pair of unfashionably politically conservative thinkers, the free-market economist Friedrich von Hayek and the renowned philosopher Karl Popper. These two men proved instrumental in setting George Soros on the intellectual path he would later pursue with great fervor in the 1980s and 1990s, as he sought to encourage the replacement of "closed" societies with "open" ones.

Hayek's 1944 book, *The Road to Serfdom,* attacked fascism, socialism, and communism, lumping them together as kindred types of collectivism that all undermined institutions that allowed freedom to flourish.

Of greater influence was Karl Popper. Though Popper was best known for his theories about scientific method, it was his 1951 book, *The Open Society and Its Enemies,* that served as the foundation for George Soros's intellectual life.

Young Soros was ripe for a book that explored the nature of human societies. He had experienced dictatorial rule, first at the hands of the Nazis, then at the hands of the communists. Now, in

England he was getting his initial taste of democracy. He was eager to put his personal experiences into some intellectual context. Popper's book provided that framework.

In *The Open Society and Its Enemies,* Popper argued that human societies had only two possible destinies. One was to become a "closed" society, where everyone was forced to believe the same thing. The second was to become an "open" society, whose inhabitants were free of the nationalisms and tribal wars that Popper found so disturbing. In this "open" society, conflicting beliefs have to be accommodated, no matter what the strains on the society. Open societies, Popper argued, however "uncertain and insecure," were vastly superior to "closed" ones.

Although Soros completed the course work for his undergraduate degree in just two years, he decided to hang around LSE for another year until he could obtain his degree in the spring of 1953. Familiar with *The Open Society and Its Enemies,* he sought out Popper to learn more from the master. He submitted a few essays to Popper, and the professor and student hit it off. Popper became Soros's mentor.

Nearly 92 years old in the spring of 1994, Karl Popper, in an interview with me, thought back more than 40 years to those days when a young George Soros first showed up at his door. "He came into my office and said, 'I'm a student at LSE. Can I ask you something?' He was a very keen student. I had written my book on open societies, and apparently it impressed him. He came frequently and presented me with his ideas. I was not his tutor officially. If he calls me his mentor today, that is very nice of him."

While Soros had been taken with Popper, the young student made no lasting mark on the professor. "I listened to what he had to say," Popper recalled, "but I didn't ask him any questions. I didn't hear much about him."

Popper's greatest impact upon Soros was in encouraging the young student to think seriously about the way the world worked, and to develop, if at all possible, a grand philosophical scheme that would help explain it.

Popper was the master philosopher seeking to pass his wisdom down to a budding intellectual. He had no interest in helping Soros get along in the practical world. Philosophy, whether the thoughts of Karl Popper or anyone else, was not supposed to be a road map for making money in the real world.

Yet for George Soros, philosophy would serve just that purpose. In time, he would go from the abstract to the practical; he would develop theories of knowledge, of how and why people think in certain ways, and from those theories he would spin new theories about the way the financial markets functioned.

Later in life, Soros constantly cited Professor Popper as the source of his inspiration for his philanthropic efforts to promote open societies in Eastern Europe and the former Soviet Union. He skipped over the contribution Popper made, however inadvertently, in helping Soros to fashion the theories he would use to amass a fortune on Wall Street.

But in the meantime, there was no fortune. Being impecunious made for embarrassing, awkward moments. But George Soros felt he had no choice. In need of financial assistance for his studies, he approached the Jewish Board of Guardians. The board turned him down, explaining that it did not provide aid to students, only to the gainfully employed. The distinction made no sense to young Soros.

Then, during one Christmas vacation, while working as a railway porter on the night shift, George broke his leg. Again, he needed money. This time he had a job working for the railroad. Surely, he could qualify now. "This is the occasion to get money out of those bastards, I decided."

Returning to the board, he decided to offer up a neat piece of fiction. He informed it that he was in a predicament: He had broken his leg, but since he was working illegally, he was not eligible for National Assistance. In fact, he was still a student. The board grudgingly agreed to give him some aid. To collect the funds, he was forced, while on crutches, to climb three flights of stairs.

In time, however, the board stopped Soros's funding. So he wrote a "heartrending" letter to the board, noting that, while he would not starve, it hurt him that this was how one Jew treated another needy one.

The answer came by return mail.

George's letter had the desired effect. His weekly allowance was reinstated—and, best of all, the funds would now be sent to him by mail, ending his arduous visits to the office. He happily took the money, but, still steaming from the earlier affront, waited some time after the cast had been removed from his leg—he was hitchhiking in southern France—before informing the board that it could stop sending the money. The Board of Guardians' treatment of him made Soros bitter about all charities long afterwards, and he had to overcome "considerable reservations" before setting up his own philanthropic program in the late 1970s.

The intellectual stimulation at the LSE helped Soros overcome some of his loneliness. He was still poor, but he seemed to be enjoying himself more. During one summer break from his studies, he found work as an attendant at an indoor swimming pool in one of London's poorer quarters. Few swimmers showed up, allowing Soros plenty of time to visit the huge public library next door. He spent a good part of the summer, therefore, reading books, caught up in the world of ideas. He later described the time as the "best summer" of his life. His professional goals were still unformed. But he enjoyed being engaged in the world of ideas, and he liked writing. Perhaps he might become a social philosopher or a journalist. He was still not sure.

He could easily imagine himself remaining at LSE and becoming an academic, perhaps a philosopher like Karl Popper. How wonderful it would be if he could stretch his mind as Popper had, and above all else present the world with some major insight, *"like Freud or Einstein."* On other occasions, he dreamed of becoming a new John Maynard Keynes, of scaling the same heights as an economic thinker as the world-famous British economist.

It was the beginning of George Soros's striving for intellectual achievement that would be one of the major themes of his life and career.

Unfortunately, Soros's grades were not good enough, and his academic pretensions seemed to founder. In late 1952 and early 1953, he wrestled with a host of philosophical questions. He was particularly interested in the gap between perception and reality. At some point, he came up with what he thought was a rather remarkable intellectual discovery: *"I came to the conclusion that basically all our views of the world are somehow flawed or distorted, and then I concentrate on the importance of this distortion in shaping events."*

He began writing a short book that he entitled *The Burden of Consciousness.* In it, he formulated notions of open and closed societies. Dissatisfied with what he had written, he put the manuscript down. Over the next decade, he sought to rework the text but eventually abandoned the effort when he "could not make head or tail of what I had written the day before."

This was not a good sign, and Soros knew it. It was unlikely he would become a professor. Soros linked his failure to finish the book with his decision to forgo the study of philosophy in favor of the pursuit of money.

However much Soros wanted to teach, it was clear to him that he needed to make a living—and fast. He was 22 years old, and, while he longed to make some great contribution to human knowledge, he had to eat. However, a degree in economics qualified him for little. He took whatever job he could find, the first as a handbag salesman in Blackpool, the coastal resort in northern England.

He had difficulty selling. To attract customers, he had to convince people early on that he was no different from them—tough for a foreigner, conversing in heavily accented English. It bothered him also to sell wholesale goods to shopkeepers who probably did not need them. Once, he made such a sale to a small shopkeeper whose shop was cluttered with unsold merchandise. This man needs my handbags like he needs a hole in the head, Soros thought to himself. Suppressing such thoughts, he convinced himself that he could not let his personal feelings surface. He sold the man the wares, but the guilt did not leave him quickly.

It could be argued that LSE was the perfect training ground for someone like Soros who would eventually take up a career as an investor. Yet, Soros had learned nothing at the school about the financial markets, barely knowing they existed. Upon graduation, he sensed there was good money to be made in investing. Needing a foot in the door of a London investment bank, he drafted a letter to all the investment banks in the city, hoping his luck would change. When Singer & Friedlander offered him a job as a trainee, he happily accepted.

Here was a firm with a flourishing stock market operation.

Enthralled, he became a trader specializing in gold-stock arbitrage, trying to take advantage of price discrepancies in the different markets. Even if he had not been terribly successful—and the evidence suggested that he was not—he felt comfortable in this world, discovering the thrill of buying and selling in the markets. It would have been more stimulating perhaps to have become a social philosopher or a journalist. But he needed to make a living. Here the prospects seemed good. Soros found this world more and more appealing.

The general estimate of George Soros's London passage has him largely a failure. Even Soros does not dispute that. He has one defender in Edgar Astaire, the London stockbroker who knew Soros then and has since become his London partner: "He was never establishment. He was only 25 and 26 years old. You couldn't do anything [in that business]. Young men were not allowed to do anything."

Whatever the case, in 1956, the young investment banker believed that it was time to move on.

To New York City.

Five

The Blind Leading the Blind

In leaving for New York, George Soros acknowledged to himself once and for all that he was serious about a career in finance. The dream of becoming a philosopher would have to remain . . . a dream.

Moving to New York automatically gave him a competitive advantage over his colleagues. Even though he did not set the world on fire in London, he had acquired knowledge of European financial markets. While experts on that subject were a dime a dozen in London, the people on Wall Street had little experience or understanding of European markets. From the moment he arrived in the United States, Soros was tagged as an expert in the field.

Soros made the journey to New York with $5,000 to his name. A relative had given him 1,000 British pounds and asked him to invest the sum on his behalf. The $5,000 represented Soros's share of the profits from that investment.

That same year, 1956, Tivadar and Elizabeth Soros left Hungary, joining their two sons in the United States. Tivadar opened an espresso stand on Coney Island. It could not have been a pleasant experience for the Great Survivor. The small business failed, and Tivadar retired. (In the early 1960s Tivadar developed cancer. His father was so poor that George Soros had to find a surgeon who would handle the case gratis.)

Soon after arriving in the United States, Soros found work through a London colleague. One phone call to one of the partners at F. M. Mayer on Soros's behalf and Soros was an arbitrageur. Though arbitrage grew into one of the hottest financial games of the 1980s, three decades earlier it was pretty dull. No one staked out large investment positions hoping to make millions of dollars from corporate takeovers. That came in the go-go eighties. In the humdrum 1950s, traders like George Soros bought and sold the same securities in different markets, hoping to exploit small price discrepancies found through meticulous research.

In time Soros became an analyst offering advice to American financial organizations about European securities. As he had expected, few on Wall Street had any interest, let alone great instinct for, investment trends in Europe. The 1950s were long before the current era of global trading, long before American investors began to sense that there was money to be made on the other side of the "pond." At the time Europeans dealt only with Europeans, and Americans talked only with Americans. This parochialism worked to Soros's advantage. Aiding him too was the fact that Western Europe's economies were slowly beginning to recuperate from the devastation wrought by World War II.

Soros was a pioneer, ahead of his time. "The things George was doing 35 years ago have only come into fashion in the last decade here," observed Stanley Druckenmiller, Soros's right-hand man since 1988.

"Nobody knew anything about [European securities] in the early 1960s," Soros recalled with a smile. "So I could impute any earnings I wanted to the European companies I followed. It was strictly a case of the blind leading the blind."

It was not surprising that during this time Soros would meet and marry someone of European background. As a newcomer to the United States, he knew relatively few American women. He met his future wife, the German-born Annalise, in Quogue, Long Island, near Westhampton. They were married in 1961. Still working at F. M. Mayer, Soros lived in a small apartment with her. (The Soroses separated in 1978 and were divorced three years after that. They had three children. In 1983, Soros married again. His bride was Susan Weber, 25 years his junior. They were married in a civil ceremony in Southampton. Late in 1985, Susan gave birth to their first son, Gregory—making George a father for the fourth time. A second son, Alexander, was born in 1987.)

In 1959, Soros moved to Wertheim & Co., where he continued to devote his energies to European securities. Fortunately for him, Wertheim was one of the few American firms that engaged in overseas trading. Soros remained one of only a handful of Wall Street traders who arbitraged between London and New York.

One of his first successful forays into the foreign financial markets occurred in 1960. Soros realized that the shares of the German insurance firm Allianz had been selling at a large discount from its asset value, thanks to the appreciation in the company's stock and real estate portfolios. He wrote a paper recommending that others invest in Allianz. Morgan Guaranty and the Dreyfus Fund liked his ideas and started to purchase sizable blocks of Allianz stock. Allianz's bosses were not pleased, and they wrote to Soros's superiors at Wertheim. Your man has come to the wrong conclusion, they essentially wrote. In fact, he had not. The value of Allianz's stock tripled. Soros's reputation grew.

Soros looked forward to continued good luck even after the new administration of John F. Kennedy took office in January 1961. Kennedy, as it turned out, would prove a serious stumbling block for young Soros. Kennedy's new Interest Equalization Tax essentially prevented American investors from purchasing foreign securities. The change of policy was earth-shattering for Soros.

But not enough to send him packing. On December 18, 1961, he had become a naturalized American citizen. He was in the United States to stay.

Soros, now 33 years old, still teetered between a career as a philosopher and a career in investments. The Kennedy policy presented Soros with one more opportunity to try his hand at the thing he seemed to love most—thinking and writing about the fundamental questions of life.

Beginning in 1961, Soros had been devoting his evenings and weekends to redrafting *The Burden of Consciousness,* hoping somehow to polish the manuscript sufficiently so that it could find a publisher. The experience was even more perplexing than when he had sat down to write the tome in the first place. Finally, in 1963, he sent the manuscript to Karl Popper. To win the master's approval would have been a feather in Soros's cap. Having the well-known Popper on his side seemed a crucial step in getting the book published.

Although he did not recall who Soros was, Popper still reacted warmly to the manuscript. When it became clear to the LSE philosopher that Soros had roots in communist Eastern Europe, however, Popper professed disappointment. He had been led to believe that

Soros was an American; the philosopher was thrilled that someone who had not experienced totalitarian rule could understand what he was talking about. Discovering that Soros was Hungarian and had met the Nazis and communists firsthand, Popper thought less of the manuscript. He encouraged Soros to continue to think through his ideas.

Soros never acknowledged what made him decide to shelve the writing project once again, though Popper's lukewarm response to the manuscript may have influenced his decision.

Writing the book was, and always would be, a labor of love for Soros. He has never revealed whether he showed the manuscript to any publishers. All that he has said was that he found the book "wanting" and therefore it never saw print.

So Soros returned to moneymaking on Wall Street. The muse, however, did not desert him entirely. In ensuing years, he relied on what he had poured into that small, unpublished book for the main ideas that went into later books that did get published.

In 1963, Soros began working at Arnhold & S. Bleichroeder. One of the leading American houses trading in foreign securities, Arnhold was a natural home for Soros. With roots in Dresden, it was founded in the early nineteenth century. The man who hired Soros, Stephen Kellen, spoke with a thick European accent, as did other members of the firm. Though the street signs said Wall Street, Soros must some days have thought he'd tapped his heels and was back in Europe.

Kellen was high on Soros from the start. "I always hope anybody I hire will be good, but he was clearly outstanding."

Hired as an analyst, Soros worked at first primarily with foreign securities. With his network of contacts in Europe, and his ability to speak a number of European languages, including French and German, Soros was the natural person to venture into this realm.

Arbitrage required both knowledge and courage, but most American traders, insular and unwilling to expand their horizons, lacked both. Not George Soros. Americans preferred selling American stocks. At least with American firms it was possible to pronounce their names. That was not the case with European firms. Soros not only could pronounce the names of the firms, he knew the owners.

In 1967, he became director of the firm's research department.

Feeling his way on the American scene, trying to make his mark, Soros displayed a certain insecurity in dealing with colleagues. One of these, insisting upon anonymity, recalled a Soros habit of taking credit for trades that went well but passing off the blame to others for those that went poorly.

Edgar Astaire, Soros's London partner in 1994, knew him in the 1960s as a complicated, secretive fellow. "You saw that he was clever, able, a very clear thinker—and very confident. You sensed that he didn't seem to be a man of particular stature. He's a bit shy. You don't know what he's thinking. He's a good psychologist. He's quite perceptive. . . . He was shy so he adopted a low profile. He made sure that others didn't get to know what his personality was like. He often says contradictory things for effect. He pontificates a lot of nonsense. He sometimes just says things for himself. He's not loveable."

Not loveable, but shrewd in his analysis of investments. Arthur Lerner, who worked with Soros in the 1960s at Arnhold & S. Bleichroeder, remembered the Soros touch in those days. Having graduated from Columbia University, Lerner in 1964 joined the Bank of New York's research department. One industry that Lerner tracked was trucking. That happened to be Soros's beat at Arnhold, and occasionally Soros, a broker for the bank, would drop by to see Lerner and his boss, Mike Danko, to discuss what stocks to buy. Somehow, Lerner recalled, Soros always steered the conversation away from the narrow field of trucking toward "the worldwide situation." George was always talking about the big picture.

Doing well with foreign securities boosted Soros's self-confidence. He began thinking about starting his own investment fund—and trying to make money for other people.

Six

Fascinated by Chaos

From the time he was a student in London in the early 1950s, George Soros had been interested in the way the world functioned. It had been his hope not only to ponder the large questions of life but to make a sizable contribution to knowledge as well.

His mentor, Karl Popper, had inspired him to think big thoughts, to develop a grand philosophical scheme. Such a scheme might benefit humanity, and it might benefit the person who came up with the scheme. Soros came to believe, in the words of his longtime friend Byron Wien, that "the more you're able to define your efforts in an abstraction, the better you'll be in practicality."

In time, Soros's interest in abstractions would lead him to the more tangible question of how financial markets worked. But to understand his theory about financial markets, the best place to begin is his general theory of life and society. One word has been key to his thinking. *Perceptions.*

Many people have asked the same questions: What is life all about? Why am I here? How do things—the big things like the Universe, the Brain, Humankind—work?

Dwelling on these questions for a moment or two, people then get on with their lives, with the practical issues of raising families, making a living, remembering to take out the trash.

Philosophers, however, have made such questions their life study. And George Soros longed to be a philosopher.

No single event triggered Soros's interest in philosophy, yet it was there for as long as he could remember. "Ever since I became conscious of my existence," he wrote in the introduction to his 1987 book, *The Alchemy of Finance,* "I have had a passionate interest in understanding it, and I regarded my own understanding as the central problem that needed to be understood."

Here then was the spark.

And yet, as young Soros figured out almost from the very start, the task of unraveling the mysteries of life was nearly an impossible one.

For one simple reason: To even begin to study who we are or what we are, we need to look at ourselves objectively.

The trouble is that we cannot.

This was a dramatic revelation for George Soros:

"What one thinks is part of what one thinks about; therefore, one's thinking lacks an independent point of reference by which it can be judged—it lacks objectivity."

Soros wrote that in his introduction to *Alchemy,* a single sentence formed the core of his theoretical analysis. Unable to achieve this independent point of reference, people cannot, in effect, get out of their skins, cannot look at the world through undistorted prisms. In the early 1950s, Soros came to the conclusion "that basically *all our views of the world are somehow flawed or distorted.*" His focus became how this distortion shaped events.

Equipped with these general notions of how the world worked, it was time for Soros to take a look at Wall Street.

The trouble was that most people who had already tried to analyze the stock market had concluded that logic prevailed in the determination of stock prices. There *had* to be some logic. It was too disquieting, not to mention too risk laden, to think otherwise when dealing in the market.

> **"All our views of the world are somehow flawed or distorted."**

Adherents of this rational school of thinking argued that because investors could have perfect knowledge of a company, every share was valued at precisely the correct price. Armed with this knowledge, investors automatically behaved rationally when presented with an array of stock choices and picked the best one. And share prices remained rationally related to estimates of company's future earnings.

This was the efficient-market hypothesis, one of the most popular theories of how the stock market works. It assumed a perfect, rational world. It assumed also that all stock prices reflected available information.

But while classical economics taught the concept of equilibrium, and made assumptions as if perfect competition and perfect knowledge were attainable, Soros believed he knew better. In the real world, he maintained, any theory that assumed perfect knowledge was attainable was flawed. In the real world, the decision to buy or sell was based—not on the ideals of classical economics—but on expectations. And in the real world, people could attain only an imperfect understanding of anything.

"The major insight I bring to understanding things in general is the role that imperfect understanding plays in shaping events. Traditional economics is based on theories of equilibrium, where supply and demand are equal. But if you realize what an important role our imperfect understanding plays, you realize that what you are dealing with is disequilibrium."

And so, he noted on another occasion, he was "fascinated by chaos. That's really how I make my money: understanding the revolutionary process in financial markets."

Ever since he played the *Monopoly*-like game of *Capital* during those summers on Lupa Island, George Soros was ensnared by the world of money. Though a part of him wandered freely in the intellectual realm, his practical side impelled him to study economics at the London School of Economics.

To his disappointment, however, he found the subject wanting.

His professors pounded home to him that economics was—or at least tried to be—a science. One could formulate theories and develop laws that governed the world of economics.

But George Soros saw right through all of this. He reasoned that if economics were a science, it would have to be objective. That is, one would have to be able to observe its activities without affecting those activities. But this, Soros concluded, was impossible.

How could economics pretend to be objective when human beings—who were, after all, at the core of all economic action—lacked objectivity? When those same human beings, by virtue of their involvement in economic life, could not help but influence that economic life?

Those who assumed that economic life was rational and logical argued as well that financial markets were always "right." Right in the sense that market prices tended to discount—or take into account—future developments, even when those developments were unclear.

Not true, said Soros.

Most investors, he once explained, had come to believe that they could "discount" what the market would do in the future, that is, take future developments into account in advance of their occurring. To Soros this was impossible. To him, "any idea of what the future will be like is by definition going to be biased and partial. I don't mean that facts and beliefs exist autonomously. On the contrary, what I have argued in expounding the theory of reflexivity is that *what beliefs do is alter facts.*"

> "**N**ot only do market participants operate with a bias, but their bias can also influence the course of events."

In effect, then, market prices were not going to be right, because they always ignored the influences that could and would come from future developments.

Market prices were always going to be "wrong" because they offered not a rational view of the future but a biased one.

"But distortion works in both directions," contended Soros. "Not only do market participants operate with a bias, but their bias can also influence the course of events. This may create the impression that markets anticipate future developments accurately, but in fact it is not present expectations that correspond to future events but future events that are shaped by present expectations. The participants' perceptions are inherently flawed, and there is a two-way connection between flawed perceptions and the actual course of events, which results in a lack of correspondence between the two. I call this two-way connection *'reflexivity'.*"

The two-way feedback between perception and reality—what Soros called reflexivity—formed the key to his theory. Soros was

"**T**he bias of investors toward a stock, whether positive or negative, causes the price to rise or fall."

convinced that what explained the behavior of financial markets was not the efficient-market hypothesis, but a reflexive relationship that existed between the biases of investors and what he called the actual course of events, another phrase for the economic fundamentals of firms.

According to Soros, the *"bias"* of investors toward a stock, whether positive or negative, caused the price to rise or fall. That bias operated as a *"self-reinforcing factor,"* which then interacted with "underlying trends" to affect investor expectations. The resulting price movement might lead management to repurchase shares or enter upon a merger, acquisition, or buyout, which in turn influences the fundamentals of the stock.

The price of a stock, then, was not determined by incisive reaction to attainable information. Rather it was a result of perceptions that were as much the outcome of emotions as of hard data. As Soros wrote in *The Alchemy of Finance:* "When events have thinking participants, the subject matter is no longer confined to facts but also includes the participants' perceptions. The chain of causation does not lead directly from fact to fact but from fact to perception and from perception to fact."

Soros's theory embraced the notion that the prices investors paid were not simply passive reflections of value; rather, they were active ingredients in making a valuation of the stock's worth.

A second key to Soros's theory, then, was grasping the role played by misconceptions in shaping events. Misconceptions, or, as

he sometimes called them, divergences between a participant's thinking and the actual state of affairs, were always there.

Sometimes, the divergence was reasonably small and could correct itself. He called this situation *near-equilibrium.*

Sometimes, the divergence was large and not self-correcting.
This situation he termed *far-from-equilibrium.*

When the divergence was large, perception and reality were far
removed from one another. No mechanism existed to push them
closer together. Indeed, forces were at play tending to keep them far
apart.

These far-from-equilibrium situations took one of two forms. At one
extreme, even though perceptions and reality were far apart, the situation was stable. Stable situations were of no interest to Soros the investor. At the other extreme, however, the situation was unstable, and
events galloped ahead so quickly that the participants' views could not
keep up with them. This situation was of extreme interest to Soros.

The gap between perception and reality was wide because
events were running out of control, a situation found typically in
boom/bust sequences in the financial markets. Soros thought of these
sequences as manias, "processes which are initially self-reinforcing
but unsustainable and therefore eventually have to be reversed."

> "Boom/bust sequences are prone to develop because markets are always in a state of flux and uncertainty."

Always the poten-
tial existed for such
boom/bust sequences. Soros's investment philosophy held that
boom/bust sequences are prone to develop because markets are
always in a state of flux and uncertainty. The way to make money
was to look for ways to capitalize on that instability, to search for the
unexpected developments.

The hard part, of course, was identifying a boom/bust sequence.
To identify one, the investor had to understood how other investors
were perceiving the economic fundamentals. Determining what the
market—the sum total of these investors—thought at any given moment was critical, the essence of George Soros's investment technique.

Once an investor knew what the "market" was thinking, it became possible to jump the other way, to bet on the unexpected happening, to bet that a boom/bust cycle was about to happen or had already begun.

How did a boom/bust sequence take hold?

When he appeared before the House Committee on Banking, Finance and Urban Affairs on April 13, 1994, Soros provided a brief explanation, suggesting that he disagreed with the "prevailing wisdom." While most believed that financial markets tended toward equilibrium and discounted the future accurately, Soros assumed that "financial markets cannot possibly discount the future correctly because they do not merely discount the future: they help to shape it."

> **"Once you know what the market is thinking, jump the other way, bet on the unexpected."**

Sometimes, he said, financial markets might *affect* the fundamentals even though they are supposed only to *reflect* them. "When that happens, markets enter into a state of dynamic disequilibrium, and behave quite differently from what would be considered normal by the theory of efficient markets."

Such boom/bust sequences do not occur frequently. When they do, because they influence the economy's fundamentals, they are disruptive. A boom/bust sequence can happen only when a market is dominated by trend-following behavior. "By trend-following behavior, I mean people buying in response to a rise in prices and selling in response to a fall in prices in a self-reinforcing manner.

"Lopsided trend-following behavior is necessary to produce a violent market crash, but it is not sufficient to bring it about. The key question you need to ask then is, what generates trend-following behavior?"

George Soros's answer:

Flawed perceptions cause markets to feed on themselves.

Feeding on themselves was another way of saying that investors had gotten themselves into a blind frenzy, or a herdlike mentality.

And markets that feed on their own frenzy always overreact, always go to the extremes. That overreaction—pushing toward the extremes—causes a boom/bust sequence.

The key to investment success, therefore, was to recognize the point at which markets began to feed on their own momentum, for when that point was identified, the investor would then know that a boom/bust sequence was either about to begin or was already in progress.

> "Flawed perceptions cause markets to feed on themselves. Markets that feed on their own frenzy always overreact."

As Soros explained: "The reason reflexive processes follow a dialectic pattern can be explained in general terms: The greater the uncertainty, the more people are influenced by the market trends; and the greater the influence of trend-following speculation, the more uncertain the situation becomes."

The main stages of a typical boom/bust sequence were:

- An as yet unrecognized trend;
- The beginning of the self-reinforcing process;
- A successful testing of the market's direction;
- An increasing conviction;
- A divergence between reality and perception;
- The climax;
- Ultimately, the start of a mirror-image self-reinforcing sequence in the opposite direction.

Soros also argued that, as a trend continued, the significance of speculative transactions grew. Moreover, bias followed the trend so that the more the trend went on, the stronger the bias became. Finally, once a trend was fixed, it would eventually run its course.

Byron Wien, U.S. equity investment strategist for Morgan Stanley in New York and a close friend of Soros, explained Soros's theory in simpler language this way:

"His idea is that things do very well and then they do badly. You should know that while they're doing well they're about to do badly and, to oversimplify his theory, the important thing is to recognize the inevitability of a trend change. The key point is the identification of the inflection point."

Examples of reflexivity abounded. In a 1988 *Wall Street Journal* article, Soros observed: "When people lose confidence in a currency, its decline tends to reinforce domestic inflation, thereby validating the decline. When investors have confidence in a company's management, the rise in share price makes it easier for management to fulfill investors' expectations. . . . I call such initially self-reinforcing but eventually self-defeating connections 'reflexive.'"

Soros's most handsome profits came when he detected "self-reinforcing" moves in stocks and stock groups. Investors suddenly changed their attitude toward an industry and bought heavily. A self-reinforcing phenomenon set in as the surge in stock buying reinforced the industry group's fortunes because the companies in that group boosted earnings through more borrowing, stock sales, and stock-based acquisitions.

This was the boom part of the boom/bust sequence.

The game was over when market saturation and rising competition hurt the industry group's prospects and the stock became overvalued. Short sellers had a field day when this process unraveled. One example in the 1960s involved conglomerates. The high price of the conglomerates' stocks encouraged these conglomerates to buy even more companies. This policy pushed prices even higher until the stocks collapsed.

> **"Detect self-reinforcing moves in the stock market and you will reap great profits."**

The reflexive relationship was evident in the use of credit as well, according to Soros:

"Loans are based on the lender's estimation of the borrower's ability to serve his debt. The valuation of the collateral is supposed to be independent of the act of lending; but in actual fact the act of lending can affect the value of the collateral. This is true of the individual case and of the economy as a whole."

In yet another example of reflexivity, this one during the mid- to late 1980s, prices offered in takeover bids led to a revaluation of a company's assets. That made bankers willing to lend more to other bidders, which in turn led to still higher bids. Ultimately prices climbed way too high; the market, unstable and overvalued, kept moving up and up. According to Soros's theory of reflexivity, collapse became inevitable.

This, then, is George Soros, the unorthodox investor.

He did not play the financial markets according to traditional rules.

That was what the other fellows did. The guys who thought the world and all that the world contained was rational.

Including the stock market.

Soros was interested in the rules of the game but only in trying to understand when those rules were about to change. Because when they were about to change, they might cause a reflexive relationship to begin, and that reflexivity could set off a boom/bust sequence.

George Soros constantly monitored the financial markets, scanning for a boom/bust sequence. In knowing that financial markets were characterized on occasion by these reflexive relationships, Soros sensed that he had a leg up on the rest of the investment community.

Possessing this investment secret, however, did not guarantee that Soros could always earn profits. Sometimes there were problems that had nothing to do with his own investing talents. Sometimes they had everything to do with those talents.

There were times, for instance, when reflexive processes simply did not exist. Or those processes were there, but Soros could not discover them in time. Worst of all were the times when Soros searched for a reflexive process, thought he had discovered one, only to find that he had misidentified it.

On some occasions Soros staked an investment position without thinking through how a certain financial market was operating—that is, whether a reflexive process was at work or not. But he was always looking for reflexive processes. When he discovered one and was able to exploit it, he racked up a row of numbers to the left of the decimal point.

While acknowledging that it was not really a full-blown theory, Soros implied that his theory of reflexivity held out the promise of explaining more than how to make money in the financial markets.

More grandiosely, he contended that his theory of reflexivity could make more clear how the world works.

This was George Soros The Philosopher speaking, not George Soros The Investor.

"I believed that the participants' bias is the key to an understanding of all historical processes that have thinking participants, just as genetic mutation is the key to biological evolution."

Soros knew, though, that it was a fantasy to pin such high expectations on his theory. However much he wished it to be different, he sensed with mounting disappointment that he had not offered the world a monumental discovery.

The theory remained flawed. He could not define what he meant by the participants' imperfect understanding. Moreover, his theory was not helpful in making sound predictions.

Ultimately, Soros admitted in frustration that, while "valid and interesting," his notion of the causative relationship of a participant's bias fell short of being a true theory. It was too broad. To be helpful, the "theory" would have to make clear when boom/bust sequences were going to appear. But it did not.

Soros was nothing if not honest about the limitations of his theory. He had some large hopes for the theory, and when those hopes did not materialize, he could have remained silent. He did not. While he did not produce a general theory, he believed that what he had devised would be partially helpful. "What I have is an approach that can help to illuminate the present precarious state of our financial system."

Reaction to Soros's theory of reflexivity varied—from those who found it too complex and difficult to understand to others who understood it and were impressed. Among the perplexed were those who had worked closely with Soros over the years. One was Robert Miller, a senior vice president at Arnhold & S. Bleichroeder who has worked with Soros since the 1960s.

The author's attempt to learn what Miller knew of Soros's theory proved frustrating.

Author: "Did you talk to him about that theory?"
Miller: "Not much."

Author: "Have you read *The Alchemy of Finance?*"

Miller: "I've read portions of it."

Author: "Can you talk about what the theory does for some-body?"

Miller: (breaking into laughter) "Probably not."

Others felt more confident discussing the theory.

William Dodge, a senior vice president for equity research and chief investment strategist at Dean Witter Reynolds in New York, admitted that he has not read *The Alchemy of Finance* but believed that Soros's theory of reflexivity made absolute sense.

"What George is pointing to is that stock prices depart from real value a lot. That creates the opportunity to make money."

In May 1994, seven years after *The Alchemy of Finance* was published. Soros was a far more widely recognized figure in the business community than ever before. As a result, a paperback version of the book appeared for the first time with a new preface. In that preface, Soros wrote that he wanted to make one new point about his theory of reflexivity to clarify what he had originally meant.

"In *The Alchemy of Finance,*" he wrote, "I put forward the theory of reflexivity as if it were relevant at all times. That is true in the sense that the two-way feedback mechanism that is the hallmark of reflexivity can come into play at any time, but it is not true in the sense that it is at play at all times. In fact, in most situations it is so feeble that it can be safely ignored."

Soros clarified a second point as well:

"The message of my book is usually summed up by saying that the participants' value judgments are always biased and the prevailing bias affects market prices." If that was all he had to write, it was not worth a whole book, he suggested. "My point is that there are occasions when the bias affects not only market prices but also the so-called fundamentals. This is when reflexivity becomes important. It does not happen all the time but when it does, market prices follow a different pattern. They also play a different role; they do not merely reflect the so-called fundamentals; they themselves become one of the fundamentals which shape the evolution of prices."

Soros faulted those who read the book in part or in whole for catching the first point—that the prevailing bias affects market prices—but missing the second—that the prevailing bias can under certain circumstances also affect the so-called fundamentals and that changes in market prices lead to changes in market prices.

He blamed himself.

What he should have done, he acknowledged, was, not to present a general theory in which the absence of reflexivity was a special case, but to suggest that reflexivity was a special case, since the key feature of reflexivity was that it occurred only sometimes.

His main excuse was that he had observed reflexivity, not in financial markets first, but prior to that as a philosophical concept. In suggesting that he had come up with a general theory of reflexivity, he acknowledged that he may have overstepped himself. It followed, he wrote, that he had erred as well in suggesting that economic theory was false. If the conditions for reflexivity occurred only intermittently, then it had to be true that economic theory was only occasionally false.

Of what value is George Soros's theory of reflexivity? This question would be much easier to answer if Soros did not cloud the issue by acknowledging that sometimes he does not adhere to his theory, that sometimes he reacts to events in the financial markets in the same way that an animal in the jungle reacts to the surroundings. He does not spell out what he means by such a statement. On other occasions, however, he adduces that bad things are about to happen in the financial markets because of the onset of . . . a backache! The backache, however, serves only the limited purpose as an early-warning system. It does not help to identify what is about to befall the markets. Once Soros identifies impending trouble, though, it is as if he had taken an aspirin.

Suddenly, his backache clears up!

Seven

Invest First and Investigate Later

George Soros's theories reveal only a part of his investment secrets, the framework that explains how he believes financial markets operate. Soros admitted as much.

The theory does not, however, reveal how George Soros operated.

Those secrets Soros kept close to his vest.

Intellectual analysis got him only so far. After that, instinct had to take over.

"We pretend [at being analytical]," observed Soros. "I can even believe it. But there is something else there also. I have a reasonably good record as a trader but I also have the theory. So there is some connection. But I don't think my success as a trader validates my theory. It is not a scientific proof. I think there must be something else."

Because Soros's theories do not provide *all* of the clues to his achievements, one might be tempted to argue that he had just been plain lucky. But few serious analysts put much credence in this explanation. I inadvertently suggested to one of Soros's most veteran associates, Robert Miller, a senior vice president at Arnhold & S. Bleichroeder, that Soros's ability to make money might be a function of his willingness to gamble large amounts. Miller responded testily:

"No. It's not his ability to gamble such large amounts. If he thinks that a situation is right, he'll make an investment of it because he's not really looking at it as gambling. He's looking at it as an economic scenario."

It was more complicated than just rolling the dice and hoping for snake eyes.

How Soros operated is a function of his abilities, the combination of which might be unique.

First, there was his *brainpower.*

While others in the market were struggling to keep up with one stock, one industry group, one commodity, Soros was absorbed at any given time in complex scenarios related to global trading.

Unlike most others, he discerned trends and movements and rhythms growing out of the public statements of world financial leaders and the decisions these leaders made. What Soros understood better than most were the cause-and-effect relationships in the world's economies. If A happened, then B must follow, and C after that. This kind of thinking was nothing to be scoffed at. Indeed, it was one of the key secrets of Soros's success.

Then, the man had *guts*.

How else to explain the dispassionate manner in which he bought and sold amounts that defied the imagination. He himself would deny that he possessed much courage, for he would assert that the key to investing is to know how to survive. And knowing how to survive meant at times playing the game conservatively, cutting losses when necessary, always keeping a large portion of assets out of play. He liked to say: "If you're doing poorly, the first move is to retrench. Don't try to recoup. And when you start again, start small."

Still, what Soros was doing required inner fortitude.

"I sat in his office when he made decisions about hundreds of millions of dollars," observed Daniel Doron, a public affairs commentator and director of the Jerusalem-based Israel Center for Social and Economic Progress. "I would shake in my boots, I wouldn't sleep. He was playing with such high stakes. You had to have nerves of steel for that. Maybe he was conditioned for that."

Soros has often been compared to Warren Buffett, another superb Wall Street investor, but often the comparison was made to show the striking differences between the two men.

While Buffett specialized in one thing and one thing only—buying solid companies at low prices—Soros was more flexible, moving in and out of financial markets according to the shifting financial winds, trying to catch swings in the markets at just the right time. Buffett purchased and sold stocks; Soros dealt with currencies and interest rates. Buffett focused on individual firms; Soros followed broad trends in the global financial markets.

One of Soros's most useful qualities has been his ability to detach his emotions from his dealings in the financial markets.

In that sense, he is something of a *stoic*.

While others permitted their egos to get in the way of making intelligent market decisions, Soros understood that the wise investor was the dispassionate investor. It made no sense to claim infallibility. Although it may have been difficult when a favorite stock suddenly took a plunge, it was far better, as Soros constantly did, to admit when he made mistakes.

One day in 1974, Soros was playing tennis with an acquaintance. The phone rang.

It was a broker in Tokyo, letting Soros in on a secret: That year President Richard Nixon was immersed in the Watergate scandal that would eventually cause his downfall. The broker was calling to let Soros know that the Japanese were reacting poorly to Nixon's troubles.

Having taken heavy positions in the Japanese stock market, Soros had to decide what to do—stay in, get out.

His tennis partner noticed that sweat had formed on Soros's forehead that had not been there during the match.

Then and there Soros decided to sell. There was no hesitation, no feeling that he needed to consult anyone else before taking such a large step.

It had taken him a fraction of a second to decide.

That was all.

Allan Raphael, who worked with Soros in the 1980s, believed that Soros's stoicism, a rare trait among investors, had served him well. "You can count them on one hand. When George is wrong, he gets the hell out. He doesn't say, 'I'm right, they're wrong.' He says, 'I'm wrong,' and he gets out, because if you have a bad position on, it eats you away. All you do is think about it—at night, at your home. It consumes you. Your eye is off the ball completely. This is a tough business. If it were easy, metermaids would be doing it. It takes an inordinate amount of discipline, self-confidence, and basically lack of emotion."

Then there was the vaunted Soros *self-confidence*.

When Soros believed he was right about an investment, nothing could stop him. No investment position was too large. Holding back was for wimps. The worst error in Soros's book was not being too bold, but too conservative. "Why so little?" was one of his favorite questions.

Finally, there was his *instinct*.

This was the immeasurable ability to know when to speculate heavily, when to pull out of an investment position—when, in effect, you were on the mark, and when you were not.

"Basically," said Soros, "the way I operate is *I have a thesis* and I test it in the market. When I'm short and the market acts a certain way, I get very nervous. I get a backache and then I cover my short and suddenly the backache goes away. I feel better. There's where the instinct comes in."

Summing up George Soros's investment skills, Morgan Stanley's Byron Wien suggested that "George's genius is that he has a certain discipline. He views the market very practically and he understands the forces that influence stock prices. He understands there is a rational and irrational side of markets. And he understands that he isn't right all the time. He is willing to take vigorous action when he is right and really take advantage of an opportunity, and to cut his losses when he's wrong. . . . He has great conviction when he's sure that he's right as he was in the sterling crisis in 1992."

> "Develop a thesis, and test it in the market."

Part of Soros's instinct was in detecting movement, one way or the other, in the stock market. This was not something one could learn in school; it was not part of the curriculum at the London School of Economics. This gift is one that few possess. And Soros had it. Edgar Astaire, his London partner, had no trouble pointing out the source of Soros's success:

"His greatest key to success is his psychology. He understands the herd instinct. He understands when lots of people are going to go for something, like a good marketing man."

Perhaps Soros's most distinctive feature, the trait that explained his investment talents best, was his ability to gain membership in a very exclusive "club," a club that included the leadership of the international financial community.

No one could apply for membership in this club. Most of the participants were the political and economic leaders in rich countries: prime ministers, finance ministers, heads of central banks. Rough estimates put the total membership at no more than 2,000 people, scattered all over the world.

Because he was not an elected leader, Soros did not have the same status as other members. But as economic power shifted away from politicians and as investors like Soros gained more and more clout in the financial markets, Soros carried increasing weight with these leaders. They wanted to get to know him, to hear what his thoughts were about the world economy. Most of all, they wanted to know what he might be up to. He, of course, had the same interest in knowing what decisions the leaders of various countries were about to make.

Few investors have been able to acquire access to this club in the way Soros has. While others were reading about these leaders, Soros had the advantage of easy access to them; he could enjoy a breakfast with a finance minister, a lunch with a central banker, or pay a courtesy call on a prime minister.

One day in the early 1980s, for example, Soros showed up at the Bank of England, invited there to share his views on reviving the financial markets through monetary restraints. He had attracted the bankers' interest after purchasing $1 billion worth of British bonds in 1980, a great moment for him, for the investment had paid off handsomely.

It was not only his financial acumen that brought Soros into the web of global financial leaders. Since the mid-1980s, when he began in earnest to establish foundations in Eastern Europe and, later, the former Soviet Union, as a means of encouraging open societies, Soros had even more reason to rub elbows with political and economic leaders, particularly in Europe.

It was not unusual for a cabinet minister to attend one of his foundation's conferences nor for him to drop in on a political leader while attending one of his foundation's board meetings. Taking writer Michael Lewis on a two-week visit to his foundations in November 1993, Soros boasted, after meeting with the president of Moldova in the morning and the president of Bulgaria in the evening, "You see, I have one president for breakfast and another for dinner."

Such encounters clearly gave Soros an advantage over other investors. Of course, breakfasting with government officials did not enable Soros to learn the precise day that a country would devalue its currency or raise its interest rates. Financial leaders were not about to make such revelations over eggs and toast, even to a George Soros— or more accurately, especially to a George Soros.

But that proximity to the leaders gave Soros a fingertip feel for events that others could not and did not possess. He might have to wait months before getting something useful from a meeting; perhaps it was an offhand remark a finance minister said at a lunch three months earlier. The point was that he had met with the finance minister and had deposited the conversation in his memory bank for further use while others had been reading the newspapers.

As George Magnus, Chief International Economist at S. G. Warburg Securities in London, noted: "Soros does have an understanding of world events and world processes. His European background makes him stand out against his contemporaries. It has given him a different perspective of how the world fits together, particularly the unification of Germany, and all sorts of other European concepts. . . . He has what the Germans call *weltanschauung,* a worldview, not tainted too much by the intricacies of domestic issues in one country or another. [What he does is] big-picture building and he translates that into opportunities."

> "A key Soros secret is gaining access to world leaders."

Having that worldview gave Soros enormous self-confidence.

"He wasn't a person who gloated over his successes," remarked James Marquez, a Soros associate from the 1980s, "except to say, 'Well, my dear boy, this *is* the way this thing should have happened.'

"You could hear him use such phrases as, 'It's quite clear,' or 'It's obvious what was going to happen,' or 'The factors that led to this were very simple and straightforward.' He could see the forest very well; others only saw the trees."

It was not merely that other investors lacked the calling card that admitted them to that exclusive club of world leaders. Even had they possessed one, few other investors would have wished to spend as much time with world leaders as did Soros.

Other investors were more accustomed to the frenzied pace of the dealing room. Most would have thought it a distraction, perhaps even a waste of time, to hang around with such people. But Soros operated on a different wave length: He could understand the need to be around the dealing room, but he also saw value in getting away from the office, not only to meet key decision makers, but also to have time to think. As Soros has suggested: "To be successful, you need leisure. You need time hanging heavily on your hands."

Soros's friend Byron Wien sensed this "laid-back" approach to life and to finances.

> "To succeed, let time hang heavily on your hands."

"He feels," said Wien, "that he should not be dependent upon other people. Some people spend all day talking to brokers. He doesn't feel that's the way to spend your time. Instead, he prefers to talk to a few people who can really be helpful and to think and read and reflect. He looks for somebody who has a kind of philosophical sensitivity. He's not interested solely in people who have made a lot of money . . . without any soul. He doesn't feel he has to do that in the office.

"He once said something to me that was very useful: 'The trouble with you, Byron, is that you go to work every day and you think that because you go to work every day you should do something. I don't go to work every day. I only go to work on the days that make sense to go to work. . . . And I really do something on that day. But you go to work and you do something every day and you don't realize when it's a special day.'"

How does George Soros spend his days?

A typical day begins at 8 or 8:30 AM. He is in and out of meetings all day, but his fund managers are free to go in and talk about a position at any time.

Soros operates on a one-to-one basis. He talks to his fund managers individually. He abhors committee meetings. Sometimes, after hearing the thoughts of one of his managers, Soros might suggest that he or she phone someone who could support the other side of an argument, according to Allan Raphael, who worked with him from 1984 to 1988. "If you liked something, he wanted you to talk to someone who didn't like it. He always wanted an intellectual rub there. He always rethinks a position. You always have to rethink it and rethink it and rethink it. Things change. The prices change. Conditions change. It was up to you as a fund manager to constantly rethink your position."

Then there would be dialogue.

Raphael might say to him: "This position is working out."

Soros: "Do you think you should be selling some here?"

Raphael: "No."

Soros: "You want to buy some more?"

Back and forth. Reviewing the positions.

"Soros," said Raphael, "has an incredible ability to ask the right questions. Then he'll look at the charts and he'll say OK."

When the time was ripe for a decision, it would never take him more than 15 minutes of study.

Fund managers like Raphael had some flexibility—not everything had to go through Soros. Small positions of say, five million dollars, could be built without a Soros OK.

"But," noted Raphael, "it was really to your benefit to talk to him about it because he was smart."

To Soros, the key to his investment success has been his skill at surviving. It might be hard to think of survival as a practical skill, but to Soros, it helped explain his accomplishments. For example, in *The Alchemy of Finance* he wrote: "When I was an adolescent, the Second World War gave me a lesson that I have never forgotten. I was fortunate enough to have a father who was highly skilled in the art of survival, having lived through the Russian Revolution as an escaped prisoner of war."

Later in the same book, he suggested that operating a hedge fund tested his training in survival to the maximum: "Using leverage can produce superior results when the going is good, but it can wipe you out when events fail to conform to your expectations. One of the hardest things to judge is what level of risk is safe. There are no universally valid yardsticks: Each situation needs to be judged on its own merit. In the final analysis, you must rely on your instincts for survival."

One illustration of this survival instinct in action occurred at the time of the October 1987 stock market crash. In hindsight, it appeared that Soros got out of some investment positions too early. But to James Marquez, that was classic George Soros—giving up the battle so that he could live to fight another day. While he absorbed heavy losses by getting out when he did, Soros was able to prevent even worse erosions in his positions. "It's hard for a lot of people to accept that kind of an outcome," suggested Marquez. "And yet Soros is able to do it because he does have enough confidence that he will be able to come back. And of course he did, and his greatest success came post-1987. I guess there's a message in that for all of us."

And so Soros has had that combination of traits—brainpower, guts, stoicism, and instinct—that took him very far. His theory of reflexivity was his Geiger counter. It did not tell him what to aim it at precisely, or most importantly when, but the theory told him where to point his gun and provided him with a way of homing in on a potential opportunity.

Then the traits took over, instructing him with greater precision, guiding him to the spot.

Soros then made his move. He would do it, not in a grandiose way, but by testing, probing, trying to determine whether what he thought was right was, in fact, correct. He would put together a hypothesis, and on the basis of that, he would take an investment position. Then he waited to see whether the hypothesis would be validated. If it was, he took an even larger position, his degree of self-confidence determining just how big a position to take. If the hypothesis happened to be invalidated, he did not delay. He got out of his investment. He was always looking for a situation in which he could develop a hypothesis.

As Marquez recalled: "George always used to say, *'Invest first and investigate later.'* That meant, form a hypothesis, take a toehold position to test the hypothesis, and wait for the market to prove you right or wrong."

In essence, this favorite Soros strategy could be called "getting a feel" of the market. Soros used the technique only occasionally, and at times he didn't even tell Marquez when the two worked together in the 1980s.

After much discussion, the two men would finally decide to take a plunge.

Marquez would then design a staged effect, setting aside a certain amount of the fund for the position.

"All right," Soros would say, "I want to buy $300 million of bonds, so start by selling $50 million."

"I want to *buy* $300 million," Marquez would remind Soros.

> "**I**nvest first, and investigate later."

"Yes," Soros would reply, "but I want to see what the market feels like first. I want to see how I feel as a seller. If it comes very easily to me as a seller, if I can lose these bonds very easily, then I even want to be more of a buyer. But if those bonds are real hard to sell, I'm not sure I should be a buyer."

All of Soros's theories and strategies were not infallible. Some indeed believed they were. They looked at his investment record and figured that anyone that good was immune from making mistakes.

Soros was amused by such thinking: "People are basically misguided in their view of my infallibility, because-and I don't mind [stressing] this—if anything, I make as many mistakes as the next guy. But where I do think that I excel is in recognizing my mistakes, you see. And that is the secret to my success. The key insight that I have reached is recognition of the inherent fallibility of human thought."

Eight

Putting My Money Where My Mouth Was

I n the late 1960s, George Soros entered the big leagues of finance. Seeking more of a leadership role within the firm, Soros managed to persuade his bosses at Arnhold & S. Bleichroeder to set up a pair of offshore funds and to let him oversee them.

The first, called the First Eagle Fund, started in 1967. It was known in Wall Street jargon as a long fund: Clients took investment positions, hoping for bullish markets.

The second, a hedge fund, was the Double Eagle Fund, begun in 1969. The fund was structured in such a way that Soros could use stocks and bonds as collateral in order to buy any number of financial instruments, including stocks, bonds, and currencies. He started the fund with his own money, a mere $250,000; soon $6 million poured in from a number of wealthy Europeans whom Soros knew.

$250,000.

That was the beginning of the Soros fortune.

Byron Wien met Soros for the first time in 1968, when Wien was a portfolio manager with a Wall Street firm that was a client of Arnhold & S. Bleichroeder. Wien's firm was intrigued with Japan; its stock market seemed undervalued, yet no one had a real handle on the Japanese economy. Wien had heard about someone named George Soros, said to be knowledgeable about Japan. Wien invited him over for a chat and listened in awe.

In the early days, this was Soros's great calling card. He seemed to know so much more about far-flung economies than did others in the big American firms.

What especially struck Wien was Soros's pioneering maneuver in establishing an offshore hedge fund that excluded American clients—

except for Soros, of course, who was permitted by the fund's rules to be a member, even though he was an American citizen. Soros, as he would be so often, was on the cutting edge of the profession, for in the late 1960s, American hedge funds with offshore funds as part of their portfolios were still novel. Soros was never afraid to rush in where others feared to tread.

While many wealthy Americans would have been all too pleased to join the Double Eagle Fund, Soros did not need them. He knew that he would be able to attract high-flying European clients despite their reputation for being fickle, for the fund's significant tax advantages were bound to enhance their loyalty. He was right; he lured an international clientele that included wealthy Europeans, Arabs, and South Americans. He operated the fund from his New York headquarters. But like many offshore funds, Double Eagle was based in Curaçao in the Dutch Antilles, where it escaped both SEC scrutiny and capital gains taxes.

Hedge funds. In the late 1960s they were little known, less understood. In 1957, Warren Buffett had started his own high-flying hedge fund. But when Soros set out in 1969, few knew what such funds did. That would of course change by the 1990s.

And George Soros would become head of the greatest hedge fund of them all.

Soros was among the first in the hedge fund field, where the profits are potentially sky-high. He was also the first to use the controversial financial instrument called derivatives, closely associated with the hedge fund crowd.

Hedge funds were created by Alexander Winslow Jones, a former journalist and academic, in 1949. Noting that some parts of an economy did well while others parts did poorly, Jones devised a scale of investing. A very bullish investor might go long with 80 percent of his positions, and short the other 20 percent. A very bearish investor might go short 75 percent of his positions, and go long the other 25 percent. The important thing was to vary one's risk.

The first hedge funds invested only in stocks, buying and selling similar securities, hoping for an overall gain. In time, the surviving hedge funds looked around and found investing opportunities elsewhere.

In the mid-1960s, some hedge funds attracted media attention, but interest slackened after 1970. It picked up again with the 1971 decision to allow exchange rates to float, but many hedge funds folded in the bear market of 1973–1974. For the next decade, hedge funds experienced a lull.

What spurred the growth of the hedge funds in the late 1980s and early 1990s—and the rise of George Soros to world-class investor status—was a decision European banks made in 1985 to lower the exchange rate of the dollar in order to increase American exports. (Lowering the dollar made U.S. exports cheaper.) The depressed dollar offered new incentives to trade in currencies. Soros and the other hedge fund managers quickly took advantage.

Had Soros hung around Europe, he might have remained just another sharp-eyed, shrewd financier, no standout, no special expert, just one of many fighting to make some money in the financial markets. But in the United States, Soros was a rare breed whose knowledge of the European financial scene would serve him well. His great advantage was his wide variety of sources in Europe and elsewhere, sources he used to get an appreciation of the big picture, of how financial and political events were impacting on the various financial markets around the world.

"George," explained Arthur Lerner, who worked with Soros in the late 1960s, "was one of the early ones who could figure out that you had to be global in your thinking rather than just being parochial. . . . You had to know how an event here would affect an event there. Currencies weren't then as important. What he took was basic information from various sources and kind of mulched it in his mind. Then he would come up with a thesis that most of the time was valid."

Lerner, an analyst at the Bank of New York, had been courted by Arnhold & S. Bleichroeder in 1967 and 1968, but had refused the first two overtures. Now, early in 1969, he finally said yes. His first job at Arnhold was as Soros's assistant, helping him run the two funds. Over the next two years they worked side by side.

Working for Soros was intense, yet intriguing. The markets fluctuated wildly in those two years, adding to the tension and drama. "George was a taskmaster," remembered Lerner. "He made you focus in. He had a command of the world that was amazing to me. He could almost take an event at point A and simultaneously take you to the consequences at point B. The logic escaped me because I wasn't at his level. He is probably the best macro investor I've ever seen. When it came to the micro, the small points, he was not as focused in or as good a he could have been."

There was something else about Soros. He seemed different from most of the others at the firm, different in fact from most of the others on Wall Street. It was his mind. He was thinking all the time, thinking big thoughts, using five-dollar words that most of the other fellows in the office could understand only if they ran to their dictionaries. Even Lerner had to make some adjustments. Among them: his writing style. "What I didn't anticipate was how much of a stickler George was for writing. He had a certain style which wasn't my style. I had been used to writing reports for general consumption. George's writing style was very literary."

So George Soros stood out. He was the office intellectual. Impressive to have around, but who could understand him?

It was around this time that Soros began writing *The Alchemy of Finance*. In 1969, he asked Lerner to read five chapters of the book. "I didn't understand a word," Lerner explained, suggesting that the problem was not with his own IQ but with Soros's ability to explain what he wanted to say. Hoping to find a brief synopsis of the theory, Lerner winced when he could not find one in the chapters.

The very word *reflexivity* bothered him. He went to the dictionary to look up it. Twenty-five years later—in the spring of 1994—Lerner acknowledged: "I still to this day have a problem with that word. I couldn't grasp what he was trying to bring across."

Feeling close to Soros, Lerner offered Soros some friendly advice. "George, don't ever be a teacher because if you want to teach someone beneath you—which most of your people would be. . . ."

He didn't finish the thought. Instead he said candidly: "You have a hard time communicating exactly what you mean."

It would have made sense for Soros to listen to what the Arthur Lerners in his life had to say to him. They weren't as brilliant as he was, but they were the ones who inevitably he wanted to impress. And if he wanted to impress them, he would have to make his written thoughts more clear. That was what Arthur Lerner was trying to tell him. It was a candid, but well-intentioned message. Get an editor, George. Get somebody who can help you get these thoughts into simple English.

It wasn't what George Soros wanted to hear. And, for that reason, most people who were asked to comment on Soros's writings made no attempt to say those things. They knew better. He wasn't about to listen to them. Why bother? Why make the man angry?

Whether or not someone like Arthur Lerner could fathom what reflexivity was all about, George Soros had decided that it was time to test his theories in the marketplace. He felt confident they would be able to give him a competitive advantage.

"I was putting my money where my mouth was and I could not afford to dissociate myself from my investment decisions. I had to use all my intellectual resources and I discovered, to my great surprise and gratification, that my abstract ideas came in very handy. It would be an exaggeration to say that they accounted for my success; but there can be no doubt that they gave me an edge."

The first industry Soros watched closely for the Double Eagle Fund was real estate investment trusts.

In 1969, Soros established a solid reputation by pointing out, in a widely circulated memo, the advantages of investing in a new vehicle called the real estate investment trust (or REIT). Sensing a boom/bust sequence, he likened the REITs' cycle to a three-act play, predicting correctly that REITs would experience a boom, but then go too far, and eventually collapse. Showing great prescience, he concluded that "since Act III was at least three years away, I could safely buy the shares." He was right, and he earned a handsome profit. When, as he had forecast, the REITs became overblown in 1974, Soros went short, making another $1 million. This early exercise in testing his marketplace theories encouraged Soros immensely.

He applied his theory as well to the conglomerate boom of the late 1960s and made money, he acknowledged, "both on the way up and on the way down." Initially, he saw that high-tech companies were going on acquisition sprees, inflating their earnings and impressing institutional investors. Soros believed that the "bias" of these "go-go fund managers" would feed conglomerate stock prices. He bought heavily. Later, he sold short and profited nicely when the decline ensued.

In 1970, Soros teamed up with Jimmy Rogers, a Yale graduate, class of 1964, who had been raised in Demapolis, Alabama.

Soros and Rogers. What an investment team they would become. One of the best ever on Wall Street.

Rogers had studied PPE—politics, philosophy, and economics— at Oxford University in England, and that had made an impression on Soros the Anglophile and would-be philosopher. During his two years in the army, Rogers acquired a reputation as a specialist in discovering good stocks. He even took charge of his commanding officer's stock portfolio.

Rogers's first job on Wall Street was with Bache & Co. In 1968, with only $600, Rogers began trading in the stock market. Two years later, he began working for Soros at Arnhold & S. Bleichroeder. Then, however, new brokerage firm regulations came into force, which did not permit Soros or Rogers to get a percentage of the profits from their company's stock trades. Arnhold & S. Bleichroeder did not want the two men to leave. But Soros and Rogers had the itch to become independent money managers. They departed and set up their own firm.

In 1973, they established Soros Fund Management (SFM), housed in rather spartan three-room offices that overlooked Central Park in New York.

Far from Wall Street.

What an odd idea in those days. Why would anyone interested in investing locate himself so far from the hub of power?

Jimmy Rogers liked to explain that since he and George Soros did not fall in line with typical Wall Street thinking, there seemed no good reason to be located within the Wall Street precincts. More important to Soros, the office was just a block from his fashionable cooperative on Central Park West.

The work style at SFM was far more relaxed than the usual hectic pace at Wall Street firms. During the summers, employees wore tennis shoes to work, and several, including Rogers himself, rode bicycles to work. Soros and Rogers liked the informal atmosphere around the office. They hoped to be able to keep it like that. No matter how much money they made. Still, everyone put in 80 hours a week on the job.

At the start it was just the two of them, Soros the trader, Rogers the researcher. Well, three—a secretary.

The office seemed small. Yet there was much the two of them could do. It turns out that there was virtue in their small size. They could concentrate on the task at hand and not worry about tripping over bodies, about having to deal with lots of paperwork, about handling the myriad chores that erupt when offices get large.

Yet, they mastered the trade. They kept the fund's capital in stocks. To bet on commodities and currencies, Soros and Rogers used futures or borrowed money. Unprecedented in its scope, the

Soros Fund traded in all of the various markets, including currencies, commodities, bonds, and stocks. From their start in 1970 until they finally parted ways in 1980, Soros and Rogers never had a losing year. Others on Wall Street talked about them with growing respect. They seemed to know much more than anyone else about where the economy was moving.

In 1971, the Fund was worth $12.5 million, a year later, $20.1 million. From December 31, 1969, until December 31, 1980, the Soros Fund gained 3,365 percent. Compare that with the Standard & Poor's composite index, which advanced in that same period only 47 percent.

By the end of 1980, the fund was worth $381 million.

Because it was a private partnership, the fund had a few advantages over other, more conventional, funds. Most important, it could sell short, an exercise that carried too much risk for some investors.

Selling short.

It sounded like a harmless enough technique. But to some, it had the ring of being unpatriotic.

They all but said: How can someone bet that a company is going to do poorly? What kind of American are you, anyway? Don't you have faith in your own economy? What kind of person are you, trying to exploit someone else's bad fortunes?

Soros didn't care. For him, the technique worked like a charm, yielding large gains in American and overseas markets. The fund also leveraged itself through the purchase of stock on margin. One dividend for the Soros Fund was its small size; freed of burdensome bureaucracies, it could move in and out of a stock position far more easily than large firms.

Soros and Rogers meshed well together. "Usually, if we disagreed," Rogers explained, "we just did nothing." Not always, however. If one felt strongly about a trade, he got his way. "Once we worked things through," said Rogers, "it was pretty clear that the trade was either right or wrong. When we thought something through, a consensus was formed. I hate to use that word, because consensus investing is a disaster, but we almost always seemed to come together."

They prided themselves on being independent-minded.

That was going to be their downfall—eventually. They were so independent-minded that they would in turn find too many things wrong with each other.

But for the time being, they functioned like a well-oiled machine. Neither thought he could learn much from other Wall Street analysts, the ones who, according to Rogers, simply followed the herd. They selected their own stocks.

And they read. Everyone read. They subscribed to 30 trade publications, including *Fertilizer Solutions* and *Textile Week*. They perused general-interest magazines, looking for social or cultural trends that might prove valuable. Hundreds of companies had SFM on their mailing lists. The fund's files included financial records of over 1,500 American and foreign firms. Each day Rogers pored through 20 or 30 annual reports, hoping to find some interesting corporate development or the glimmering of a long-range trend—something that others couldn't quite see.

> "Look for a sudden change in the stock market, a change not yet identified by anyone else."

The "something" they searched so assiduously for was a sudden change.

Soros was on the lookout for sudden changes in a stock group, changes that no one else had yet identified in order to test his theory. As Rogers put it, "We aren't as much interested in what a company is going to earn next quarter, or what 1975 aluminum shipments are going to be, as we are in how broad social, economic, and political factors will alter the destiny of an industry or stock group for some time to come. If there is a wide difference between what we see and the market price of a stock, all the better, because then we can make money."

One example, in the early 1970s, was the "sudden change" Soros found in the banking industry.

In 1972, Soros sensed that change was about to occur in that sphere. Banks had the worst of reputations then. Their employees were considered stodgy and dull, and few believed that the banks would rouse themselves from their deep slumber. Understandably, investors showed no interest in their shares.

Soros, however, had done his homework and found that a whole new generation of bankers, fresh from the top business schools and ready to act aggressively on behalf of their employers, was taking over, quietly but decisively. These new bank managers were focusing on the bottom line—and that was bound to help the prospects of bank stocks. The managers were using new financial instruments, and the banks' earnings performances were looking up. Bank stocks, however, sold at virtually no premium. Many of these banks had reached the limit of their leveraging capabilities. To continue to grow, they needed more equity capital.

In 1972, the First National City Bank hosted a dinner for security analysts in an unprecedented display of aggressiveness. To his obvious chagrin, George Soros did not receive an invitation. But the dinner spurred him into action. He wrote a brokerage report and called it "The Case for Growth Banks," arguing that while bank shares had been going nowhere, they were about to take off—contrary to what others thought. Timing the publication of the report to coincide with the bank's dinner, Soros laid out his arguments for getting behind the bank stocks. He recommended some of the better-managed banks. In time, bank stocks began to rise, and Soros garnered a 50 percent profit.

The bank turnaround marked the beginning of the great lending boom of the 1970s, a boom that fueled the expansion and amalgamation of corporate America in the 1980s. In accordance with his theory of reflexivity, Soros had identified the start of a boom in a boom/bust cycle.

Searching as well for foreign economies about to take a giant leap forward, Soros sought to capitalize on foreign stock markets. Which countries were opening their markets to foreign investment, which were promoting new policies for economic stabilization, which were committed to market reform?

Soros hoped to reap an advantage for himself by getting in at the wholesale level. "Like any good investor," said one former associate, "he was trying to buy a quarter for a nickel." If there were immature markets, like those in France, Italy, and Japan, Soros took a bead on them. He hoped to invest 6 to 18 months before other investors.

Accordingly, he purchased Japanese, Canadian, Dutch, and French securities. During one period of 1971, one quarter of Soros Fund assets were invested in Japanese stocks, a gamble that paid off when the fund doubled its money.

Soros and Rogers made shrewd stock selections. On one occasion in 1972, an acquaintance informed Soros that a private Commerce Department report described the growing American dependence on foreign fuel sources. Accordingly, the Soros Fund purchased large amounts of stock in oil-drilling, oil-field equipment, and coal companies. A year later, in 1973, came the Arab oil boycott, which caused energy stocks to soar.

In 1972, Soros and Rogers also foresaw the food crisis, and after purchasing stock in fertilizer, farm equipment, and grain-processing companies, earned impressive profits.

And the beat went on. Around this time, Soros and Rogers craftily identified the American defense industry as a potentially profitable source of investment.

In October 1973, Israel was caught by surprise when Egyptian and Syrian armed forces launched major attacks against the Jewish state. In the opening days of that war, Israel was on the defensive, suffering thousands of casualties and losing many planes and tanks. There was some indication that Israel's military technology was antiquated. It occurred to Soros that American technology must be antiquated as well. And, realizing that its hardware was obsolete, the Pentagon would have to spend large amounts of money to revitalize it.

This thesis had little appeal to most investors. Defense firms had lost so much money once the war in Vietnam ended that financial analysts did not want to hear anything more about them.

Early in 1974, however, Rogers began to keep a special eye on the industry. The potential in the defense industry encouraged Rogers to hit the road. He traveled to Washington, talked with Pentagon officials, and journeyed to defense contractors around America. Soros and Rogers grew even more convinced that they were right—and the others were going to miss out on something big.

In mid-1974, George Soros began scooping up defense stocks.

He bought Northrop, United Aircraft, and Gruman. And, though Lockheed seemed threatened with extinction, Soros took a bet on that company, investing in the firm in late 1974.

He and Rogers had acquired one vital piece of information about these companies. They all had major contracts that would, when renewed, provide fresh earnings over the next few years.

Early in 1975, the Soros Fund began investing in firms that supplied electronic warfare equipment. Israeli air losses during the Yom Kippur War had been due largely to the lack of sophisticated electronic countermeasures needed to neutralize the Soviet-manufactured weaponry in Arab hands.

Soros and Rogers took note of that fact.

They also noted that the modern battlefield was fundamentally changing. A whole new arsenal of modern equipment was now state-of-the-art: sensors and laser-directed artillery shells and "smart bombs."

All of this was going to cost a good deal of money. Soros and Rogers were right, resulting in large earnings for the fund.

What was Soros's secret at this juncture?

Infinite patience, to start with.

Then, a highly developed sense of where to find "gold" in the stock market. Everyone looked for the "gold," everyone had a theory where it could be found. Soros, however, had his antennae attuned to the movements of the financial market, searching all the time for some mysterious signal that something was afoot.

When he picked up the signal, he homed in on it, never letting on to anyone why he was moving in one direction and not another, testing his instincts against the reality of the market.

He knew he was good.

All he had to do was look at the bottom line year in and year out.

Nine

A Quantum Leap

By 1975 George Soros was beginning to be noticed within the Wall Street community. More precisely, his talent for making money was attracting attention. Few had any doubts that he was destined for greatness.

As Allan Raphael, who worked with Soros in the 1980s, noted: "He worked hard. He saw things. He was aggressive. He just excelled at his profession. This is a business that doesn't necessarily lend itself to logical, rational thinking. It's an intuitive process. It's a business where the sum of your experience can make the difference and I think George is endowed with those skills."

Though some on Wall Street were getting to know him, Soros remained virtually anonymous to the outside world.

With good reason.

Unlike the late 1980s and 1990s, marquee investors went almost unnoticed in those days. At that time, however, the business media was far less zealous in charting every twist and turn on Wall Street. Consequently, it was much less interested in the major personalities in the financial markets—unlike today, when their careers along with their personal lives are intensely scrutinized.

Even if the media had acted more persistently, Soros and most of his colleagues on Wall Street harbored great suspicion toward the media. They wanted as little publicity as possible. Investing was considered a very private act.

Moreover, it was widely assumed on Wall Street that the mere act of attracting publicity would prove a jinx, a kiss of death that, while initially seductive, would lead eventually to the abyss. The conventional wisdom had it that the worst fate that could befall a Wall Street investor would be to get his or her face on the cover of a widely circulated magazine. Fame not only had its price, it could be fatal.

So George Soros stayed out of the limelight, a posture with which he seemed perfectly comfortable. "George," said his longtime friend Byron Wien, "has never in my experience with him been self-promoting even when it would have done him some good to be self-promoting."

But on May 28, 1975, *The Wall Street Journal* beamed a bright light on George Soros in a largely laudatory front-page story. The headline gave Soros an early taste of public glory:

Bucking Trends: Securities Fund
Shuns Wall Street's Fashions,
Prospers in Hard Years

Soros Fund Gives Foreigners Big Profits
by Spotting Basic Shifts in Industries:
Israeli Weapons Yield Clues

Would the *Journal* article doom Soros? Would he find his luck changing? He himself had a premonition that the media attention would prove damaging—though actually, Soros had every reason to be pleased about the *Journal* article. Its thrust was to tout Soros for his independent financial mind, asserting that this independence had garnered huge profits for the Soros Fund.

The preparation for the article had put Soros in a foul mood. When the *Journal* reporter sat down with him for an interview, the investor complained of a chronic bad back, which, he said, grew worse whenever the Soros Fund ran into difficulty. "Money management is about the most merciless business around," he asserted, sounding bitter. "You can't fake it or even let up because the score is kept every single day."

Then, in an intriguing comment, given the incredible and enduring success his fund later achieved, Soros sounded a pessimistic note about the future.

"Who knows how long the Fund will continue to do well? History shows that fund managers all eventually burn out, and I'm sure we will, too, someday. I just hope that it isn't this afternoon."

The story led off with Soros smiling into his stock-quote machine. He was in the midst of selling short numerous shares of a well-known building-products firm. He expected the stock price to drop. The big institutions were trying to buy all the stock he sold.

"Look at the bank trust departments go after it," Soros smiled. "Why, I just offered to sell some of the stock half a point above the price of the last sale and somebody jumped the gap to grab it."

Over the next few weeks, the stock declined, providing Soros with a nice paper profit. The eager buyers took a loss on that trade.

Point of the story? This kind of independence on George Soros's part was standard operating procedure.

In praise of Soros and Rogers, the *Journal* intoned:

"Over the years the pair has shown a knack for buying stocks before they come into vogue and unloading them at the peak of their popularity. They generally ignore stocks widely held by the major mutual funds, bank trust departments and other institutions— except as short-sale opportunities."

Then it was Soros's turn to blow his horn:

"We start with the assumption that the stock market is always wrong, so that if you copy everybody else on Wall Street, you're doomed to do poorly. Most Wall Street security analysts are mere propagandists for company managements, cribbing their investment reports from company annual reports or each other, and rarely uncover anything worthwhile."

> "The stock market is always wrong, so that if you copy everybody else on Wall Street, you're doomed to do poorly."

Where does that leave George Soros?

Free to engage in his own brand of independent thinking. And was he ever successful!

The large institutions watched in dismay as the value of their holdings was sliced in half in 1973 and 1974. Soros, meanwhile, had marvelous years, showing gains of 8.4 percent in 1973 and 17.5 percent in 1974.

Robert Miller, a close associate of Soros at the time, remembers that Soros "had a knack for finding ideas before they were well-known and being able to see through all the gray clouds to where the silver linings were. . . . He would know exactly why he should or shouldn't buy. The other great ability George has is that when he finds he's in the wrong situation, he'll get out."

One of the Soros Fund's favorite games was shorting. He admitted that he took "malicious pleasure" in making money by selling short stocks that had been institutional favorites. The fund bet against several large institutions and shorted a number of favorites. Ultimately these stocks nosedived, making a good deal of money for the fund.

Soros's play on Avon has been considered a classic example of reaping benefits from going short. To sell the shares short, the Soros Fund borrowed 10,000 Avon shares at the market price of $120. Then the stock plummeted. Two years later, Soros bought the shares back . . . at $20 each, turning on its head the old saw by selling a nickel for a quarter. That $100-a-share profit earned the fund $1 million. He did it by spotting a cultural trend: Long before Avon's earnings started to plunge, he recognized that an aging population would mean far less sales for the cosmetics industry.

Soros gleefully explained: "In the case of Avon, the banks failed to realize that the post–World War II boom in cosmetics was over because the market was finally saturated and the kids aren't using the stuff. It was another basic change that they just missed."

Soros was able to anticipate mergers in the American railroad industry. And, when others were predicting that New York City would go bankrupt, Soros earned profits in New York City–related bonds. But there were failures, to be sure. At times he placed too much store in the upbeat assessments of company managers during factory tours. The only reason he purchased Olivetti stock was a meeting he held with company officers. He regretted the session. The stock did not fare well.

Speculating in foreign currencies also turned out to be a losing proposition; so did the purchase of stock options. The Soros-Rogers team lost $750,000 on Sprague Electric, believing mistakenly that semiconductor stocks would grow bullish. Explained Rogers: "It was just a case of poor analysis plus the fact that we bought a fringe company in the semiconductor industry rather than one of the major concerns."

Still, their system worked. If the early 1970s proved hazardous for many on Wall Street, George Soros was one of the remarkable exceptions. From January 1969 to December 1974, the fund's shares nearly tripled in value, going from $6.1 million to $18 million. For each of those years it showed a positive record.

Compare this with Standard & Poor's 500 stock index, which, during that period, fell 3.4 percent.

In 1976, the Soros Fund was up 61.9 percent. Then in 1977, while the Dow was losing 13 percent, the Soros Fund was up 31.2 percent.

In late 1977 and early 1978, Soros and Rogers decided again to take positions on technology and defense stocks, a most contrarian view, since most Wall Street traders would not touch those issues. "Remember," said Morgan and Stanley's Barton Biggs, "you had Jimmy Carter as president talking about human rights. George was talking about those stocks 18 months before the street was." Soros faulted himself for arriving late to these stocks, but still he was virtually alone.

In 1978, the fund posted a return of 55.1 percent as its assets grew to $103 million; the following year, 1979, it had a 59.1 percent hike with assets of $178 million. Soros's high-tech strategy was still very much alive—and showing no signs of burning out.

In 1979, Soros renamed his fund. It was now called the Quantum Fund, in tribute to Heisenberg's uncertainty principle in quantum mechanics. That principle asserts that it is impossible to predict the behavior of subatomic particles in quantum mechanics, an idea that meshed with Soros's conviction that markets were always in a state of uncertainty and flux and that it was possible to make money by discounting the obvious, betting on the unexpected. The fund did so well that it charged a premium based on the supply of and demand for its shares.

Inevitably, when someone makes as much money as George Soros has, questions arise as to whether all of his financial activities have been above board. Now and then over the years he has had his run-ins with the Securities and Exchange Commission, none significant setbacks.

One, however, in the late 1970s, seemed serious.

The SEC brought charges against him in United States District Court in New York, alleging stock manipulation. The specific charges were civil fraud and violating antimanipulation provisions of federal securities law.

According to the SEC's complaint, Soros drove the price of Computer Sciences stock down 50 cents a share the day before a public offering in October 1977. He allegedly urged a broker to sell Computer Sciences shares aggressively, the SEC said. The broker sold 22,400 of the fund's 40,100 shares, accounting for 70 percent of the activity in Computer Sciences that day, October 11, 1977, according to the suit.

The SEC added that the price of the previously announced offering had been based on the "artificially low" price of trading at the end of the day, $8.375 a share. The Jones Foundation, a California-based nonprofit corporation, had made the offering, agreeing in June 1977 to sell 1.5 million of its shares to the public and another 1.5 million shares to Computer Sciences at the same price as the public offering.

Thus the alleged manipulation could have cost the foundation about $7.5 million.

The SEC said that the Soros Fund bought 155,000 shares from the manager of the offering and another 10,000 shares from other brokers at the lower prices. On the day of the offering and later that month, Soros ordered the purchase of another 75,000 shares of Computer Sciences stock to keep the price at or above $8.375 a share and to induce "others to purchase" the stock, the SEC charged.

The case concluded when Soros signed a consent decree in which he neither admitted nor denied the charges. He contended that it would have cost him too much time and money to fight the SEC. Soros was quoted in a 1981 magazine article, arguing that "the SEC can't believe that one can perform as well as I did without doing something wrong, so they looked for something to latch on to."

The Fletcher Jones Foundation of California also brought suit against Soros, claiming it had suffered a substantial loss because of the declining stock value. Soros and the foundation eventually reached a $1 million settlement.

The case did not shut Soros down. Indeed, it had no discernible effect on his earnings.

Soros did well in the British currency market. He sold the British pound short at the top. He made large moves into British gilts—bonds, then in large demand, that could be bought for a mere fraction of their full value. Soros bought a huge number of them, reportedly $1 billion worth. He eventually earned $100 million from that move.

In 1980, 10 years after the Soros fund started, it had an incredible year, with an increase of 102.6 percent; by this time, the fund had grown to $381 million. Soros's personal wealth by the end of 1980 was put at $100 million.

Ironically, the major beneficiaries of Soros's investment prowess, apart from George Soros himself, were a few wealthy Europeans, the same people who had provided the capital for the Soros Fund at its start. "These people didn't need us to make them rich," Jimmy Rogers declared. "But we made them stinking rich."

Ten

The Identity Crisis

B y the late 1970s, with the Soros Fund doing magnificently, George Soros seemed to be riding high. By all logic, he should have been able to relax and achieve a certain balance in his life. He could not. While his own parents had doted on him and his brother, he, in contrast, could not do the same with his wife and children. Totally wrapped up in his work, he had little time for his wife, even less for his children.

In 1977, his marriage began to fall apart. According to Soros, "I identified with my fund; it lived off me and I lived with it, slept with it . . . it was my mistress. It was a fear of losing and the distress of being wrong that I was trying to avoid. It was a miserable way to live."

A year later, in 1978, he separated from his wife.

On the very day of his separation, he ran into a 22-year-old woman named Susan Weber, whom he had met some time before at a dinner party. Her father made handbags, shoes, and shoe accessories in New York. Susan had studied art history at Barnard College, afterwards helping produce documentaries on Mark Rothko and Willem de Kooning, 20th-century painters. "I just got separated from my wife today," announced Soros. "Would you like to have lunch?" He and Susan Weber were married five years later in a civil ceremony in Southampton, Long Island.

In 1979, Soros was only 49 years old. He had all the money he would ever need, but he began to suffer from the first strains of his work. The fund had grown so large that more employees were needed. The original staff of three was now up to a dozen. He no longer was part of a small shop where he had to talk to only one or two other people. Now he had to worry about something new: delegating responsibility to others, an ability that, according to some of his associates, he had in small measure.

With cash piling up, more and more decisions had to be made about how to invest it. It was not easy to come up with the right array of promising stocks.

What was more, Rogers was getting on his nerves. They had always been able to overcome their differences, but now, new tensions arose. Rogers was not thrilled with the idea of running such a large establishment. The crunch came when Soros tried to bring in another partner, someone he could train as his successor. Rogers balked at the idea. "He didn't approve of anybody I considered and he didn't tolerate anyone else around," Soros said. "He made life extremely difficult for the other people."

The unraveling of their partnership was ironic, for in 1980 Soros and Rogers enjoyed their most successful year. But in May of that year, Rogers left the firm, taking with him his 20 percent interest valued at $14 million; Soros's 80 percent was worth $56 million.

For the record, Rogers explained his departure by suggesting that the fund had grown too big, that with so many employees, he had to spend too much of his time deciding when to give them vacations and raises. Neither Soros nor Rogers have talked publicly at great length about what caused the rift. In a brief conversation with me, Rogers exhibited little interest in dredging up the past. From the tone of his voice, it was all too evident that the memory was still too much alive, too bitter.

Soros wondered whether continuing the business was worth it.

He had made more money than he could possibly spend. The day-to-day grind was getting to him; he felt the pressure of gambling with other people's money, of presiding over more employees than he had bargained for. And for what? Where were the rewards? Where were the joys? Soros admitted to being "in fact, somewhat burned out." After 12 incredible years, after fighting his way to the top of the heap, he realized that life as an investor was just not enough to satisfy him.

"Eventually, in 1980, when I could no longer deny my success, I had a kind of identity crisis. What is the point of undergoing all this pain and tension if I cannot enjoy my success? I asked myself. I must start enjoying the fruits of my labor even if it means destroying the goose that lays the golden egg."

Soros's identity crisis affected his business. He was increasingly quick to change his mind when an investment appeared to be turning sour. He kept positions too long. He had long benefited from high-level contacts, but now he appeared to be talking to the wrong people, or at least so his critics charged. He was in fact spending a good deal of time with government officials, especially the chairman of the Federal Reserve Board, Paul Volcker. "If you are getting your investment advice from people in government," observed money manager Gerry Manolovici, who later joined the Soros Fund, "it will only put you in the poorhouse."

In the summer of 1981, no one thought the Soros Fund was heading for the poorhouse. Some had genuine concerns, however, that all was not well. Then along came the American bond market fiasco.

Soros's problems with the American bond market had started toward the end of 1979, when Paul Volcker decided to break the back of inflation. Interest rates had risen from 9 to 21 percent, and Soros had been reasonably certain that the economy would suffer as a result. When bonds rallied early that summer, Soros began buying them. Long-term treasuries maturing in 2011 increased to 109 in June. Prices fell, however, to 93 by summer's end.

Soros had been banking on short-term interest rates rising above long-term interest rates; this would harm the economy, forcing the Federal Reserve Board to lower interest rates, improving his bond positions. The economy, however, remained strong far longer than he anticipated, and rates went even higher.

Soros would have been all right had he been able to sustain a "positive yield carry" on bond positions that he had taken on leverage. As long as the bond's yield was higher than the cost of borrowing from the broker, the yield carry was positive and hence profitable. Soros had apparently put his positions on when the rates were at 12 percent. When, however, the yield on his bonds rose to 14 percent, and briefly to 15 percent, yet interest rates climbed to 20 percent, it created a "negative yield carry," and the profits ceased. Soros was losing three to five percentage points on every bond he held that year. Estimates were that he had cost clients $80 million.

Heavily leveraged, he encountered clients who began getting cold feet; several key European clients decided to pull out of the fund. One Soros associate recalled that "he felt defeated. He felt forced to make the wrong decisions at the wrong point. He always says that you shouldn't be in the market unless you're willing to take the pain. He was willing emotionally and psychologically to take the pain, but his investors were not. He realized that his Achilles heel was this set of unreliable investors. Being beaten by the markets bothered him a lot, it bothered him losing the money but it didn't come close to the disillusion he felt toward the people walking out on him. He couldn't decide whether to stay in business or get out."

Ironically, Soros's prediction that the economy would sour proved correct—but his timing was off by six to nine months. His prediction that high interest rates would lead to a recession was validated, but not until 1982, well after Soros had taken heavy hits in his bond positions.

Magnifying the pain, intensifying the embarrassment Soros felt during that horrific summer of 1981, was the ironic fact that a major business magazine had published a flattering cover story on him, describing him in glowing terms—on the very eve of the summer setback.

It was in June 1981 that Soros appeared on the cover of *Institutional Investor.* Next to his smiling face on the magazine's cover was the phrase "The world's greatest money manager."

The subhead read: "George Soros has never had a down year, and his up years have been awesome. Here's a look at how he has bucked the money-management trends of the past decade and built himself a personal fortune worth $100 million in the process."

The story's lead suggested that Soros was a business superstar: "As Borg is to tennis, Jack Nicklaus is to golf and Fred Astaire is to tap dancing, so is George Soros to money management."

The article explained how Soros had built his fortune. From assets of only $15 million in 1974, the Soros Fund had grown to $381 million by the end of 1980. "In a dozen years of running money for such clients as Heldring & Pierson in Amsterdam and Banque Rothschild in Paris, Soros has never had a down year; in 1980 the fund was up a staggering 102 percent. Soros has turned his fee income into a personal fortune worth $100 million."

Those who read the article were supposed to think of Soros as something of an enigma, a magician who did not reveal his secrets, tricky but not dishonest, clever, even brilliant. As the writer noted: "Adding to the mystery surrounding [Soros's] record is the fact that no one is ever quite sure where Soros is making a move or how long he stays with an investment. As a manager of offshore funds, he is not required to register with the SEC. He avoids Wall Street professionals. And those in the business who *do* know him personally admit that they have never felt particularly close to the man. As for fame, it's widely agreed that he can happily do without it." For a long time Soros had refused to grant an interview to *Institutional Investor* for its cover story. Acceding to be interviewed, he noted that "you're dealing with a market. You should be anonymous."

How Soros wished he could have remained anonymous that summer. Yet there he was, a newly emergent public figure. The world's greatest money manager was having a great deal of trouble managing money.

Soros's losses that summer hurt him deeply. For as *Forbes* magazine wrote in its October 12, 1981, edition, "A world that didn't know about his triumphs wouldn't care about his setbacks." Thanks to that cover story in *Institutional Investor,* the world knew all about George Soros's triumphs. And so the world seemed to be watching him that summer.

The danger of a massive client revolt appeared to be growing. Though Soros made numerous trips to Europe to talk one important Swiss investor out of quitting, the client threw in the towel on the fund. Others followed. Said one associate from that time: "It was his first experience with what had heretofore been loyal clients, partners walking out on him at that point. He was very bitter that summer toward people he had made a great deal of money for in the previous 10 or 15 years. He felt very vulnerable to the process of having money called back, and for a long, long time he didn't actively solicit money."

The year 1981 was the fund's worst year. Quantum shares fell 22.9 percent, the first and only year that the fund had not shown a profit over the previous year. Many of Soros's investors were what one observer called "flighty European performance-chasers." They were concerned that Soros was losing his grip, and so fully one-third of them withdrew. Soros admitted later that he could not blame them. Their departure sliced the value of the fund almost in half—to $193.3 million.

It seemed only natural that George Soros would talk of quitting. He thought long and hard about what to do. He was tempted to drop all of his clients. At least by doing that he would not have to face future walkouts.

The time seemed ripe to get started on the book he had long wanted to write. He even had a tentative title. He was going to call it *The Imperial Circle*.

Eleven

The Imperial Circle

A fter Ronald Reagan assumed the presidency in January 1981, Soros was fascinated to see the new conservative-leaning president embarking on a campaign to beef up America's defenses—without raising taxes—as part of a renewed effort to get tough with the Soviets. How would the new Reagan policies affect the American economy? Could this be the start of another boom/bust sequence?

Yes, Soros believed, it certainly could be.

The television commentator Adam Smith asked Soros to explain when he knew that one of these boom/bust sequences was starting. "Does a bell go off when you read the morning paper?" Smith asked the investor. "How does it work?"

First, said Soros, such sequences don't occur every day. The new Reagan policies, however, what he dubbed "Reagan's imperial circle," promised to set one in motion. The Imperial Circle, he wrote, was "a benign circle at the center and a vicious circle at the periphery of a worldwide system based on a strong dollar, a strong U.S. economy, a growing budget deficit, a growing trade deficit and high real estate interest rates." And, noted Soros, "you had a self-reinforcing process . . . which was, however, unsustainable, and had eventually to be reversed. So it was a boom-bust kind of sequence."

Perhaps on to something, Soros was enthusiastic, but not enough to continue running the fund full-time. Before lowering his profile, he knew he had to put the fund into capable hands.

He spent much of 1982 searching for the right person. He finally found him in faraway Minnesota. Jim Marquez was then a 33-year-old whiz kid who had been running a large Minneapolis-based mutual fund called the IDS Progressive Fund. Marquez was no slouch. That year, the fund had grown to $150 million, up 69 percent, making it the champion mutual fund for 1982. Soros and Marquez first met early that year, then off and on another 15 times throughout 1982.

With each session, as Soros put the young fund manager through "mental gymnastics," Marquez sensed he was getting closer and closer to hearing a job offer. But first Marquez sat through George Soros's set of seminars, as the master investor probed and challenged, always asking himself whether the whiz kid from the Midwest was the right person.

"George is a good thinker," Marquez told me in the spring of 1994, taking time off at the end of the day at his Park Avenue office in Manhattan where he was running his own investment fund. "A lot of times he likes to see if you can keep up with where he's going and what he's doing. And then there are times when he . . . wants to see the tenor of your own thinking and how well you jump through the hoops. He would take an economic scenario, something that was happening currently, describe it. Then he would say, 'Given those stimuli and inputs, what's your response to that? What would you do?'"

> "To be in the game, you have to be willing to endure the pain."

Even as he searched for a replacement, Soros continued to agonize over whether to slip into part-time work. To Marquez, there seemed little doubt that Soros wanted to lighten his personal burden. "To be in the game, you have to be willing to endure the pain," Soros told him more than once. Marquez sensed that Soros no longer wanted to be in the game. He wanted a surrogate. "So I guess I was the first surrogate," Marquez said.

Ironically, for all the troubles Soros seemed to be going through, his fund had an excellent year in 1982. As Soros had predicted, Reagan's policies boosted the American economy, and the financial markets turned bullish that summer as interest rates fell and stocks rose. The boom part of the boom/bust sequence was distinctly visible. By the end of that year, the Quantum Fund was up 56.9 percent, climbing from $193.3 million to $302.8 million in net asset value. Soros was nearly back to his 1980 level ($381.2 million). Still, he wanted out—at least for a while.

Marquez reported for work on January 1, 1983. Soros turned over half of the fund's pool money to him; the other half was given over to 10 outside managers. Apart from handling all of the domestic trading, Marquez backed Soros in international investing. And so it was Soros on a back burner, Marquez at full flame, and three others who kept the heat up in the trading room.

Though Soros adopted a lower profile, he managed to come into the office a great deal. Still, he spent long periods abroad—six weeks in the late spring in London, a month in the Far East or Europe in the fall. Summers were reserved for Southampton, Long Island.

Soros and Marquez seemed well attuned to one another. Soros engaged in macro analysis, scanning the big picture: international politics, monetary policies around the globe, changes in inflation, interest rates, and currencies; Marquez, for his part, sought out industries and firms that would best take advantage of these expected new alignments.

If the expectation was that interest rates would rise, for example, Soros had Marquez scout out industries that would be hurt in order to short stocks in those industries. Soros employed the technique of selecting two companies in an industry for investment. But not just *any* two.

One had to be the *best* company in the industry. As the preeminent player, this firm's

> **"When choosing stocks in an industry, pick two, but not just any two. Pick the best and the worst."**

stock would be purchased first and most frequently, pushing the price up. The other had to be the *worst* company in the industry, the most highly leveraged, the one with the worst balance sheet. Investing in this company afforded the best chance to make large profits once the stock finally caught on with investors.

The first four months of 1983 were "sort of a culture shock" to Marquez, a time when the new man came to realize that "this august fellow had really given me all the autonomy and authority—and money—and the rope to hang myself."

To prepare for work each morning, Marquez went through a ritual, sometimes in the shower, sometimes riding to work: He mapped out scenarios of what might happen that day in the financial markets. He called these his "framework of expectations," and from that framework he drew conclusions on what to buy.

Once the trading day was over in New York, Soros and Marquez engaged in rigorous review sessions, often lasting well into the evening. "It was exhilarating," observed Marquez, "but very straining. The one thing George Soros is very good at is that he can look at you when you're explaining something and he can tell when you're rationalizing."

Soros never let up, grilling his right-hand man as if he were giving an oral exam to a doctoral student. "Do you have any different thoughts than you did this morning?" he often began, and then rattled off an endless stream of questions—probing, searching for reasons why Marquez might have guessed wrong. Marquez remembered the review sessions as harrowing experiences: "Because he was constantly looking for the soft underbelly, he was constantly trying to find out what was wrong with your story.

"George would try to find out if the market was acting differently from what you expected. Let's say I expected bank stocks to go up and if bank stocks were sideways to down for any amount of time, he would say: 'Let's go over our assumptions. Let's go over the reasons why you're doing this, why the perceptions are that this should happen, and then try to reconcile [that] with what the market is saying.'"

If at first Soros appeared to be playing the gray eminence around the office, he gradually got on Marquez' nerves "because you felt like you were constantly being second-guessed. You constantly had to stand up to a level of intellectual nitpicking. I shouldn't say nitpicking, just a picking away, constantly probing, and after a while, it's very wearying. Very wearying.

"A lot of times you would do things exactly as you thought he wanted them done, and he would come back to you like a teacher talking to a pupil, and say, 'You didn't understand that. That's not what I meant.' Then you'd be totally discombobulated because you thought you had a perfect understanding.

"It was very easy for him to lose his temper. He had a way of looking at you with such penetrating eyes that you felt you were under a laser gun. He could see straight through you. He always felt he wanted you around, but he never thought you were going to get it right, he would just tolerate you. Almost like you were a lesser being.

"All he asked of you is that you believe what you're telling him, that you constantly examine and cross-examine. He would try to go to the jugular, and say, 'Do you still believe what you told me yesterday?'"

Soros was not quick to lavish praise on others, or share credit when investments paid off.

"Sharing [credit] with him is a constant fight," asserted Marquez. "He figures this is the major leagues, and this is after all an economic, not an academic exercise. Your success is being determined in dollar and cents, and you're being paid to win."

Working with Soros could be intoxicating as well.

For a thirty-something like Jim Marquez, the life that George Soros led was . . . well, different from his own.

He remembered with great fondness the time that Soros asked him to come along to a board meeting of the Soros Fund in Ireland. The site was a castle, the same one Ronald Reagan later visited as president. "It was a very rarified atmosphere." Over dinner with the directors, Marquez listened, enthralled as Soros moved easily from one language to another, English to French to German, depending upon what language a certain director spoke.

But the danger existed that one could be mesmerized by working with such a genius. "He could be so intellectually dominating that if you became intimidated, if you became a yes-man, clearly you were not doing him any good, and you were not doing yourself any good," observed Marquez.

"If you said, I want to be a little Soros, I want to be a world thinker, to think great thoughts, to be a great portfolio manager, and I'm going to do and act the way he does, it was clear that he didn't need that in the office. He may need it now [1994] but he didn't need it then. That's a real siren call, to want to be like this fellow, because if you really think he's a paradigm in the business, you quickly realize you're not equipped, you're just not equipped."

Soros and Marquez enjoyed a good year in 1983. The fund now stood at $385,532,688, a net increase of $75,410,714 million, or 24.9 percent over 1982.

That same year George Soros married for the second time. His bride was 28-year-old Susan Weber. According to newspaper reports, Soros showed up late for the wedding because he had been playing tennis.

Other articles in the media reported an embarrassing moment at the wedding ceremony—one that Soros might have avoided had he taken the time to rehearse the ceremony. According to these articles, when the minister asked Soros if he was willing to give all his worldly goods to his new wife, Soros turned white. One of Soros's sons pretended to cut his throat, apparently trying to suggest to his father, perhaps half jokingly, "There goes the fortune." Soros quickly looked behind him at his personal attorney William Zabel, as if to say: "If I repeat the traditional vow 'For better or worse, I do endow thee with all my worldly goods' would I really be bound to give everything to Susan?" Zabel saved the day by indicating to Soros that no harm would be done by his answering. Just to be on the safe side, Soros mumbled in Hungarian, "Subject to my prior agreements with my heirs." With that, the ceremony carried on.

While 1983 had been a good year, 1984 was not. The fund was up, but only 9.4 percent, to $448,998,187.

The lower profit put Soros under pressure from board directors at Quantum to return full-time to investing. He agreed. Late in the summer of 1984, Soros broke the news to Marquez.

"Like it or not, I'm the captain of this ship, and I see a hundred-year storm coming. In a hundred-year storm, you want the ablest, best, most experienced hand at the helm. And let's face it, between the two of us, that's me."

What exactly was the hundred-year storm?

Essentially, it was the collapse of the American economy in the wake of Reagan's high-spending, no-taxing policies from the early 1980s. The United States, Soros believed, was heading for a depression.

Marquez recalled: "All this pressure was building in the world system at that point. The dollar was getting stronger and stronger. Reagan kept saying: 'This is fine. The sign of a country's true strength is the strength of its currency.' And George Soros thought this would just blow the lid off at some point."

Soros announced his plan to hire two other people. To Soros, the ideal organization had four or five professionals, providing a depth and discipline that could not exist in a one- or two-person shop. Marquez could, if he wished, stay on in a lesser position and run a subgroup. Marquez decided to leave, believing that he was being shunted aside and would have less authority. He acknowledged, though, that "the truth of the matter is that George wasn't wrong. There were times at night I'd get these thromboses of the head where I couldn't deal with it all. There was so much going on—and pressure."

Meanwhile, Soros had canvased his 10 outside fund managers for fresh blood. The name Allan Raphael came up.

"I was his first draft choice," said Raphael.

From 1980 to 1984, Raphael had been codirector of research at Arnhold & S. Bleichroeder, the firm that had employed Soros in the 1960s and early 1970s. Raphael returned to Bleichroeder in December 1992 as senior vice president, director of global strategy, and senior portfolio manager.

In early August 1984, Soros decided to seek out Raphael. The two men had never met, though Raphael knew Soros by reputation. Several of Soros's outside managers had phoned Raphael to inform him that they had recommended him to Soros as a candidate for the number two job. His background in global economic research made him a natural.

"Would you be interested in talking with George?" one manager asked Raphael.

It took Raphael only "a nanosecond," as he recalled. "Of course," he replied to the manager.

Raphael believed Soros to be the best investor on Wall Street. "His triumphs were just phenomenal." The possible job offer seemed to Raphael too good to be true.

Then came the phone call from Soros himself. Could Raphael come over for breakfast to his Central Park West apartment the following Thursday?

Another nanosecond flashed by, and Raphael said yes.

Raphael arrived at the breakfast convinced that his chances of getting a job offer were one in a million. He assumed that another 75 candidates were in line, that the job selection process would take another year—at which time he would be passed over.

Ninety minutes passed, but Raphael attributed little significance to the length of the breakfast. Then the two men rose from the table. Raphael thought it a good time to sum himself up for Soros.

"It's very important for you to know what I do and what I don't do," he said, hoping he didn't sound too aggressive, too forward. He was not sure Soros had absorbed his words.

"Perfect," came the response to the summary. "I do all the other things. We would be a good team."

Raphael was taken aback. "I guess so" was all he could say in a small, faint voice.

Soros flashed his big smile and said with a degree of finality: "You think it over the weekend. We'll meet on Monday or Tuesday. Call me up. You'll come over again for breakfast."

Walking out the apartment door and on to the street, Raphael began mulling over the last few minutes of the breakfast. He hailed a cab and sat down inside it, a big grin on his face. Perhaps he was dreaming. Making sure the cabdriver wasn't looking, Raphael pinched himself. He decided he had not been dreaming. He just might be going to work for George Soros as his number two.

The following Tuesday found Raphael once again eating breakfast with George Soros. A formal job offer was actually made.

It was, as Raphael recalled, "basically, 'Let's get engaged before we get married. I'll keep you for the rest of the year. Let's see how it works out.'"

Again, a nanosecond passed. But for some reason that, years later, Raphael found hard to comprehend, he did not accept right there on the spot.

"Let me think about it," he answered. Reliving that meeting in the spring of 1994, Raphael could only say: "It seemed the right thing to say."

Recalling the warnings from others ("This guy is tough," "He fires people"), Raphael decided to overlook them: "Who cared? This was my chance. So I'd get knocked around a bit; it was just an extraordinary opportunity." Raphael went for the phone and accepted the offer. In early September 1984, Raphael signed on with Soros.

Twelve

Killing of a Lifetime

eorge Soros stepped up his role in the fund during late 1984. As much as he might have wanted to pass the baton on to others at the Quantum Fund, he was not yet ready to step down entirely. He still believed a storm threatened the world's economies. He could not guess its nature or when it would begin. But he wanted to be there when it happened, to ride its rough waves, to exploit it, perhaps. Meanwhile, he paid careful attention to the fund, spending more time in the office, trying to make sure that 1984 and 1985 would be good years.

In December 1984, he had his eye on Great Britain, which was just launching a major privatization drive. Three of the companies in question were British Telecom, British Gas, and Jaguar. Soros understood that the British prime minister, Margaret Thatcher, wanted each British citizen to own shares in British stocks. The way to accomplish that? Underprice the securities.

Soros asked Allan Raphael to look at Jaguar and British Telecom. Raphael's studies of Jaguar convinced him that its chairman, Sir John Egan, was doing a brilliant job, turning the Jaguar into the hot new import car in the United States. With the stock at 160 pence, Quantum took a position that represented 5 percent of its nearly $449 million portfolio, around $20 million. That would be a big position for other people, but not for George Soros.

Raphael met with Soros.

"I've done the research on Jaguar."

"What do you think?"

"I really like the way the company is performing. We'll be OK, I think, in the position we've taken."

To Raphael's shock, Soros picked up the telephone and ordered his traders: "Buy another quarter of a million shares of Jaguar."

Raphael didn't want to spoil Soros's mood, but he still felt duty-bound to utter a word of reservation. "Excuse me. Maybe I didn't make myself clear. I said: 'We'll be OK.' "

OK apparently meant different things to Raphael and Soros. To Allan Raphael it meant "What we've done so far is OK. But let's not commit ourselves to anything more until we see how the land lies." To Soros it meant that if you like the situation now, why not follow your instincts and go with all you've got? Soros spelled it out for his associate:

> **"If your investment is going well, follow your instincts and go with all you've got."**

"Look, Allan, you tell me the company is doing a brilliant job of turning around. This is what they're going to earn on a cash-flow and earnings-per-share basis. You think the stock is going to get rerated upward. International investors are going to catch on to it. American investors are going to catch on to it. And you say the stock is going to go up."

To Soros, this was another one of those tailor-made situations in which he could apply his theory of reflexivity. He sensed that the price of the stock would rise, that investor frenzy would soon take hold, propelling it upward even more.

Raphael found nothing in Soros's words with which to quarrel.

"Yeah," he agreed, "the stock is definitely going to go up."

"Buy more."

Raphael said "yeah" but wondered whether Soros really knew what he was doing.

"*If the stock goes up,*" Soros went on, "*you buy more.* You don't care how big the position gets as part of your portfolio. If you get it right, then build."

Soros smiled and then said, to indicate that he wasn't interested in debating the point, "Next."

Soros had confidence that Jaguar and British Telecom were sure bets. He understood that much more was at play than the balance sheets of these companies. What was really at play was the single, crucial fact that Margaret Thatcher was going to make sure that British privatization would be underpriced.

Raphael was in mild shock. He was concerned that Soros was betting the store.

He need not have worried. Quantum's profit on Jaguar was $25 million.

Part of the concept of hedging that Soros would come to be identified with was shorting. The biggest short position Soros took in the mid-1980s involved Western Union.

The year was 1985. It was a time when the fax machine was becoming popular in the United States. Western Union's stock, which had been much higher in earlier years, was now selling in the high teens and low 20s. Soros and his associates, however, took special note that the company still carried a great deal of telex equipment on its balance sheet at its depreciated value. Because the equipment was electromechanical, it was no longer state-of-the-art and therefore had almost no value in the marketplace. Western Union was also carrying debt.

Soros doubted the company could repay that debt or the rearages in preferred stock.

"What we thought in so many words," recalled Allen Raphael, "was: 'What Western Union did to pony express, the fax machine would do to Western Union.'"

A number of big-time institutional analysts were recommending Western Union as an asset play without taking into account that the value of its assets was considerably less than Western Union was suggesting. Soros, however, understood that. He took a short position of a million shares. The profit, Allan Raphael said, was "in the millions."

Well into 1985, Soros still worried that the U.S. economy was headed for collapse. In August he believed that the "Imperial Circle" was in a final round of credit expansion in order to stimulate the U.S. economy and pay for the military expansion. Relief was about to appear and, fortunately for Soros, he was able to recognize it in time and exploit the opportunity. The relief would come as the United States and other economic giants realized that the currency market had turned into a monster that was working against their interests.

Picking up on this point, Anthony Sampson, writing in *The Midas Touch,* noted that "back in the sixties enthusiasts for global deregulation had looked forward to the world's currencies gradually and rationally adjusting their values against each other, as nations with weak exports and economies devalued until they met levels where they became competitive: dollars, yen or pounds would accurately reflect each country's industrial efficiency.

"When President Nixon disconnected the dollar from gold in 1971, and when currencies began floating independently, no one anticipated the hectic movements which were to follow in the seventies and eighties." Currencies shifted with each new rumor. Exchange rates no longer seemed linked to exports. By the late 1980s, the dollar's value in yen could alter by 4 percent a day.

At first Soros had not had good luck at all trading currencies. During the early 1980s, he had actually lost money. His reading of the situation in the mid-1980s, however, renewed his confidence. He knew that the dollar—and its relationship to the Japanese yen and the German mark—would furnish the main drama in the financial world, and he was paying attention.

The value of the dollar had been going through all sorts of twists and turns in the early 1980s, leaving a world that depended on a stable dollar weary and breathless.

In the first few years of the 1980s, the Reagan administration had been committed to a strong dollar, hoping that it would beat back high inflation by permitting cheap imports and by attracting foreign investors to finance the trade deficit.

Eventually, Reagan turned to tax cuts, which, coupled with the defense buildup, had touched off a boom in both the dollar and the stock market. Foreign money was attracted to the United States, and that lifted the dollar and the capital markets. More economic expansion attracted even greater amounts of money, all of which pushed up the dollar—again, what Soros called "Reagan's Imperial Circle."

Inherently unstable, though, the Imperial Circle was eventually doomed, Soros believed, "because the strong dollar and high real interest rates were bound to outweigh the stimulating effect of the budget deficit and weaken the U.S. economy." So as Soros had guessed, by 1985, the U.S. trade deficit was increasing at an alarming rate, and U.S. exports were terribly handicapped by the highly valued dollar. America's domestic industries were threatened as well by cheap Japanese imports. Soros had watched all this and detected the first stage of a typical boom/bust sequence.

In the meantime other analysts were touting cyclical stocks. Not Soros. True to his contrarian nature, he leaned toward takeover stocks and financial services—and both took off. The Quantum Fund, for instance, had 600,000 shares of the ABC television network when Capital Cities took it over. One afternoon that March, Capital Cities announced that it would bid $118 a share for ABC. The Quantum Fund made $18 million on that bet.

Soon thereafter, Soros phoned Allan Raphael, who had handled the deal. "That's very good," Soros said. "But what do we do now?"

In telling the story years later, Raphael imitated a Hungarian accent in recounting what Soros had to say. Raphael knew very well that Soros wasn't really asking him a question. He was testing him. It was as if Soros were saying, "I'm very happy, but don't get carried away."

"It's quite clear," said Raphael. "We buy more Capital Cities."

Raphael could tell by Soros's silence that he had aced the test.

Soros believed that Reagan's policies toward the dollar would eventually lead to the "bust" part of the sequence. The president might seem to have good reason to keep the dollar high, but he had better reasons to lower it. During the early 1980s, short-term interest rates had risen to 19 percent. Gold had reached $900 an ounce. Inflation was soaring—at 20 percent levels. The sky-high dollar could fetch 240 Japanese yen, 3.25 German marks.

Finally, it now seemed clear to Soros that with OPEC about to fall apart, oil prices were about to drop. That would put additional pressure on the U.S. government to lower the dollar's value. Oil had lately reached $40 a barrel, and projections were that it could climb to $80 a barrel. OPEC's breakup would cause inflation to drop around the world. With the drop in inflation would come a parallel drop in interest rates. As a result of these changes, the dollar would come down dramatically.

Raphael explained Soros's strategy: "The position obviously to take was to short crude oil, go long the short end of the U.S. interest rate curve, and go long the long end of the Japanese interest rate curve as Japan is dependent on imported oil. In addition, the U.S. dollar was to be shorted against the mark and the yen. As commodity, fixed income, and currency markets are much deeper in size and volume than equity markets, an investor or speculator can accumulate very large positions in a relatively short time. Also, as these securities have relatively small margin requirements, a great deal of leverage can be utilized. Therefore, although the fund was only $400 million at the time, the ability to leverage the fund was enormous.

"George Soros had big, big positions in all these things. You can only do that once in a lifetime."

Beginning in August 1985, Soros kept an investment diary; it recorded the background thinking that went into his investment decisions in what he called his "real-time experiment" as he sought to answer how long the Imperial Circle would endure. He saw the diary as a test of his ability to predict the movements of the financial markets—and a chance to put his theories to the test as well. Thanks to the diary, Soros's views and his investment strategies between August 1985 and November 1986 are carefully documented. The diary appeared in Soros's 1987 book *The Alchemy of Finance.*

The first big test for Soros came in September 1985. On September 6 of that year, Soros was betting that the mark and yen would go up. But they had been declining. He was beginning to doubt his notion of the Imperial Circle. He had long positions on both currencies amounting to $700 million—more than the entire value of the Quantum Fund. Although he had lost some money, he was still confident that events would prove him right, so he raised his position on both currencies to just under $800 million—$200 million more than the fund's value.

Then on September 22, 1985, Soros's scenario began to materialize. James Baker, the new U.S. Secretary of the Treasury, decided that the dollar had to come down, for Americans were beginning to demand protection for their industries. Baker and the key finance ministers of France, West Germany, Japan, and Britain—the so-called

Group of Five—huddled in New York City at the Plaza Hotel. Soros learned about the meeting and quickly realized what the finance ministers were about to do. He worked through the night, buying millions of yen.

The ministers indeed decided to try to bring the price of the dollar down, producing what came to be called "the Plaza agreement." It proposed the "orderly appreciation of nondollar currencies" by "cooperating more closely." This meant that the central banks would now feel obligated to devalue the dollar.

The day after the accord was announced the dollar fell from 239 yen to 222.5, or 4.3 percent. It was the largest one-day drop in history. To Soros's glee, he made $40 million overnight. Raphael saw him that morning and said, "Nice hit, George. I'm impressed." Soros kept buying yen.

In his diary entry of September 28, 1985, Soros called the Plaza accord coup "the killing of a lifetime . . . the profits of the last week more than made up for the accumulated losses on currency trading in the last four years. . . ."

The Plaza accord investment has taken on the status of folklore around the Quantum Fund. Stanley Druckenmiller, who began working for Soros in 1988, recounted that in the fall of 1985 other traders, piggybacking Soros, were long the yen just before the Plaza meetings. When the yen opened 800 points higher that Monday morning, these traders began taking profits, thrilled at making so much money so quickly. Soros, however, was looking at the bigger picture. "Supposedly, George came bolting out of the door, directing the other traders to stop selling the yen, telling them that he would assume their position. The government had just told him that the dollar was going to go down for the next year, so why shouldn't he be a pig and buy more [yen]?"

For the next six weeks, the central banks kept pushing the dollar down. By late October, the dollar had fallen 13 percent, to 205 yen. By September 1986, it was down to 153 yen. Foreign currencies rose on average 24 to 28 percent against the dollar.

Altogether, Soros had made a $1.5 billion bet. Using leverage, he placed most of his money on the mark and the yen. It proved to be a shrewd move. He made, over time, an estimated $150 million.

Clearly, the trend had been established. And Soros was not worried. He could not help himself. He kept making money.

By the first week of November, the fund had grown to $850 million and Soros was holding $1.5 billion in yen and marks, almost double the value of the fund. In his diary he wrote: "The reason I am nevertheless willing to increase my exposure is that I believe the scope for a reversal has diminished. One of the generalizations I established about freely floating exchange rates is that short-term volatility is greatest at turning points and diminishes as a trend becomes established." He was short $87 million in British pounds and over $200 million in oil, long $1 billion in stocks and futures, and nearly $1.5 billion in bonds. Altogether, he had nearly $4 billion long and short in various markets.

> "**S**hort-term volatility is greatest at turning points and diminishes as a trend becomes established."

He displayed incredible confidence that he was right. On December 8, 1985, he wrote in his diary: "I have about as firm a conviction about the shape of things to come as I shall ever have, as witnessed by the level of exposure I am willing to assume." Having worried the previous August that economic collapse was around the corner, Soros now felt reassured. The government was trying to bring the dollar down—and succeeding. The stock and bond markets were rising. A great stock market boom seemed possible, he believed. In December Soros was heady with optimism. He called this period "the Golden Age of Capitalism" and announced "the bull market of a lifetime."

The year 1985 was a marvelous one for Soros.

Compared to 1984, the Quantum Fund was up an amazing 122.2 percent. Its assets rose from $448.9 million at the end of 1984 to $1.003 billion at the end of 1985. That advance was nearly four times larger than the Dow's 1985 rise of nearly 34 percent (including dividends).

Soros's overall record was remarkable.

A dollar invested with him when he launched his fund in 1969 would have been worth $164 at the end of 1985 after all fees and expenses. Soros proudly explained to journalist Dan Dorfman that the same dollar invested in Standard & Poor's 500 stock index would have gone up to just $4.57 during the same time.

Soros would not tell Dorfman how much of the fund he owned other than to acknowledge that it contained most of his personal assets. Dorfman's sources, however, guessed that Soros owned 15 to 30 percent of the fund. With Quantum's 1985 profit at $548 million, Soros would have made between $83 million and $166 million. "False—way, way off," Soros retorted when *New York Magazine* asked for a comment on these figures.

In an interview with Dorfman over breakfast in his Fifth Avenue apartment overlooking Central Park, Soros explained that he had done so well in 1985 because of:

- Large killings in the German mark and Japanese yen.
- A strong showing in bonds, such as long-term Treasuries.
- Large gains in foreign stocks.

Soros had not done as well in American stocks. "I'm not particularly good at playing the takeover game," he admitted. His off-and-on investment in Disney in the mid-1980s seemed to substantiate his point. Ultimately, he triumphed, but the path had not been smooth.

In 1984, the Quantum Fund was one of Disney's largest shareholders outside the Disney family. The stock looked increasingly attractive because of several failed takeover attempts against the big entertainment firm. When takeover artist Saul Steinberg cast his eye on Disney, few believed that Disney would allow the takeover.

Few also believed that Disney would agree to Steinberg's greenmail either. Yet, that is precisely what happened, and Soros, along with others, lost a bundle when Disney stock plunged $20 a share. Weakened by the greenmail, Disney nonetheless bounced back, and Soros reinvested in the company. Marquez credited Raphael with sensing the trends at Disney: "Allan was very quick to understand what was happening. We had been looking at Disney as an undervalued asset base that was going to be monetized for various reasons. He looked at it as an asset base that was rich and could be grown and milked and wasn't to be shot through the head and put out of its misery." Accordingly, the Quantum Fund made a fivefold profit.

Crowning Soros's year in 1985 was the fact that *Financial World* ranked him number 2 among the 100 highest-paid people on Wall

Street. According to the magazine, Soros made $66 million from his personal stake in the Quantum Fund's profits, along with $17.5 million in fees and a $10 million bonus from his fund's clients. He made that year, according to the magazine, $93.5 million.

By early January 1986, Soros had altered his portfolio dramatically. More bullish about the U.S. stock market, he increased U.S. stocks and stock-index futures and raised his foreign stock position so that together the American and foreign stocks totaled $2 billion in value. He dropped his position against the dollar from $500 million to zero.

In February he took his stock position down to $1.2 billion. On March 26, he felt good about his bullish thesis; the fall in oil suggested to him that he was right. Accordingly, he took his American and foreign stocks back up to $1.8 billion. Since early January the fund had improved its net asset value from $942 million to $1.3 billion.

On April 4, Soros reduced his stock position, taking it down by $831 million. Ten days later he bought back $709 million. On May 20, he sold $687 million, mostly in index futures.

Forty percent of his stock positions and two-thirds of his foreign stock positions were tied up in the Finnish market, Japanese railroad and real estate stocks, and Hong Kong real estate stocks.

July 1986 brought two perplexing, contradictory trends, a continuing bull market and the fall of oil prices. The fall of oil prices could set off deflation, causing an economic collapse.

Finally, in September, Soros wrote with some degree of finality: "It is better to declare the phase I have called the 'Golden Age of Capitalism' as complete and try to identify the next phase."

Soros did very well in his real-time experiment. He took the Quantum Fund from $449 million—where it stood at the start of 1985—to $1.5 billion by the end of 1986. Yet he found the experiment more problematic as time wore on. The more he wrote in his diary, the more he felt compelled to justify to himself why he was making a certain investment move. He came to look at the experiment as a burden.

Thirteen

Philosophical Speculator

W hat motivated George Soros?

Money? Few of his friends and associates thought so. "If he made another billion dollars," suggested his close friend Byron Wien, "that wouldn't make him happy. Making the first billion didn't make him all that happy."

Well, it must have brought him some joy.

But not much. George Soros was far too complex. He had more than just that one dimension. No matter how much money flowed into his bank account, he would never be satisfied as simply a man of leisure. In that sense, he was like many other wealthy people in the 1990s.

In previous generations, the very wealthy valued their spare time. They spent as much time as they could doing as little as possible. But as the British writer Anthony Sampson has pointed out, "The rich no longer aspire to a life of leisure, and work has become an essential part of their status. . . ."

As for favored status symbols, the luxury hotel suite, the yacht, and the private jet had replaced the fancy house, garden, and park. But what most distinguished the newly rich from earlier generations of the wealthy was mobility. Aspiring to something beyond a life of leisure, Soros has felt far more comfortable in jet planes than yachts, far more useful in hotel suites than in huge mansions, far more productive globe-trotting than sitting by a pool.

Yet Soros is different from many of the contemporary rich in one significant way: the degree to which he has engaged in intellectual life. Apart from Karl Popper's writings, the two books that influenced Soros most were, predictably, a pair of esoteric mind-benders called *Gödel, Escher, Bach,* by Douglas Hofstadter and *Step to an Ecology of Mind* by Gregory Bateson. He has viewed himself not just as a speculator but as a philosopher. Or, perhaps more accurately, a failed philosopher who happened to be a speculator. When he was admitted to the Chancellor's Court of Benefactors at Oxford University in England in the autumn of 1992, he asked to be listed as "a financial and philosophical speculator." "I would really like to be recognized as a practical philosopher," Soros has said, "but I am quite happy to be recognized as a philosopher manqué."

By the 1990s, however, he had become a billionaire—and no matter what he did outside of the world of finance, he was frequently described as "the Hungarian entrepreneur," "the master money manager," "billionaire speculator," and even once as "the bad boy of global finance" (*The Wall Street Journal*, June 1, 1994). He tried to escape such labels. The press release issued by the Soros Foundations in New York described him as an "international philanthropist." It was his way of saying: If I can't be called a philosopher, at least don't describe me as a financier.

More than anything else, though, he sought respect—for his mind, for his ideas, for his contributions to society through his philanthropic efforts. Had he called himself a philosopher, and nothing else, he might not have been taken seriously. He said more than once that being a success on Wall Street had at least afforded him the chance to be listened to, and that was the beginning of being taken seriously.

For he saw himself as an intellectual in the European tradition. Wall Street was a decent enough place to make money, but beyond that its inner precincts and the people who inhabited its offices were of little interest to Soros. "I don't spend much time with the people in the stock market," he confided to journalist Dan Dorfman. "I find them boring." He felt more comfortable with intellectuals, he said, than with businesspeople.

He might have yearned to cease his investment activities in favor of philosophizing as a full-time vocation. It was never to be. He had done far too well on Wall Street for that. If moneymaking was hardly an end unto itself, it did present opportunities that few philosophers sitting in their ivory towers would ever experience.

Though making money came easily to him, Soros could not, at first, admit to himself that he had chosen a profession other than an academic or intellectual one. Gradually, though, he got used to the idea. "For many years I refused to identify with my performance. It was a means to an end. Now I'm much more willing to accept it—

that this is, in fact, my life's work." When he was asked in the early 1980s how it felt to be the world's most successful money manager, he admitted, "It's a pretty good feeling."

However satisfied he had become with doing well on Wall Street, Soros was not, by any means, pleased with the anguish that went into the day-to-day decision making of investing: "My ego was really put on the line, and this turned out to be a very painful experience. For one thing, my ego suffered an incredible battering whenever I made the wrong move in the market. For another, I did not really want to identify myself with moneymaking to the extent that was necessary in order to be successful. I had to deny my own success in order to maintain the discipline that was responsible for that success."

The problem with investing, what made it so painful, he explained on another occasion, was losing money. And, as he liked to point out, it wasn't possible to make money without the threat of losing it. His "identity crisis" in the early 1980s was the result of his feeling that making so much money was not enough in life.

He worried, as men of ideas often worry, that the accumulation of money could have a corrupting influence on him and that people paid attention to him only because he had made so much money. "I have to accept my success with its power and influence. . . . My biggest risk lies in the process of acknowledging that I am becoming powerful and influential because I have a lot of money." The identity crisis came almost as a relief.

He enjoyed the good life. He has four residences, in Manhattan; Southampton, Long Island; Bedford, New York; and London. Yet he was far more modest than other people of great wealth. He neither smoked nor drank, and did not seem to enjoy huge amounts of food.

Edgar Astaire, his London partner, often saw Soros outside the office. Soros's tastes were not pretentious, he asserted: "He likes the theater, music. He doesn't collect things. He doesn't collect paintings. He has had a bit of Hungarian art. He likes his clothes. He's always been well turned out."

"I used to collect but actually I don't have great material needs," Soros told a reporter in 1993. "I like my comfort. But, really, I am a very abstract person."

When traveling abroad to visit his philanthropic foundations, especially in the 1980s and early 1990s, Soros eschewed a chauffeur or bodyguard. He sometimes stayed in student quarters when visiting a university campus. He sometimes hailed his own taxicabs, or walked from one part of town to another, or even took public transportation.

Many of his friends have their favorite story about how George Soros rejected the life of a billionaire. Tibor Vamos, one of the Hungarian intellectuals attached to Soros's philanthropic foundation in Budapest, recalled the time he and Soros were sitting in the building that housed the Hungarian Academy of Sciences.

"How can I reach the university?" Soros asked.

"You can take a taxi," Vamos told him.

"Why not a streetcar?" Soros asked in all seriousness.

Soros was not trying to save money, Vamos explained. It was simply that he was practical. If a streetcar was the fastest way to get from one place to another at that moment, why not take it?

The house in Southampton is a whitewashed Spanish-tiled villa with a swimming pool and tennis court. Soros celebrated his 60th birthday at a party there in 1990. On the lawn was a large white marquee for the supper dance. Among the 500 guests were important business figures, plus, according to one guest, "millions of Hungarians."

Though he sought to give the impression of living a modest life, it was sometimes a bit misleading. There *were* the seaplane rides from Southampton to Manhattan and the four houses. But there was no yacht, no Rolls Royce. When Soros traveled, it was more often on commercial airliners (business class), than in private jets. Soros once had a yen for buying a plane to take him back and forth between New York and Europe. He asked Byron Wien what he thought. It was a bad idea, Wien told him: "If you have a plane, you will find yourself using it just because the pilots want to use the plane." Wien suggested he could charter a plane whenever necessary. Soros took his advice.

To some Soros seemed exceptionally shy. Yet he loved having people around. Wien observed that "he likes to live in a nice place comfortably. George doesn't take you around his house and say, 'Look at this clock. Or look at this statue, or painting.' He appreciates material things. He likes to live well. He likes to have people to his house, to serve them nice dinners, to have enough help to make it go smoothly."

He often gave parties. Sometimes he would phone Susan at the last minute. He'd invited some friends over for dinner. How many? Susan was bound to ask. Oh, maybe 50 or 75, Soros would respond. Susan then found herself preparing a meal for 70 Russian dissidents and their partners.

On New Year's Eve each year he hosted a party in his New York City apartment. Every Saturday night during the summer at Southampton, the Soroses entertained, and for George the evenings were as much business meetings as social events. Wien, who attended some of those parties, observed that Soros was "good in crowds. He says hello to everyone. He remembers their names. The people who go to these parties are from the arts, they are people he plays tennis with, businesspeople, government people. There are always more people there than he can interact with. He gets something from these experiences, but more importantly they interact with one another."

As a natural extension of his gregariousness, Soros had no interest in living a sedentary life. He wanted to be on the move, to see other parts of the world, to keep his mind active, to interact with people who were doing important things. In short, he wanted, indeed he aggressively sought, adventure in his life. It was no wonder that he found businesspeople and dealing rooms boring.

He kept up a frenetic pace out of a conviction that he was someone special, someone endowed with a special purpose in life. This was a man, let us remember, who believed as a child he was God.

As an adult, he seemed to understand that such thoughts could get him into trouble; they could, for instance, turn him into an egomaniac. "The only thing that could hurt me," he wrote in 1987, "is if my success encouraged me to return to my childhood fantasies of omnipotence—but that is not likely to happen as long as I remain engaged in the financial markets, because they constantly remind me of my limitations."

They also reminded him that he seemed to have the Midas touch—that, while he was hardly infallible, he was literally in a league of his own. When he enjoyed his most spectacular year in investing in

1985, journalist Dan Dorfman asked him what he planned to do for an encore. "It's basically a nonrecurring event," he said, "which in my case just happens to recur." The point was, for George Soros, even nonrecurring events recur.

If he could make nonrecurring events recur, what was to stop him from using his intellectual powers in the same way? What was to stop him from making some great contribution to human knowledge? At one stage in his life, back in the 1950s, he had run into a stumbling block and abandoned plans for an academic life, for a life as a philosopher. Yet the more money he made, the more convinced he became that he might be able to return to the intellectual realm.

From such thoughts, he spun theories—about knowledge, about history, about the financial markets—and he came to believe that his ideas had merit. He proclaimed that his "discovery" regarding the role that participants' bias plays in the quest for human knowledge was a key to understanding all historical processes that have thinking participants, "just as genetic mutation is the key to biological evolution."

Thinking himself extraordinary, Soros had a hard time abiding people he thought less gifted. After all, he believed that he had insight into things that others did not share. Of his ability to understand financial markets, for example, he noted: "I think that I really understand the process that is occurring, this revolutionary process, better than most people because I have a theory, an intellectual framework, in which I deal with it. It's my specialty, really, because I deal with similar processes in financial markets."

As for others who tried to plumb the markets: "I had a very low regard for the sagacity of professional investors, and the more influential their position the less I considered them capable of making the right decisions."

Jim Marquez saw this up close when he and Soros worked together in the mid-1980s: "He was imbued with the feeling that he could understand things better than you can, and it was always a struggle, not because he was converting his mind from Hungarian to English, but because he was trying to bring you along.

"It was clear to him that he couldn't bring you along fast enough. He had the feeling that when he understood something, it was as if he were talking to God. That he was so sure what would happen, and he was the most surprised person in the world when it didn't happen that way. And if it did, well that was just the way it should be."

Fourteen

A Cheap Price for Freedom

arly in his business career, philanthropy was the farthest thing from George Soros's mind. He disliked the very notion of philanthropy. Philanthropy, he told a reporter in 1993, "goes against the grain because our civilization is built upon the pursuits of self-interest, not on any preoccupation with the interests of others." So no one around him ever remembered Soros talking about how important it was to feed or house the poor. He was willing to give away large sums of money. But not to individuals. He wanted to have a more powerful impact. But to do that, he had to target whole groups, even societies. He thought on a grand scale.

His memory of the treatment he had received from the Jewish Board of Guardians in London still rankled; and that memory shaped his attitude toward all aid giving in general. "You should understand that I am actually opposed to philanthropic foundations," he told the reporter. "There is a sense of potential corruption because of the influence of the founder. The only justification that I see for a foundation is where there is something we want to accomplish that matters more than the foundation itself." He believes that any organization, including his, is subject to "erosion and corruption" as people within it pursue wealth, power, and comfort.

He never tired of telling people about the "foundation" that he had once organized, a small group called the Central Park Community Fund, whose goal was the renovation of New York City's Central Park. It so happened that another organization called the Central Park Conservancy had much the same mandate as his own, but was far more successful. When the Soros "foundation" began attacking the other one, Soros was appalled. He not only put a stop to the practice, he "killed" (his own word) the Community Fund. He took more pride, he said, in destroying it than in creating it.

119

And yet, he knew he had no choice, not if he were going to try to do some good. He would have to create foundations. He would just have to make sure they performed effectively.

Then the question was, How should he disperse his money? Since Soros was Jewish, would it not be natural for him to help out his fellow Jews?

Soros had never denied or cloaked his Judaism; he simply put it aside. He deliberately avoided giving any of his wealth to Israel until 1986, when he befriended Daniel Doron, the Israeli public affairs commentator, and provided a small amount of funds to Doron's Jerusalem think tank. Later, Gur Ofer, a professor of economics at Jerusalem's Hebrew University, approached Soros to try to get the investor to establish a foundation for the 500,000 Soviet Jews who had streamed into Israel in the previous two years. But Soros was dead set against the idea and cut the conversation short.

Why was Soros so opposed to helping Israel? "It was," recalled Ofer, "a mixture of his considering Israel too socialist and feeling that until Israel reforms itself there's no point supporting Israel. There's a non-Zionist or anti-Zionist element in his thinking. He believes that Jews should act within the societies where they live."

As Soros searched for a place where he could be a "man on a white horse," he realized that the watershed event of his life had been his escape from the "closed society" that had taken hold in his native Hungary. Since leaving Hungary, he had tasted freedom, first in England, then in the United States. Why not try to give others in Eastern Europe and the Soviet Union that same opportunity?

Soros decided that he would use his financial muscle to promote open societies, places where people could be autonomous, where they could speak their minds and pursue their own objectives.

By bankrolling efforts to undermine communism, George Soros was in effect financing revolt throughout Eastern Europe and the Soviet Union. The revolution would be conducted not at the barricades, not in the streets, but in the minds of the citizenry. It would be peaceful, slow, gradual, but unremitting. And eventually it would lead to the birth of democracy in these countries.

What Soros planned to do would not be easy. The obstacles would be formidable. Communist governments would not automatically fall into his embrace. And he understood that he could not bulldoze his way into each country. Some efforts might work, some might not. He knew that his power was limited; hence it was important to choose those points where he and his philanthropy could have the greatest impact. Like the Rothschilds, he would use his wealth to redraw Europe's political map.

At first, when communism still ruled these countries, it was easier to have an impact than later, after communism disappeared. Soros noted that "if you expose a dogma to alternatives, it will crumble because it will be seen to be false once you have something to compare it with."

Yet Soros knew that he could not make over Eastern Europe and the ex-Soviet Union by simply handing out money. Beyond that, he needed to imbue the East with an appreciation of Western ideas. It was in the West, after all, where the notion of an open society had flourished.

Soros went up against people who were not used to someone tossing his money around so freely. Said Jeffrey Sachs, professor of international trade at Harvard University and economic adviser to the governments of Poland, Russia, and Estonia, among others: "George Soros is seen through all different kinds of prisms and some are not very attractive. Among the governmental leaders the reaction to him is much more positive than it is among the anti-Semitic groups, the extreme nationalists, and other xenophobic groups. Among them it's negative."

Indeed, it has not been easy for Soros to establish beachheads in these Eastern European countries. Romanians disliked him because he was Hungarian. Hungarians disliked him for being Jewish. And in Slovakia, a Hungarian Jew had two strikes against him.

He has not gotten away unscathed in the West either, where he has had to live down accusations of being a modern-day Robin Hood, of "taking" from the rich West and giving the money to the poor East. When he put all his chips on the pound in September 1992—and won—it was noted nastily that Soros had "stolen" the equivalent of 12 and a half pounds from each British resident. Soros took the attack in good humor. "I really think that the West ought to have done and ought to do more for the East so I'm happy to do it on their behalf."

Not every British citizen, though, was bothered by Soros's charitable acts. Asked what he thought of the accusation that Soros had "taken" 12 and a half pounds from each British citizen and given it away to Eastern Europe, Neil MacKinnon, chief economist for Citibank in London, responded, "It was a cheap price to pay for freedom."

Soros actually began his forays into philanthropy in 1979 in South Africa. He had identified Capetown University as a place that seemed devoted to the notion of an open society. Accordingly, he offered to provide scholarships for black students. The effort backfired: Soros discovered that his money was being used largely to finance already enrolled students, and only in small part new students. He withdrew his support from the school. "South Africa was a vale of tears," he explained later. "It was very difficult to do anything without in some way becoming part of the system." In communist Eastern Europe, though, he felt he had more leverage against the system: "It was heroic, exciting, rewarding—and it was great fun. We were in the business of undermining the system. We would support anything. We gave out large numbers of very small grants because any autonomous operations would undermine the dogma of totalitarianism."

Once he decided to concentrate on Eastern Europe, Soros sensed that he needed a showcase. He chose his native Hungary. It so happened some of the reform-minded members of the hardline government of Janos Kadar had an eye on Soros as well. They wanted his foreign currency for their ailing government.

One was Ferenc Bartha, who at that time was responsible for the government's economic relationships. When Bartha and Soros met in 1984, Soros explained that he was interested in establishing a philanthropic foundation. Negotiations ensued. Conducting them for the government was George Aczel, the only Jewish member of Hungary's Politburo, and the unofficial cultural czar of Hungary and confidante of Prime Minister Kadar.

As his own personal representative in Hungary, Soros chose a formidable Hungarian dissident, Miklos Vasarhelyi. Soros and Vasarhelyi had met for the first time in 1983, when Vasarhelyi was working at the Institute on International Change at Columbia University in New York. Vasarhelyi had been a spokesman and member of the inner circle of

Hungary's prime minister Imre Nagy at the time of the 1956 uprising. After the Soviets crushed the revolt, Nagy was hanged and Vasarhelyi was expelled from the Communist party and sentenced to five years in jail.

Vasarhelyi guessed that the chances of setting up such an institution were no better than 50-50. On the plus side for Soros was the Hungarian government's wish to burnish its image abroad in order to obtain Western credit and hard currency. On the minus side, however, Soros confronted a communist state that had no experience with outsiders running philanthropic foundations, let alone outsiders seeking to encourage an "open society."

Even if the Hungarian regime agreed to Soros's plan to set up a foundation, it was not going to give him much of a free hand. Soros, for his part, insisted on independence. "I am coming to Hungary and I will give money to whomever I consider worthy," he said defiantly. The politicians reacted: "Mr. Soros, bring your money here, and we will distribute it for you."

The talks dragged on for a year. Soros wanted to contribute only $2 or $3 million, but that figure was too paltry for the politicians. The government favored aid for scientific research, but Soros preferred that the foundation sponsor individuals who would travel, write, or perform in the arts. The government wanted the foundation to finance equipment; Soros wanted to finance people.

Finally, it appeared that Soros and Bartha had overcome their differences. After the Hungarians signed the relevant documents, one of them said, "Great! Your secretariat can tell our foreign cultural-relations department what it wants to do, and we'll do it."

In other words, the Hungarian government was now insisting that the new Soros foundation fall within the purview of the Ministry of Culture. To the shock of the Hungarian negotiators, Soros rose from his chair and walked to the door. He would not sign the documents.

"What a pity to have wasted all that time and effort for nothing," he said, ever the good negotiator. His hand actually was on the door handle when the bureaucrats relented. They would allow the Soros Foundation a great degree of independence.

With that concession, Soros signed the documents. Soros promised to give $1 million a year to run the foundation for the foreseeable future. By 1993 the figure had grown to $9 million a year.

In an intriguing twist, Kadar's government apparently hoped that Soros's foundation, by improving scientific research, would somehow quash discontent among the country's scientist intellectuals. Things didn't quite work out that way. Those academics who had been sent abroad to study through Soros Foundation scholarships returned to their native country armed with fresh Western ideas about a market economy and democracy.

It was the photocopy machine episode that served as the great breakthrough for the Soros Foundation in Hungary, establishing its reputation as an aggressive force for reform. Until that time, the Hungarian authorities had kept a tight grip on any machine that, if available to the underground press, could be used for subversive purposes. Few in Hungary had ever seen a photocopy machine. Soros decided to provide 400 photocopiers to Hungarian libraries, universities, and scientific institutes, stipulating that he would donate the photocopiers only if the government agreed not to monitor their use. Somehow he won the government's approval, stipulation and all, perhaps because it needed the hard currency.

Soros and his foundation faced continuing mistrust on the part of the government. For its first four years—from 1984 until 1988—the foundation was barred from advertising its programs in most of the Hungarian media. Nor could most of the media print the name George Soros or the phrase "the Soros Foundation." What little publicity Soros and his foundation received proved too much for the government. Trouble reached a peak in 1987.

The foundation had given a scholarship to a young journalist who wanted to write a biography of Matyas Racozi, Hungary's prime minister in the early 1950s. An item related to the forthcoming biography appeared in the *World Economy* magazine, the only Hungarian journal permitted to carry foundation advertising. Janos Kadar, the current prime minister, saw the item and thought, "This is impossible. Tomorrow Soros will give a scholarship to someone to write *my* biography." Kadar extended the media ban to include *World Economy*.

Irritated at the way he and the foundation were being treated, Soros appeared ready to close the Soros Foundation. "For the next two or three weeks there was much tension," noted Miklos Vasarhelyi. "Finally matters cooled down." Once again, *World Economy* magazine became accessible to Soros and his foundation. The biography of Racozi was eventually published, but by then the storm had died down.

In 1988, Kadar and nearly all of the party leaders were swept from power. Soon after the new leaders took over, Soros was invited to meet Karoly Gros, the new general secretary of the party, a sign that the foundation was back in the government's good graces, for he had never been granted a meeting with the previous leadership.

The improved relations were short-lived, lasting only until 1989. By that time the government's anti-Semitic sentiments had became visible, and the foundation's position in Hungary grew more tenuous. Nowhere in Eastern Europe was right-wing criticism of Soros sharper than in Hungary. One eight-page article published on September 3, 1992, was headlined: "Termites are devouring our nation, reflections on the Soros regime and the Soros empire." It spoke of "The . . . common role played by Communists and Jews in the Hungarian power struggle." Soros made clear that he would not be intimidated by the nationalists. "These people are actually trying to establish a closed society based on ethnic identity. So I'm really genuinely opposed to them and I'm happy to have them as my enemies."

By 1994, a decade after its birth, the Soros Foundation in Budapest was operating 40 programs, supporting libraries and health education, and providing scholarships. Travel abroad was a priority. So were youth projects. One Soros Foundation program even supported debates in schools. "The notion of debate wasn't familiar here," said Laszlo Kados, the foundation's dark-bearded director. "The atmosphere was more one in which you received orders and you didn't argue."

But despite its success, the foundation's directors sensed that they had much more work to do. "Hungary is still not an open society, " said Kados. "There are lots of structures, lots of mentalities that we have to change. You can found a party, have parliamentary life, free elections. These things already exist in Hungary. But this does not make for an open society. It is only the starting point."

Soros was candid about what he hoped to accomplish through the foundation's grants. "Instead of going at our goal directly, through political action against the government, we indirectly undermine the dogmatic system of thinking. The struggle between different ideas is the stuff of democracy."

After setting up the foundation in Hungary in 1984, Soros decided to expand his philanthropic activities. He had moved into China in 1986, mesmerized by the thought of establishing a foundation in the largest communist country in the world. His investment was small, only a few million dollars, and for three years Soros tried to penetrate the "inscrutable" Orient. He failed miserably. He had various excuses. He accused the Chinese secret police of hijacking his local organization. He also had trouble with the Chinese culture. "There is a Confucian ethic rather than a Judaeo-Christian ethic. If you give someone some support he becomes beholden to you, he looks to you to look after him for the rest of his life and he owes you loyalty. That is totally contrary to the concept of an open society." Despite the setback in China, Soros was undeterred from pushing ahead in Eastern Europe and the former Soviet Union.

In 1987, he had begun efforts in the Soviet Union; then in 1988, he moved into Poland, and in 1989, Czechoslovakia. But one of his most imposing challenges was Romania.

Among the worst effects of the communist regime in Romania had been the grinding poverty. Romanians have an average monthly wage of $50. When I visited there in March 1994, I saw Romanians lined up in large numbers outside drab-looking stores to buy cheap, subsidized milk. The stores offered few of the products available in the West. Inflation, as high as 400 percent a few years earlier, had been eating away at Romanian purchasing power; many young people were seeking to leave the country.

In 1989, revolution overtook Romania, the "events," as Romanians have come to call what happened in a six-day span in December. Soros spoke to officials at the New York Human Rights Watch office, insisting: "We've got to do something. We've got to do something. Those people are going to kill themselves."

Fighting had not yet broken out, but Soros sensed that a conflagration impended. He was right. On December 16, 1989, Romanian security forces fired on demonstrators in Timisoara; hundreds were buried in mass graves. Ceauşescu declared a state of emergency as the protests spread to other cities.

Five days later, on December 21, protests began in Bucharest, where security forces fired on the demonstrators. The next day army units joined the rebels. A group calling itself the "Council of National Salvation" declared that it had overthrown the government.

Ceauşescu fled, and fresh fighting erupted, as the army, now backed by the new government, tried to put down forces loyal to Ceauşescu. The fleeing dictator was captured on December 23, and two days later, following a quick trial at which he and his wife were found guilty of genocide, he was executed.

It seemed an ideal time for Soros to get involved.

The Helsinki Watch group organized a fact-finding mission to Romania for January 1. Joining as guide and translator was Romanian-born Sandra Pralong, who, as a 15-year-old in 1974, had reached Switzerland and then had attended the Fletcher School of Diplomacy at Tufts University in Boston. She became associated with the Human Rights Watch effort in New York. As she was about to leave the United States, she received a phone call from George Soros, who said he was about to help a Philadelphia-based organization called Brothers' Brother, which was sending medicine and other items to Romania. "I would like to pay for them to send shipments of medicine, but I don't want the shipments to fall into the wrong hands." Soros asked if she would try to see that the medicine was distributed directly to those in need, bypassing official channels. Pralong promised to do her best.

Soros then decided to visit Romania in January with the hope of setting up a foundation there. To head the foundation, he had in mind one of the country's leading dissidents, Alin Teodoresco, the 39-year-old leader of an organization of former dissidents called the Group for Social Dialogue. On December 22, 1989, the day that the revolt began in earnest, Teodoresco had discovered five cars filled with secret police outside his home. His phone line was cut, and he was briefly confined to his home, a virtual prisoner.

Teodoresco had never heard of George Soros—and had no idea what a foundation was or what one was supposed to do. Not surprisingly, his first meeting with Soros on January 6, 1990, did not go smoothly. Soros showed up at Teodoresco's doorstep without an appointment. He was accompanied by Miklos Vasarhelyi, his personal representative to the Soros Foundation in Hungary.

Teodoresco was busy with meeting after meeting, and when a colleague announced that "there are two Americans waiting for you outside, one of them is saying he is a billionaire," Teodoresco was not suitably moved. "Oh, come on. Fuck them" was his less-than-polite response. Americans had been arriving by the busload after the revolution, telling Teodoresco and the other dissidents that they had money and wanted to help. So he kept Soros waiting for two hours. Finally a secretary popped into Teodoresco's office to let him know that the two men were still around.

"Let them come in."

In walked the billionaire and his associate.

"Hi, I'm George Soros."

"OK," Teodoresco said, unimpressed.

Then Vasarhelyi was introduced.

Teodoresco had heard of Vasarhelyi, a great dissident himself, a person who had been jailed and become something of a hero to many around Eastern Europe. Vasarhelyi's presence convinced Teodoresco to give Soros some time. Billionaires did not impress the Romanian dissident. Other dissidents did.

The three men met for breakfast the next day at Bucharest's Intercontinental Hotel. First came a half hour of small talk between the Romanian and Hungarian.

Finally, George Soros elbowed into the conversation.

"*I'm a billionaire,*" he began.

"OK," was all Teodoresco could think of by way of reply.

"I would like to set up a foundation here in Romania."

"What is a foundation?" Teodoresco asked in all sincerity.

Soros explained patiently. "You receive money from me. You have a board. You advertise that you have money and people come to apply for this money. And you give out the money."

Soros said he wanted Teodoresco to head up the foundation and that he would put $1 million at his disposal. Teodoresco sensed that it would be strange and difficult to introduce the idea of an outside foundation into his country. A month later, when Soros was back in Romania, he was eager to learn why Teodoresco seemed hesitant to accept the post. Soros asked, "Do you need help to set up this foundation?"

"Yes," the former dissident said, "I need help. I don't know how to set up a foundation."

Fine, said Soros. He had just the person in mind. Sandra Pralong. "You have to see her. She's the most creative person I've ever seen, a little bit neurotic."

When he returned to New York, Soros called Sandra Pralong.

"What do you think of my foundation?"

"What foundation?" she answered perplexedly. She had no idea what he was talking about. "It's not functioning yet."

"Do you want to go to Romania and fix it?"

Soros seemed to be offering her a job, and Sandra Pralong grew excited. Finally, he asked her formally to become the foundation's first executive director, and she agreed. In April 1990, Soros met again with Teodoresco, and together they agreed that he would become the foundation's first president.

Now that the top two jobs had been staffed, the foundation could get under way.

The foundation began functioning in June 1990. It was called the Foundation for an Open Society. Sandra Pralong arrived in Romania in September to take up her new duties.

For Alin Teodoresco, getting on with Soros was not simple, for Soros displayed little patience. He wanted to get the money spent and move on to other countries, other projects. Teodoresco was used to dialogue. "When I first met him, he was like a boss," Teodoresco recalled. He used the word "boss" pejoratively, to signify someone who expected his employees to function without too much instruction and without the chance to ask the boss questions.

As time wore on, though, Teodoresco became totally awestruck by the investor. He developed a theory about George Soros: that he was on a higher moral plane than most other people. He thought the secret to understanding Soros was to think of him as competing with himself, not against others, a concept that Teodoresco had drawn from the philosopher Immanuel Kant.

It was not easy creating the foundation from scratch. Just advertising for foundation staff in the newspaper was precedent setting. So was advertising the first scholarships. Despite its break with communism, Romania remained secretive, suspicious. When the first group of 60 Soros scholars arrived at the Bucharest train station on January 3, 1991, headed for the University of Edinburgh, one was crying. She confessed that when she had seen the newspaper advertisement she had thought it was a trick. The only Romanians who had gone abroad until then had been in high places, and she was decidedly not. That was why she was crying.

Even the foundation staff found it hard to function in the "open" atmosphere at the foundation. Anca Haracim, a tall, attractive 30-year-old, began working at the foundation as program coordinator in October 1990, but in 1993 she succeeded Sandra Pralong as executive director. Her budget that year was a hefty $6 million.

Haracim had grown up believing that every activity required a centralized body to make decisions. Working at the foundation shattered that mind-set. Her constant smile masked the fear she felt at first. But by 1994 she was able to say, "I'm completely infused with the foundation ideology. I can even apply what I've learned to my private life. I take charge more. Now I'm at the next stage. I have to delegate. That's more difficult than taking charge."

Soros could not live down his Hungarian past, not at least in Romania. With a population of 23.1 million, Romania had in its midst 2.4 million Hungarians. For a Hungarian-born billionaire to arrive in Romania, preaching capitalism, economic reform, and an open society seemed, to some Romanians, simply a disguised way to turn Romania's Hungarian population against the government.

Attacks on Soros began soon after the foundation was launched. Soros was accused in some newspapers of trying to "sell" Transylvania, where 1.8 million Hungarians lived, to Hungary. The foundation sought to be fair, not to discriminate in favor of Hungarian residents of Romania—or against them. It was not easy. In the city of Cluge, Hungarian residents had applied in large numbers, and the foundation had no choice but to award them what seemed like a disproportionate number of grants.

Soros ignored the attacks. In the absence of any guidelines from Soros, foundation officials fought back by being as open as possible with the public. Before the attacks, the foundation had never published the names of scholarship winners. Once the attacks began, it did. "This was a way to show others that we were not just selling Transylvania to the Hungarians, but also doing good things," said Anca Haracim.

Even the name the foundation had taken for itself—the Foundation for an Open Society—created the suspicion that the staff had something to hide. After all, the foundation did not carry Soros's name. So Pralong asked Teodoresco to rename it the Soros Foundation for an Open Society. Hopefully, Soros's name on the marquee would convince people that the foundation was not an underhanded tool for using Hungarian money to support Hungarians in Romania.

And yet there is no marquee. Standing in the large Vittoria Square in Bucharest, outside the building that houses the Soros Foundation, one immediately notices the lack of a sign indicating that the Soros Foundation for an Open Society is inside. Nor is there a sign in the third-floor corridor outside the foundation offices. This hardly seems an oversight.

One searches similarly in vain for photographs of George Soros on the walls. Though he pays the bills, and the place bears his name, there is a refreshing absence of signs meant to exalt him. No one talks of him personally; or makes jokes about him. But George Soros is always there. He hangs about ethereally, his name popping into conversations once every four or five sentences. The Open Society embodies Soros's all-encompassing strategy and mission. The staff knows that if it thinks up a program that can impact on this mission, Soros will go for it.

Though the lives of all of the Bucharest Foundation staff are wrapped up in George Soros, no one seems worried that he might, even on a whim, close the place down. Only a few weeks before I visited Bucharest, Soros had lost $600 million by making an incorrect financial gamble on the yen. Anca Haracim said she was not concerned at Soros's loss or that he would shut down the foundation. The loss was all part of The Game George Soros played. Some days the horse came in, some days it never left the gate.

In 1987, Soros decided to open a new philanthropic front in the Soviet Union, "the quintessential closed society," as he called it. In March of that year, three months after Soviet officials freed Andrei

Sakharov, the great symbol of Russian dissent, Soros began negotiating with the Soviets to allow him to establish a foothold in the Soviet Union. His great hope was to promote economic reform.

That year he sought out members of the Soviet emigré community in the United States for advice. Alex Goldfarb, a Moscow-born scientist and veteran dissident, was at the first meeting at Soros's New York City apartment. Goldfarb and his friends were skeptical. "We were actually quite negative. We said that such an effort will immediately be consumed by the KGB and they will outsmart you however smart you are." Soros dismissed their negativism.

And in fact, he pulled it off. In 1990, he established the Open Estonia Foundation and similar foundations in Latvia and Lithuania to provide business and management training, travel grants to scholars, scholarships, and English-language training. One such effort was the Management Training Program directed by his longtime friend Herta Seidman. Her program trained adult workforces—from Albania to the former Soviet Union—in business management techniques. In April 1994, the Management Training Program had just completed an accounting program for 35 Russians. "As the economies of these countries develop," said Seidman, "they will need local professionals to supply the services. That's what we're trying to do."

In December 1992, Soros announced one of his biggest aid programs, donating $100 million in support of scientists and scientific research in the former USSR. Having scored big against the pound in September 1992, Soros said, "I was looking for a megaproject that would make a bigger impact." The grant was designed to slow down the brain drain; already, 50,000 scientists had left the former Soviet republics, abandoning their research for better-paying jobs in places like Libya or Iraq. Here was a telling illustration of Soros at work. While the United States and the European Community were dithering about how to help Russia's disintegrating scientific community, Soros just went ahead and started a program.

Since 1987 Soros has opened Soros Foundation offices throughout the East. Each year his expenditures ballooned. His efforts in Eastern Europe grew in 1990, when he founded the Central European University with campuses in both Prague and Budapest. With 400 students from 22 countries, the CEU was Soros's dream, the project that meant the most to him. By the spring of 1994, the Soros philanthropic empire had spread to include 89 offices in 26 countries. He had given away $500 million in the previous two years, and he had made commitments to give another half billion dollars.

Some Soros-watchers believed cynically that the sole purpose of Soros's philanthropy was to give him better access to information so that he could invest more prudently. One skeptic noted that conferences Soros hosted for his foundations in Europe were attended by cabinet ministers who represented countries where he invested. Even Teodoresco believed Soros had a dual agenda in promoting his philanthropy, asserting that the contacts Soros made through his Foundation work gave him a better understanding of how the world economy functioned. "It's not at all random that he was more successful after he started to spend money through his foundations," said Teodoresco.

Soros attracted a great deal of publicity for his September 1992 coup against the British pound. The media wanted to know all about his investment style. He had no interest in giving away his secrets, so he used a diversionary tactic: By having reporters spend time with him in Eastern Europe, Soros was able to get the media to diffuse the focus. Less time was spent on his investments, that much more on his aid programs.

One British television documentary team, which aired its report on December 3, 1992, seemed happy to dwell on his aid efforts. They caught Soros talking on a plane to Prague about how little investing he was doing at that time. "Most of my effort goes into [the aid programs], probably 80 to 90 percent. I'm in touch with my office every day but I don't actually make any of the decisions. There's a team running the business. . . . I find it easier to make [money] than to spend it, actually,"

With that George Soros broke into a huge grin.

The jet landed in Prague and Soros deplaned. A Czech television crew caught up with him, and its reporter asked what sort of a capitalist he was: "I don't feel that I'm a business. I invest in businesses run by other people. So I'm really a critic. In a way you could say I'm the highest-paid critic in the world." Again, the camera caught that big Soros smile.

As he moved around Prague, checking on his foundation and the Central European University campus, he radiated enormous satisfaction. "I've got all the money I need, and therefore I intend to step up my philanthropic activities. I'm thinking of setting aside something like a quarter of a billion dollars to be spent as fast as possible."

A quarter of a billion dollars?

Few people gave away as much money with such little fuss as George Soros.

The next scene of the television documentary showed the opening of the academic year at the Central European University. Soros stood next to Vaclav Havel, the dissident who became president, behind a microphone that was too tall for him, that seemed to be hanging over his nose. He kept his right hand in his coat pocket, gesturing with the left.

"Originally I committed five million dollars a year for five years. That was 25 million dollars. To the university. Our current level of spending is already well in excess of that figure."

The students in the crowd understood enough English to know that this was a good time to applaud.

To his credit, Soros has avoided trying to make himself into a cult figure through his aid programs. Certainly he wants recognition and respect, but he does not insist that his name and photo be placed prominently on every institution he finances. Nor does he seem particularly interested in using the foundations to disseminate his ideas. During my visit to Soros foundations in Eastern Europe in the spring of 1994, it was virtually impossible to find copies of Soros's books. Even the library of the Central European University in Budapest, which boasted a well-stocked library, had none of his books. The school itself was called the Central European University, not the Soros University. *"I don't want to have a memorial of my name after my death,"* he once snapped. *"I want to influence what's happening now."*

Soros the aid-giver was a far happier person than Soros the money-maker. His life seemed to have a fresh purpose. If many in Eastern Europe and the former Soviet Union considered him a saint or Santa Claus, that was fine with him. When his critics hurled epithets his way, he brushed them off, as if they were harmless flies buzzing around him. He was a man on a mission, trying to make a difference, acting in a very hands-on way, having the time of his life. His foundation work, Soros said gleefully, "has brought me closer to realizing a real sense of satisfaction than making large amounts of money."

Soros's satisfaction was evident in late 1993. Michael Lewis, author of *Liar's Poker,* accompanied him on a two-week tour through Eastern Europe and said: "When I wonder aloud from the back of his jet how to illustrate . . . the comically complex web of his activities between Germany and China he will swivel around in his seat at the front and say, 'Just write that the former Soviet Empire is now called the Soros Empire.' Then he will turn back around and smile to himself."

With his empire so spread out, so active in so many places, Soros seems to feel as if he should be everywhere at once. He has trouble sticking to a schedule. A whim will overtake him and he will change his plans at the last minute, to the exasperation of those who have already set his original plans in motion. In late 1992, he was scheduled to fly from Tirane, Albania, to Vienna, but when he boarded the plane, he suddenly shifted gears. "Let's fly to London," he told the pilot.

The pilot grimaced, smiled, and recalled the two hours he had spent preparing for the Vienna trip.

"Mr. Soros," the pilot said, "you are the most challenging customer we have." Soros laughed.

Racing from one project to another, Soros seems to be trying to make up for lost time. Nitty-gritty projects, however important, fail to capture his attention as much as the large ones. He wants to have an impact, and to have it immediately. "He always wants to begin new projects," explained Miklos Vasarhelyi. "If something is already on its way and is working, he's not so much interested in it. His decisions are not quite the best choices, but he's able to correct himself, because if he sees that something is not good, he'll admit it."

Tibor Vamos, who has been associated with Soros's aid program in Hungary, traced Soros's impulsiveness in his aid efforts to his "little stock-exchange brain. . . . He can change his mind while speaking a sentence. That's really a stock-exchange mind. At 9:30 AM you buy some textile industry, and 15 minutes later you sell everything and buy something very different. So he is somehow impatient if we are speaking about long-range effects and not very visible work."

By the spring of 1994, Soros had earned a good deal of credit in the West for his aid efforts. His "one-Man Marshall Plan," as *Newsweek* had dubbed it, was getting generally good grades. Yet Soros understood that far more needed to be done before Eastern Europe and the former Soviet Union could be considered truly open.

While he and his foundation staff often profess to wish that Western governmental and nongovernmental agencies will eventually supplant Soros Foundation efforts, the truth is that Soros has little confidence that others will be able to accomplish what he has. He thinks little of government aid, believing it "the last instance of a command economy, because the help is given to benefit the donors and not the recipients." He told an official from the Council of Europe in Strasbourg, "You really can't do anything. You don't have enough power to change Eastern Europe."

Soros has had the advantage of being a lone wolf, able to make his own decisions, not having to submit his ideas to others for approval. Jeffrey Sachs, a Harvard University economist who has served as an adviser to the Polish and Russian governments on economic reform, said: "George Soros . . . operates in a very flexible way. There isn't in these crisis cases a lot of cash around. So a small amount of money can help tremendously, paying for someone's airfare, a trip. The World Bank might take two years to get something going. George will give the air ticket overnight."

Due to the largesse Soros had spread around Eastern European and to the former Soviet republics, *The New Republic* has called him "the single most powerful foreign influence in the whole of the former Soviet empire." A *Business Week* cover story described him as the "single most influential citizen between the Rhine and the Urals."

But even with all that praise, by the early 1990s Soros seemed depressed at the slow progress of his aid efforts. He had, at first, hoped that he could simply light a match and ignite a revolution. "I feel that I have gotten sucked in a little deeper than I am really prepared for, because it is, in the end, very draining, and very exhausting."

Fifteen

An Urge to Reveal Oneself

I n the early phases of his business career, George Soros thought that fame was the worst thing that could befall him. Fame meant instant recognition, it meant telephone calls from the media, it meant an end to the joys of privacy. Fame was considered a death blow to one's investment career.

No wonder the profile of choice on Wall Street was invisibility.

According to James Grant, editor of *Grant's Interest Rate Observer* in New York, Soros was not alone in the shadows; most of Wall Street was with him. The popular view was that "like mushrooms, fortunes seem to grow best in the dark. People on Wall Street don't want to explain some day in the business section of the *New York Times* how they make money. They don't want the world to know how much money they have because they know that from time to time political winds change, admiration turns to envy, and there are hearings."

In earlier days it was easy to avoid the media. Business stories and business personalities carried little appeal for journalists. They might be titans on Wall Street, wheelers and dealers in their corporate boardrooms, but the media thought them to be faceless, uninteresting, lacking in controversy and reader interest. Then in 1984 the publication of controversial automobile executive Lee Iacocca's autobiography gave a mass audience a glimpse into his business career, and for the first time business personalities seemed an interesting breed. In the wake of the Iacocca book, the media decided to probe more intensively into the country's businesses and its leaders.

In the 1970s and 1980s, Soros seemed uninterested in publicity. The media responded by largely ignoring him. Every once in a while, *The Wall Street Journal* wrote a story summarizing his career, as it did in a flattering front-page story in 1975. But even when given the chance to project himself as a public figure, he seemed to shy away. In the late 1970s and early 1980s *Barron's* invited him to participate in a series of panels to make stock predictions. Except on a few occasions, Soros restrained himself from giving away much information.

To friends of Soros, the silence surrounding the investor came less from Soros than from Wall Street. Some argued that the investment community, jealous of his brilliant record, imposed a conspiracy of silence on him; they rarely mentioned him around reporters, so Soros, according to these friends, was hardly known to the business media. The flaw in this view is that when Soros did receive media attention, it was almost entirely sympathetic. If there was a conspiracy of silence in those days, it surrounded not just George Soros but most Wall Street business personalities.

Though articles on him had appeared before, it was only when he made the cover of *Institutional Investor* in June 1981 that George Soros attracted widespread public notice.

Full of bombast and grandiose verbiage, the magazine crowned Soros "The world's greatest money manager." This was no small praise, and the phrase had such a ring to it that it remained in people's minds. Even as the magazine heightened Soros's profile, it reminded its readers that Soros was very much an enigma. "For all his personal and professional success . . . Soros has remained something of a mystery man, a Howard Hughes of investment. Aside from his occasional—and uncharacteristic—appearances in *Barron's* annual forecast panel, few on Wall Street or in the financial community at large know much about the reclusive fund manager. Yet few haven't heard of his record.

". . . Adding to the mystery surrounding his record is the fact that no one is ever quite sure where Soros is making a move or how long he stays with an investment. As a manager of offshore funds, he is not required to register with the SEC. He avoids Wall Street professionals. And those in the business who *do* know him personally admit that they have never felt particularly close to the man. As for fame, it's widely agreed that he can happily do without it."

While the *Institutional Investor* story was certainly positive, what happened in its wake was certain to make Soros wonder whether media attention was desirable. In the months immediately following the story, Soros suffered through the only losing year of his career. In conversations with James Marquez in 1982 before hiring him, Soros made clear how distasteful he had found the whole experience of "coming out."

"To George this [publicity followed by the financial setback] was almost a causal relationship," remarked Marquez. "George knew the risk of believing one's own press clippings and knew it causes one to sit back on one's laurels and watch rather than participate. He thought that he had shared . . . what he knew and how to invest with others through the media, and look what it got him. Not only that. He had lost some of his long-term investors and friends in the process. So he went into a very secretive phase."

Marquez experienced the "secretive phase" up front as Soros's right-hand man in 1983 and 1984.

Business journalists often phoned the Quantum Fund during that period, wanting to know what it was doing or how Soros and Marquez thought some piece of news would impact on Wall Street. When Marquez joined the firm, Soros made clear that he was not to talk to the press. "The last time I went on the record," said Marquez, "was the day I went to work for George Soros, January 1, 1983."

Marquez, a friendly type who obviously enjoyed talking with reporters, took the phone calls, despite Soros's orders. To Marquez, it was important to get certain issues before the public. But he made it clear to journalists that his remarks were to be reported only on a background basis. "I would say to the reporters: 'I'll tell you the things I know, or that I think I know, but it's absolutely not for attribution.'" Neither he nor the Quantum Fund could be quoted. Those were his rules.

Soros probably sensed that Marquez was talking to reporters, but he never asked Marquez to leak information. Sometimes Marquez was sure that Soros knew he had been the source of a story. "He always had a way of acknowledging that I was behind something— he would say, 'Gee, this sounds almost like you wrote this.' I would be espousing something one day to him and the next thing it would appear in the newspapers."

When Allan Raphael joined Soros in 1984, he was told never to speak to the press. And he obeyed. "We were known as the secretive Soros Fund, which in my opinion is the right way to do it. We generally took good-sized positions, and the last thing you want is for anybody to know what you're doing."

Why?

"Because people front-run. If you're running a fund that's global and people want to know what you're doing, you don't want people tracking you very easily because if you want to buy something, and everyone else finds out about it, they buy it ahead of you; it just messes you up."

Also, Soros's clients were all outside the United States and "very secretive," according to Raphael. "They just don't want to see their name in the newspaper."

And so in the early and mid-1980s, Soros's press policy was to have none. He had no spokesperson; no press releases were issued. "We wanted," said Raphael, "to come and go quietly."

One critical exception came in September 1987, when Soros was interviewed for the *Fortune* magazine cover story entitled "Are Stocks Too High?" Soros predicted that the American stock market would not suffer a setback. The Japanese market, however, would. Soon thereafter, Wall Street collapsed.

"It was like appearing on the cover of *Sports Illustrated,* said Raphael. "Your team is favored to win the World Cup and then it's immediately eliminated. We sort of joked that it's almost like a jinx to be on the cover."

To achieve some of his other goals, especially fostering open societies in Eastern Europe and elsewhere, Soros could not remain entirely secretive. For he wanted respect. He wanted the cynics to take him seriously as a thinker. He understood that his philanthropic efforts in Eastern Europe would be helped if he became more of a public figure and spoke out on behalf of them.

It was as if he were in a tug-of-war with himself. One side, the investment side, was tugging in the direction of secretiveness; the other side, the philanthropic side, was tugging in the direction of openness. This tension was best illustrated when he noted that "there is a point beyond which self-revelation can be damaging, and one of the flaws in my character, which I have not fully fathomed, is the urge to reveal myself."

His theory of reflexivity had vaulted him into the stratosphere of investing, and now—in 1987—he was ready for the public to get to know him better. He had used his most powerful resource, his mind, liked the results, and was now confident that the time was right for him to carve out a place for himself in the world of ideas. That place had been denied to him in the past. But what about now?

He had long wanted to publish a book that would make some contribution to human knowledge, but he knew he would have to make his ideas clearer to the public. "They are not understood," he said once, "because I have not been very good at explaining them and they are complex."

While publishing a book of his philosophy remained an elusive dream, he could produce a book that would explain his financial theories. He hesitated, though, before taking the plunge; he worried that, in exposing his financial theories to public scrutiny, he would appear to be boasting. What if, after the book was published, he suffered more financial setbacks? What would the public say then? What would it think of his financial theories?

He decided to take the plunge anyhow.

The manuscript for what eventually became *The Alchemy of Finance* basically existed. He simply had to prepare it for publication. As far back as 1969, he had shown chapters of the book to colleagues. Some had digested it and said nothing to him. Some had remarked about how difficult it was to understand. Few made any concrete suggestions. They understood that Soros wanted praise for his writing, not a critique.

One who saw an early version of the book—actually loose notes in manuscript in a bound volume—was Jim Marquez. "He gave me a number of these notes to read and it was very heavy slogging, very heavy slogging. It's great sleeping material for a lot of people." James Grant, editor of *Grant's Interest Rate Observer* in New York, one of the more astute minds on Wall Street, thought little of *Alchemy:* "I tried to read [the book] and I came away slightly empty-handed, or I guess, empty-headed. I did not find it a particularly lucid exposition."

Another who saw some early chapters was Allan Raphael. "The book is meant for graduate students, not popular reading. We had to read every draft of every chapter that he did. In all candor, it's not so stimulating. From the reader's point of view, it wasn't how to make a zillion dollars in 10 days. It wasn't a diary of what he did. He jumped back and forth. He didn't let anyone edit the book, which I think was a mistake." Simon & Schuster wanted to provide a professional editor to go over the book, a standard publishing practice, but Soros refused, according to Raphael.

It was not entirely true that the manuscript lacked an editor. Byron Wien, Soros's longtime friend and U.S. investment strategist at Morgan Stanley, did some serious editing on it. "He would write drafts of it, and I would make suggestions for rewriting and I would also edit pretty severely. . . . Some people say it's still unreadable, and I said to them: 'You should have seen it before.'"

Soros originally wanted to call the book *Boom and Bust*. But Byron Wien talked him out of it. "It was such a cliché. It sort of demeaned what the book was all about."

Soros was very concerned that readers not misunderstand the purpose of the book. He did not want to publish yet one more how-to guide about getting rich on Wall Street. Readers might search for investment tips on every page. But he was not trying to help others make money. He was writing for one purpose only: to explain to readers how his financial theories were part of a wider set of general theories about how the world functioned. He wrote that he was using his "experiences in the financial markets to develop an approach to the study of historical processes in general and the present historical moment in particular."

To be taken seriously, to get the public interested in his ideas, Soros had to make himself understood. He had to set out his theories in a way that others would have no trouble comprehending. He would also have to make clear how he had applied his theory to his decision making as an investor.

If he could do that, he would open a window to his mind, and the respect that he so longed for might follow. If he did not do that, he would simply confuse people, and inevitably turn off most or all of those who waited eagerly to be enlightened. But while the book was taken seriously, particularly by book reviewers, it did little to win Soros great respect within the financial community.

The reason was simple.

Soros did not make clear to these people what his financial theories were all about. He obfuscated in ways that were apparently not obvious to him. For anyone who took the time to plow through it, the book was heavy, difficult reading.

Soros genuinely believed that, even with his amazing financial acumen becoming more and more a matter of public record, he could remain in the shadows. He genuinely believed that the publication of *Alchemy* would buttress his reputation without thrusting him too much into the public spotlight.

He was about to find out how wrong he was.

When *The Alchemy of Finance* was published in 1987, Soros hoped that the financial community and those outside of it would treat him with the respect he felt he deserved as an intellectual. It did not dawn on him that the media would treat the ideas contained in the book with indifference. When Soros realized that his theories were of less interest than his investment positions, the experience proved jarring to him.

When Simon & Schuster talked to him about promoting the book, he thought he was embarking on a journey of exploring ideas with the media, not exposing himself to the kinds of questions he had avoided throughout his business career.

"You've got to go out and publicize the book," a senior figure at the publishing house told him.

"OK, I guess so," Soros said grudgingly. "What should I do?"

Well, the publicity folks explained, you should seek interviews with *Fortune,* the *New York Times,* and others. We'll set them up for you.

Soros comforted himself with the notion that the interviews would focus on his book. It was a naive presumption, and some of his associates tried to steer him right: No, they're not going to want to talk about your book. They'll want to find out what you bought last. That's what they'll ask about, that's what they'll want to know.

One Friday afternoon, Soros was sitting in a conference with his fund managers when suddenly he announced that he had to catch a train to Washington.

"I'm going on this 'Wall Street Week' program," he declared with seeming pride. "They're going to discuss my book."

Allan Raphael, one of the fund managers at that meeting, knew that Soros never watched television. He tried to be helpful.

"You know what this program is all about?"

"Yes, they want to discuss my book." Soros seemed so insistent. Still Raphael plunged on.

"George, they don't want to discuss your book. They want to know what you're buying, what your favorite stocks are. They're going to ask you a lot of things which you don't want to respond to."

"No," said Soros, this time with less insistence in his voice. "They're going to discuss my book."

That evening Soros appeared on the program. Sure enough, after two minutes of pleasantries, the question was put to him:

"What are your favorite stocks?"

Soros, however, was prepared.

"I'm not going to tell you."

And he didn't.

Nonetheless, this encounter was his initial entry into the world of public life. And he was not entirely comfortable with it.

But Soros was in for yet another surprise.

Donald Katz wanted to interview Soros for *Esquire*. But Soros had been hard to pin down. The writer seemed at his wit's end until he learned that Soros had written a book, which he later described as "an impenetrably dense but at times breathtakingly brilliant book."

Katz wrote the investor a long letter, begging for an interview. Who could deny an audience, he asked Soros in seeming good humor, to someone who claims to have read your book? A few days later Soros granted Katz only 10 minutes. Evidently he was not entirely convinced Katz had read *The Alchemy of Finance*.

Katz arrived at the Soros Fund offices and was escorted into a waiting room filled with books with such titles as *Quantitative Risk Assessment in Regulation* and *The Political Economy of Socialism: A Marxist View*. He also found a book in Chinese and a work about a painter. Then Soros arrived, wearing a beautiful gray suit, looking cheerful. He escorted Katz into his spacious office.

Then Soros popped the question. It came out as more of a statement, tinged with cynicism or doubt.

"So, you say you've actually read my book."

Katz said he had, but he sensed Soros was skeptical.

"And you understood it?"

Whatever Katz answered—he offered no clue—it convinced Soros that the conversation with the writer was worth pursuing. Soros sought to make the same point he had hoped to make on the Washington talk show, that he cared only about philosophy, not at all about moneymaking.

"My real interest is genuinely analytical," he explained to Katz. "It's the theory I care for. My success in the market merely provides me with a platform so people will take me seriously. I have no interest in getting new clients."

Then a grin flashed across Soros's face. "And I certainly don't want to get rich on this book."

Sixteen

The Big Crash

The incredible bull market of the mid-1980s had showered investors with billions of dollars of profits. None had done better than George Soros.

In 1986, the Quantum Fund was up 42.1 percent—to $1.5 billion, adding to Soros's luster. His own income from the fund was $200 million.

In 1985 and 1986, he had amassed a staggering $2.5 billion for himself and his small group of foreign investors.

The Dow Jones average had risen steadily, from 776.92 in August 1982 to a high of 2722.42 in August 1987. According to Soros's theory of reflexivity, the market would climb even higher. The sheer enthusiasm and frenzy of investors would carry it aloft.

Yet, in the back of his mind, Soros knew that sooner or later, if his theory of reflexivity was correct, *the bust aspect of the boom/bust sequence would take hold.* It was only a matter of time. But it need not happen immediately.

Meanwhile, Soros appeared on the cover of *Fortune* magazine on September 28 and proclaimed that things never looked better, particularly in Japan.

"That stocks have moved up, up and away from the fundamental measures of value does not mean they must tumble," Soros observed in an interview for that cover story. "Just because the market is overvalued does not mean it is not sustainable. If you want to know how much more overvalued American stocks can become, just look at Japan." He reiterated these views on "Wall Street Week."

Even after adjusting for the peculiarities of Japanese accounting, Japanese stocks were selling in October 1987 at profit/earning ratios of 48.5 compared to 17.3 in England and 19.7 in the United States. Soros thought that those multiples were bad omens for the Tokyo market. He knew of the soaring land prices in Tokyo, knew that too much money was chasing too few assets. And he believed that the high ratios and low dividends could not be sustained.

He also knew that many Japanese firms, particularly banks and insurance companies, had invested heavily in the stocks of other Japanese companies. Some of these firms had even issued debt to finance their stock market activities. That amount of stock market exposure had increased the value of those companies as the Tokyo market soared—but the threat of a major collapse if things went wrong always loomed. With his theory of reflexivity in mind, Soros sensed that investor frenzy, now racing wildly, would probably set off an implosion of Japanese stock values. Because the Japanese market accounted for 36 percent of all stocks values around the world, the effect would be felt everywhere. Soros grew deeply pessimistic about the Japanese stock market. "There's no turning back for the Tokyo market. The perception of value has become so extended, an orderly retreat seems impossible. There may be a crash coming."

The U.S. market would not be affected very much, however, if the Japanese market collapsed, he guessed. U.S. stocks had values that were nowhere near the absurd levels in Japan. While he saw on Wall Street some of the same processes that had led to the extreme Japanese valuations, Soros was not overly worried about the U.S. market. Accordingly, that fall he transferred several billion dollars of investments from Tokyo to Wall Street. He sounded an optimistic note: "The American market has only recently gotten carried away, and it can still correct these excesses in a mild, orderly fashion."

Not everyone agreed. In mid-October Robert S. Prechter, a popular market forecaster who had been riding a bull market run for five years, reversed himself, warning clients to pull out of the market. Soros, along with other investors, was stunned by Prechter's comments. On October 14, Soros wrote an article in the *Financial Times* of London, predicting again that it was the Japanese market that was headed for collapse.

Then came the dramatic week of October 19.

Anatole Kaletsky, bureau chief for the *Financial Times* in New York at the time, spoke regularly with Soros. On October 19, he called the investor to find out what was happening in the markets.

"Considering the scale of his positions, he showed remarkable sangfroid. He was extraordinarily articulate, and gave me a historical, philosophical account. We talked about the analogies between what was happening that week and what happened in 1929. I wouldn't have suspected for a moment that he had anything at stake at all. I remember him saying in a very relaxed way, 'Well, technically this is 1929, what's going on today.' What he meant was that this was the sort of ultimate meltdown in the financial markets which he had been expecting for some time."

But then the New York market crashed, falling a record 508.32 points that Monday. Soros expected the Japanese stock market to crash even harder. Instead, it held firm overnight Tuesday. The crash on Wall Street marked the end of the five-year bull market.

On Thursday, October 22, the market rebounded by 300 points, but then grew bearish again. Reports of large margin calls were heard. American stocks opened dramatically down on foreign stock exchanges. Soros decided to sell large chunks of his long positions.

An account in *Barron's* describes what happened: "The other pit traders, picking up the sound of a whale in trouble, hung back, but circled the prey. The offer went from 230 down to 220 to 215 to 205 to 200. Then, the pit traders attacked. The Soros block sold from 195 to 210. The spiral was ghastly. It was Soros's block and not program trading that drove the futures to a cash discount some 50 points, or 20 percent, below the cash value of the S&P contract. The discount on the 5,000 contracts represented some $250 million. The futures fund manager covered these, as did a number of local traders who made millions off the immediate snapback in price."

Once the Soros block had vanished, the irony was that the S&P futures market recovered quickly, closing at 244.50. Soros lost $200 million in one day.

Soros, as it turned out, was one of the biggest single losers in the Wall Street crash.

He admitted to making an error of judgment. "I expected the break to come in stocks, but in retrospect it obviously began in the bond market, particularly the Japanese bond market, where yields more than doubled in just a matter of weeks earlier this year." As a result, the U.S. bond market had gone into a tailspin during the spring of 1987. Failing to see the downturn coming on Wall Street, Soros had still expected to see a healthy U.S. stock market.

Adam Smith, the television economics commentator, wondered how it had happened that Soros saw the crash coming and still got caught.

Soros replied with disarming candor: "I made a very big mistake, because I expected the crash to come in Japan, and I was prepared for that, and it would have given me an opportunity to prepare for the falloff in this country, and actually it occurred on Wall Street and not in Japan. So I was wrong."

The conventional wisdom in newspaper articles published soon after the '87 crash has it that Soros lost anywhere from $650 million to $800 million.

The *New York Times,* for example, reported on October 28, 1987, that the Quantum Fund's net asset value per share had risen $41.25 in 1969 to $9,793.36 the day before the crash. The *Times* wrote: "This could be the second year Quantum loses money. . . . Since the market started its decline in August, the Quantum Fund has lost more than 30 percent of its value, sliding to less than $1.8 billion from more than $2.6 billion. Last week alone, Soros sold hundreds of millions of dollars' worth of stocks."

Barron's, in Floyd Norris's "The Trader" column on November 2, 1987, reported that Quantum had suffered a 32 percent loss in net asset value as a result of the crash, dropping from $2.6 billion at the end of the third quarter—up 60 percent on the year—to $1.8 billion. According to *Barron's,* "Soros had lost some $840 million in less than two weeks." In a brief phone interview with *Barron's,* Soros conceded that he had some trading losses but noted that the fund was still up 2.5 percent for the year.

The question of how much Soros actually lost in the 1987 crash has plagued him ever since. According to Allan Raphael, Soros sought to persuade the media that he had lost far less than the rumored $800 million.

"It's very unfortunate, " observed Raphael. "Others like to look at your misery as their joy. We were asked for an interview by the *New York Times.*

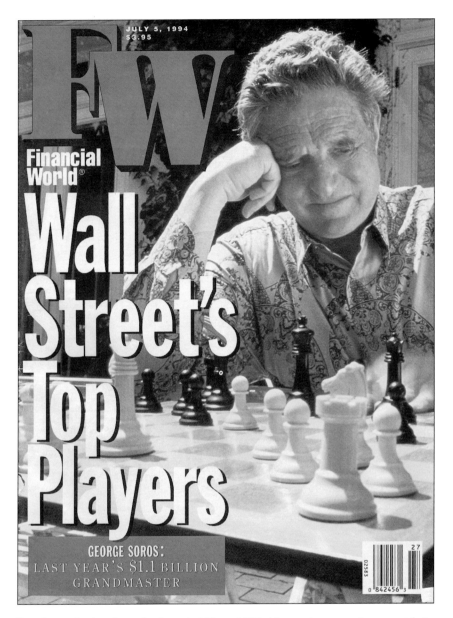

Soros' expertise is not exactly chess, but *Financial World* magazine seems to suggest that he reads the financial markets the way a chess expert reads a chess board.

Byron Wien

Stories like this one gave Soros the reputation of someone with vast powers over the financial markets.

Allan Raphael

Benny Landa

As part of the Soros Foundation aid efforts, computers have been donated to high schools in Eastern Europe.

Despite strong concerns over Russia's future, Soros has provided much aid to the former Soviet Union. Here he is shown in Moscow.

Adopting a low profile for years, Soros became well-known only in 1992 when he earned nearly $2 billion in his "coup" against the British pound.

Due to the largesse Soros has spread around Eastern Europe and the former Soviet republics, he has been called "the single most influential citizen between the Rhine and the Urals."

Called the world's greatest investor, Soros watches his investments from afar in the mid 1990s, preferring to devote his time to his aid programs.

Soros at first wanted to be a
philosopher, but then turned
to investing—and became a
superstar!

Soros likes to say that he finds it easier to make money than to spend it.

Soros, eager to burnish his image of "world statesman," talks here with South African leader Nelson Mandela.

A secretive, mysterious figure for a long time, Soros, by the early 1990's, was pleased to appear at press conferences as a way of promoting his philanthropic activities.

Soros and his wife Susan in a relaxed pose.

"Now there's much more information about the price of the fund, but back in 1987 the only information the outside world had of the price of the fund was . . . the quotation . . . in the *Financial Times* under 'other overseas investment trusts.'

"But that was not the net asset value of the fund. If you wanted to buy into the fund you had to pay the net asset value plus a premium. . . . The net asset value, which reflects the asset value of the fund, is not the price you see in the *Financial Times* and people didn't realize it. And that's how they computed the $800 million.

"These people said you went into October at $20,000 dollars a share and you finished the month at $16,000 a share. Therefore you must have lost $4,000 a share. . . . But their calculation, we argued, included the premium. Our loss turned out to be $350 to 400 million. Everyone thought it was really $650 to 800 million. It was bad enough. Gary Gladstein, speaking in George's name, explained to the *New York Times* about the premium, but they basically had already reached their conclusions. It did not make Soros happy.

" 'This isn't true,' he said. 'How can they print this? How do they do this?'

"I told him: 'George, you don't get into a peeing contest with people who buy ink by the barrel. That's all there is to it.'

"But it really soured him. After that it made no sense for him to talk to the press."

In effect, the crash wiped out Soros's entire profit for 1987. A week after the crash, Quantum's net asset value had dropped 26.2 percent to $10,432.75 a share. This was even larger than the 17 percent drop in the U.S. stock market. It was also reported that Quantum was off 31.9 percent since October 8, suggesting that Soros had lost $100 million of his own money.

A reporter from *Time* magazine asked his reaction to the setback: "I'm amused," was all he would, or could, say. Realizing apparently that things could have been a lot worse, he said, "I'm still smiling."

Though the October crash marked one of Soros's worst setbacks—not since the 1981 bond fiasco had he suffered so much—he took the blow with great equanimity. "He was perfectly calm during the crash," said one investor friend of his. "He takes a loss better than anyone I have ever met. He may think that the market did not react as it should have, which is to say as he predicted. But once the mistake is made, he understands it and goes on."

To Soros, the bust was not over. He thought another major financial collapse could occur. Then, he noted dourly, many investors would find out just how complex playing the market actually is. "A lot of people have been riding this thing up," he said. "But just as the decline of 1960 and 1970 melted away many of the fortunes built during the 1950s and 1960s, the testing will come in the face of adversity."

In an article he wrote in early 1988, Soros noted the striking similarities between the 1987 crash and the one in 1929.

"Reflexive connections do not operate with equal force in all markets at all times. Nevertheless, the patterns often show similarities. For instance, the resemblance between the crashes of 1987 and 1929 is uncanny. The tendency for the dollar to overshoot, both on the up and the down side, is equally noteworthy.

> "**R**eflexive connections do not operate with equal force in all markets at all times."

"In currency markets there has been a mutually reinforcing connection between the relative importance of international capital movements, which have become progressively more trend-following, and excessive exchange-rate fluctuations. . . .

"In the stock market, however, the growth of a trend-following bias has largely escaped attention. . . . When one is judged in comparison with market averages, it is difficult to keep one's own judgment independent of the market trend. . . .

"Eventually, the reliance on trend-following devices became greater than the capacity of the market to accommodate them. When the market started to fall, it continued to accelerate until it became disorganized, and some of the supposedly automatic programs could not be executed. . . .

"Much of the discussion about liquidity or its lack is misplaced; what matters is the balance between buyers and sellers. Trend-following speculation (such as indexing, performance measure, and technical analysis) and trend-following devices (such as portfolio insurance and option-writing) disrupt the balance. Financial markets need a measure of liquidity to permit execution of buy and sell orders without excessive transaction costs; but be-
yond a certain point,
liquidity, or its illusion,
can be harmful because
it encourages trend-fol-
lowing behavior."

Incredibly, by the
end of 1987, the Quan-
tum Fund was still up
14.1 percent to $1.8
billion.

> "The reliance on trend-following devices became greater than the capacity of the market to accommodate them."

Indeed, the crash barely caused a ripple in Soros's standing on Wall Street.

When *Financial World* published its annual survey of the highest paid people on Wall Street, there was Soros ranked number two behind the leader, Paul Tudor Jones II. Tudor Jones's estimated earnings were put at between $80 million and $100 million. Soros's 1987 income, even with the crash, was $75 million. No wonder he accepted the losses from the crash calmly!

Seventeen

It Takes Courage to Be a Pig

With his heart and mind focused on Eastern Europe and the Soviet Union, George Soros felt less and less inclined to keep up with the day-to-day operations of the Quantum Fund. He could afford the diversion. From the mid-1980s on, the fund had a net asset value of over $1 billion. Soros was on his way to becoming one of the richest men in America. He wished to spend most of his time promoting open societies in Europe, as little as possible worrying about making a buck.

By the fall of 1988, Soros was determined to choose someone who could not only take over the day-to-day running of the fund but one day take over the entire operation, someone who could make decisions over a wide realm of investment choices. Finding that person and putting him at the helm marked one of the most important decisions George Soros would ever have to make.

The person he selected was Stanley Druckenmiller.

Like Soros, Druckenmiller, a Philadelphia native, had attracted virtually no media attention in the early years of his career. He had been an investment whiz, but few knew anything about him. He had obtained his undergraduate degree in English and economics *magna cum laude* at Bowdoin College in Maine. He went on to study economics at the graduate level at the University of Michigan but found the program overly quantitative and theoretical—and boring. It seemed to place too little stress on the real world.

Druckenmiller had begun his career in 1977 as a stock analyst for the Pittsburgh National Bank. His salary was $10,800 a year. When he was promoted to director of equity research soon afterwards, his salary was raised to $23,000 a year. Less than a year after that he became division head at $48,000 a year. Two years later, in 1980, he left the bank at age 28 to begin his own money management firm. Prompting the move was a call he had received from a securities-firm executive who had offered him $10,000 a month just to talk with him about investments. Druckenmiller called his fund Duquesne Capital Management.

Six years later, in 1986, Druckenmiller was recruited by Dreyfus to become a fund manager, though he was permitted to continue managing his Duquesne fund. At Dreyfus he managed stocks, bonds, and currencies, moving in and out of markets both on the long and short side. His talents highly appreciated, Druckenmiller was given responsibility for several funds developed just for him. The most popular, established in March 1987, was the Strategic Aggressive Investing Fund. For the next 17 months, it was the best-performing fund in the industry.

Druckenmiller's success with the Strategic Fund came to George Soros's attention. According to Soros, Druckenmiller sought him out after having been intrigued by *The Alchemy of Finance*. Soros was in search of the best, and Druckenmiller seemed to fill the bill. Though Druckenmiller had been thinking about going back to managing his own fund full-time, Soros was an idol of his: "He seemed to be about 20 years ahead of me in implementing the trading philosophy I had adopted." That philosophy was to hold a core group of stocks long and a core group of stocks short and then to use leverage to trade S&P futures, bonds, and currencies.

Soros invited Druckenmiller for some meetings.

He was torn. Should he go back to Duquesne? Or take a chance and work for the Master?

Druckenmiller had heard all the stories about Soros, that George liked to fire people on a whim, that the turnover at Quantum was rapid. When he mentioned to his friends in the investment community that he was considering going over to the Quantum Fund, they advised him not to take the job.

The rumors did not bother him that much. What could happen? In his worst-case scenario, he would last a year before Soros fired him. During that year, at least, he would get one hell of an education, and the year would only work to his advantage once he returned to Duquesne.

Determined to attract Druckenmiller, Soros applied a full-court press. Even before he officially hired him, Soros would refer to him as "my successor." It was all very flattering to Druckenmiller, and frightening. "When I went to Soros's home to be interviewed, his son informed me that I was his tenth 'successor.' None of the others had lasted too long. . . . And when I arrived at Soros's office the next day, the staff all referred to me as 'the successor.' They also thought it was funny."

In September 1988, Soros offered him the job, and Druckenmiller accepted it. Soros's replacement had been found. Now all Druckenmiller had to do was demonstrate that he was up to the job.

The first six months were—as Druckenmiller had feared—brutal. The two men may have had similar trading philosophies, but their strategies for implementing those philosophies differed. Druckenmiller wanted to be able to operate independently. He did not want George standing over him, second-guessing his every move. For his part, Soros had no desire to give Druckenmiller a great deal of freedom at the outset. He had to earn it. Then Soros would see about turning over the reins to him.

The new man had no wish to clash with the boss. So when Soros proposed something, Druckenmiller went along. Druckenmiller was unquestionably intimidated by his mentor, the man he had often described as the greatest investor of the era.

But capitulating to Soros eventually got to Druckenmiller. It seemed almost idiotic to disagree with anything that came out of Soros's mouth, and yet he had no desire to be a mere clerk. Druckenmiller finally told Soros: "You just can't have two cooks in the kitchen; it doesn't work." Soros made noises about promising to change, but not much happened. For a while Druckenmiller took a grin-and-bear-it attitude.

Then in August 1989, nearly a year after he joined Quantum, the two men had their first open quarrel.

Druckenmiller, acting on his own, had taken a position in bonds. Without consulting him, Soros sold the bonds. It was the first time Soros had gone behind Druckenmiller's back.

Druckenmiller exploded. The two exchanged angry words. Eventually, Soros calmed down and promised that he would keep his distance.

Soros acknowledged that he and Druckenmiller went through some early rough spots. "At the beginning, he found it difficult to work with me. Although I gave him a great deal of authority, he was inhibited by my presence and felt that he was not doing as well as he had before joining my firm."

Would Soros live up to this new arrangement? Druckenmiller had his doubts. Soros hadn't managed to keep a low profile in the previous year. Why should he turn over a new leaf now?

But a few months later—in late 1989—Druckenmiller got a break.

Events took a dramatic turn in Eastern Europe as the Velvet Revolution began. Communist regimes began to fall. The Berlin Wall came tumbling down that November. Soros was following events there on a day-to-day basis. "With George off in Eastern Europe," beamed Druckenmiller, "he couldn't meddle even if he wanted to." Soros gave his version: "In the summer of 1989, I told Stan that he must take full charge of running the fund. Since then we have had no difficulties. I became the coach, and he became the competitor. Our performance improved. . . ."

The newfound independence proved a boon to Druckenmiller. With Soros away, he made his first big trade for Quantum, based on his conviction that the German mark would strengthen after the fall of the Berlin Wall. Although Soros might have been out of sight, he was not, however, out of Druckenmiller's mind. The young fund manager recalled *The Alchemy of Finance,* specifically Soros's theory about currencies. One part of that theory had it that if a huge deficit arose at the same time as an expansionary fiscal policy and a tight monetary policy, a country's currency would rise. This seemed the right time to bet on the German mark.

In practice, Soros's theory appeared to fly in the face of reality. In the first two days after the wall came down, the mark went down with it. People believed that the deficit would grow but that its growth would hurt the German currency. Nonetheless, Druckenmiller followed the Master's advice, establishing a $2 billion position in marks over the next few days and reaping large profits.

He also believed the Nikkei index was overextended; the Bank of Japan was tightening its monetary policy. Seeing the handwriting on the wall, Druckenmiller shorted the Japanese stock market in late 1989—again, scoring a hit for Quantum.

In the late 1980s, the borrowing climate in the United States helped big league investors like Soros and Druckenmiller enormously.

Beginning in late 1989, short-term rates became profitably lower than long-term rates. "Profitably," James Grant, editor of *Grant's*

Interest Rate Observer in New York, explained, "because you can borrow at say 3.5 percent and you can go out and buy a government security that yields you 5.5 percent. And those humble-sounding two percentage points can earn gigantic amounts of money providing that daylight exists through the length of your trade."

In theory those "humble-sounding two percentage points" were available to anyone. Hedge funds, however, had the means to exploit the opportunity to the hilt. "Hedge funds," observed Grant, "have the kind of balance sheets that allow them to demand banking lines of credit. You and I can't go in and borrow a billion dollars like these guys can. . . ."

Grant continued: "What is happening differently over the last few years . . . is that individual partnerships can and have been borrowing. If you start with a billion dollars of capital, you can borrow a whole lot of money and make very big footprints. . . . Well, if you do that with a billion dollars, or five billion dollars, all you got to do is show up in the morning! . . . This financial climate was tailor-made for speculation, and speculation on a big scale."

In early 1991, Stanley Druckenmiller took short positions of $3 billion in the U.S. and Japanese markets; he was also short with large positions in the U.S. and world bond markets. During the first two weeks of the year, with the United States rattling its sabers against Iraq, it appeared that the market would dip seriously once the fighting erupted.

Disagreeing, Druckenmiller switched the Quantum Fund's S&P futures positions from short to long. He kept a large short position in stocks, especially bank and real estate stocks. By the time the war broke out, Quantum was fully long. As it turned out, Druckenmiller had guessed right, despite going into January 1991 with all the wrong positions: a $3 billion short position in equities around the world, a $3 billion short position in the dollar against the mark, plus a big short position in Japanese and American bonds. Accordingly, Quantum wound up at the end of January 1991 on the plus side.

Quantum racked up a 53.4 percent gain that year. Its total assets were $3,157,259,730. A spokesman for the fund was quoted as saying: "We had a lucky year; we're not this good. We made good money in stocks, currencies, bonds—and it's unusual to hit on every cylinder like that." Earlier in the year, in the aftermath of the Gulf War, they had been bullish. Later in the year, Soros's money managers became bearish and dumped billions of dollars of short- and longer-term Treasury bonds.

Druckenmiller's largest and most successful play in 1991 was his $12 billion stake in European, Japanese, and U.S. bonds and in currencies. When bonds rose amid indications of economic weakness in August and September, Quantum made hundreds of millions of dollars. Quantum also did very well in biotechnology stocks and made $200 million in Mexican telephone and other stocks. Druckenmiller did so well for his boss that Soros was the top American income earner in 1991, at $117 million.

> "Attain superior long-term returns through 'preservation of capital and home runs.' "

And Druckenmiller had done well enough to earn from Soros the ultimate compliment. He calls him his "alter ego."

Technically, Druckenmiller was one of 12 managing directors. But in fact, he ran the entire operation. And what a run it's had: Since Druckenmiller has taken over at Quantum, the fund has averaged 40 percent annual gains in net asset value, higher than Soros's record of 30 percent annual gains from 1969 to 1988. In 1989, the first full year under Druckenmiller's leadership, Quantum rose 31.6 percent; in 1990, 29.6 percent; in 1991, 53.4 percent; in 1992, 68.6 percent; and in 1993, 72 percent.

In the rare interviews he has given, Druckenmiller has attributed his great track record to George Soros. He has followed Soros's philosophy about how to build long-term returns, and it has worked.

Soros, explained Druckenmiller, argued that the way to build long-term returns was "through preservation of capital and home runs. You can be far more aggressive when you're making good profits. Many managers, once they're up 30 to 40 percent, will book their year (i.e., trade very cautiously for the remainder of the year so as not to jeopardize the very good return that has already been realized). The way to attain truly superior long-term returns is to grind it out until you're up 30 to 40 percent, and then if you have the convictions, go for a 100 percent year. If you can put together a few near-100 percent years and avoid down years, then you can achieve really outstanding long-term returns."

The most significant lesson Soros taught him, Druckenmiller suggested, was "that it's not whether you're right or wrong that's important, but how much money you make when you're right and how much you lose when you're wrong. The few times that Soros has ever criticized me was when I was really right on a market and didn't maximize the opportunity."

> "It's not whether you're right or wrong, but how much money you make when you're right and how much you lose when you're wrong."

He learned this soon after he began work at Quantum. He had been unenthusiastic about the dollar and he took a large short position against the German mark. The position began to go in his favor, and he was quite pleased with himself. Soros dropped in on him in his office and discussed the trade.

"How big a position do you have?" he asked.

"One billion dollars," Druckenmiller answered.

"You call that a position?" Soros said, a question that has become part of Wall Street folklore.

Soros suggested that Druckenmiller double his position. He did. And, just as Soros had predicted, even more profits poured into Quantum.

"Soros has taught me," noted Druckenmiller, "that when you have tremendous conviction on a trade, you have to go for the jugular. It takes courage to be a pig. It takes courage to ride a profit with huge leverage. As far as Soros is concerned, when you're right on something, you can't own enough."

One of the great influences on George Soros's life—he has made this point often—has been his wife Susan. He has said in public and in private that "she has managed to keep me human."

At one stage Soros wanted to live in London, where he would be closer to Eastern Europe and the former Soviet Union, the scenes of his greatest interests in the 1980s and early 1990s. Susan wanted them to live in New York for the sake of the children. For the most part, she has won that argument, though Soros still travels a good part of the time.

> **"It takes courage to be a pig. When you're right on something, you can't own enough."**

She has been a lightning rod for some of the most negative publicity surrounding Soros. The most controversial incident, in 1991, had to do with Susan's dissatisfaction with the Soros's British butler and cook, who were, according to one newspaper, paid 70,000 British pounds a year between them and were married to one another.

Newspaper accounts at the time indicated that while Soros was away, Susan decided that Nicki Davison's English-style cooking was not good enough. She flew in American chef Miriam Sanchez. According to the *New York Post,* "Tempers soon flared like a grease fire as highly trained butler Patrick Davison noticed Sanchez 'splashing' a $840 bottle of Chateau Lafite into her goulash after he advised her to use a Chardonnay or 'youngish' Beaujolais," according to testimony reported in Britain's *Daily Mail.* "I thought it was outrageous," Davison told the court.

One day, the *Daily Mail* reported, Sanchez and Davison got into a tiff over which spoon to use for a soufflé. Susan fired Davison and the cook. The married couple complained to a British tribunal. In response, Susan told the court she preferred Sanchez's cooking and that Davison's food was "overdone." Davison contended that the row between Susan and himself was a trick on Susan's part to get George to spend more time in New York, less in London.

"Mrs. Soros is 25 years younger than Mr. Soros, and I'm afraid she gets anything she wants," claimed Davison. "She fired us while he was away, and I've since tried to call him, but he won't even talk to me." Again according to newspaper accounts, the British court in May 1991 ordered Soros to pay the Davisons about $40,000, the maximum amount of compensation the law provided.

One of Soros's close acquaintances, British journalist Anatole Kaletsky, told me that the "Chateau Lafite" episode seemed totally implausible to him and that he was embarrassed over the British media's coverage of the incident. "It didn't have the ring of truth. . . . The descriptions of this palace which Soros was alleged to live in were out of kilter with the house in which he actually lived. His wife insisting on using Chateau Lafite for the stew was totally implausible. I've eaten dinner at their house in London a number of times. It's quite inconceivable that they would send someone to buy the most expensive wine to pour it in a stew. It wasn't the style they lived in. . . . George and his wife Susan both said to me that most of the specifics of the incident were not true."

Whether the "Chateau Lafite" episode was true or not, it was to plague Soros into the future. For a time, when articles appeared about him, writers reminded readers who George Soros was by relating the story of the butler, the wine, and the goulash.

Two years later, in 1993, Susan Soros launched her own graduate school, the Bard Graduate Center for Studies in the Decorative Arts. The Center, located on West Eighty-sixth Street in New York, is part of Bard College and offers a two-year master's degree in the study of decorative objects, furniture, and fabrics. She was helped by a $6.6 million grant from her husband.

The Quantum Fund was growing so rapidly that Soros and Drucken-miller believed it was time to spin off several smaller ones. So in 1991 and 1992, the Soros operation expanded. Like Quantum, the Quasar Fund, founded by Soros in 1991, invested in anything from currencies to commodities. Quasar was run by 15 outside managers; Soros, however, managed currency trading for the fund.

In 1992, the Quantum Emerging Growth Fund and the Quota Funds were set up. The former focused on emerging stock markets in Asia and Latin America; it could, though, invest in the United States and Europe, and in currencies and bonds as well as stocks. The Quota Fund was known as a "fund of funds." Its investments were handled by 10 outside managers. Taken together, by the start of 1993 the funds held portfolios of more than $50 billion. Drucken-miller directly controlled the Quantum Fund and oversaw the others.

Eighteen

Taming the Snake

G eorge Soros's greatest coup—the one act that made him a world-famous investor—occurred in September 1992.

It was then that he made his remarkable bet against the pound. In doing so, he had taken on two of the most formidable institutions in all of England.

One was the once almighty pound itself. For 200 years the pound had been the world's key currency, anchored to gold, as strong a symbol of British power as the British navy. But then, the cost of World War I plus the 1929 stock market crash eroded its power. The British let it float and took it off the gold standard. Its value changed every day.

The other venerable institution that Soros took on was the Bank of England. For years the bank stood for prosperity and power, a veritable Rock of Gibraltar of British Finance. Nothing could dislodge it from its solid place as the country's most durable bulwark against turmoil in the marketplace.

George Soros would test the strength of these institutions in ways that no one had ever dared to imagine. What he was about to do had never before been tried. He had been preparing himself for a good long while.

Before he could act, several ingredients had to come together.

The ERM—Exchange Rate Mechanism—system organized in 1979 was supposed to be the first installment of a broader program to create a single European currency. A single currency would stabilize European business. It would also diminish the power of traders and speculators who might make life difficult for government bankers—

especially when those governments acted as if they were not part of a monetary union.

With the ERM in force, the nations of Western Europe would be linked together, their currencies pegged not to gold or the dollar— but to one other. Each currency would trade within a certain range called a band. If any currency hit the top or bottom of that band, the central banks in the individual countries would be obligated to bring it back in line by selling at the top or buying at the bottom. Within these bands, the currencies of member countries would be permitted to fluctuate relative to the currencies of the other member countries and a central rate based on the German mark.

Hope for tighter European unity had risen on February 7, 1992, when the Maastricht Treaty was signed. That treaty, signed by the European Community's 12 member nations, was meant to prepare the region's monetary and economic systems for gradual full-scale union. The plan was to create a single central bank and single currency by the year 2000. It was also supposed to launch Europe toward a political union.

What a grand hope—and an illusion, as it turned out.

Implied in the hope was the notion that the European states would act in concert, suppressing national interests for the good of the united community.

The trouble was: Someone had forgotten to tell the Europeans that they were supposed to act in unison.

The success of the effort was highly dependent on each country coordinating its economic policies with one another. But no matter how many documents they signed, no matter how many grand speeches they made, the politicians of Western Europe could not bring themselves to do the things that a unified Western Europe required them to do.

The billions that George Soros would eventually risk in the fall of 1992 in his bet against the British pound were only a small part of the swelling waves of capital washing along the shores of the world's financial markets. With advances in technology and deregulation, $1 trillion in currency was being exchanged every day, more than triple the level of 1986. The pension funds of American workers had $150 billion invested overseas, 20 times the level of 1983. All kinds of institutions, from Japanese insurance companies to American mutual funds, were scouring the world for investments.

Since 1987 the major European currencies had been "anchored" to the German mark. The British pound, for example, had been pegged to the mark at about 2.95 marks to the pound, which made the cost of joining the ERM quite high. In 1992 it was becoming increasingly clear that a number of European currencies—not just the pound but the Italian lira as well—were significantly overvalued in relation to stronger ones such as the French franc and the German mark. Because of the British recession, and because there seemed little reason to believe that Britain would be able to keep the pound pegged so high vis-à-vis the mark, speculators began to smell blood. They began to believe that the British would be forced to abandon the ERM.

> **"George's genius is in seeing the trend long before anyone else does."**

George Soros gambled that the ERM, colloquially known as "the snake," would not be able to maintain a unified stance. Soros understood that the only way the Europeans could keep speculators at bay was to maintain interest rates at the same level in all countries. And should those rates vary, speculators like Soros would be ready to move in—to exploit the weaker currencies. And that essentially was what started to happen in the summer of 1992.

Soros had seen all this coming for some time.

"George's genius," noted Gary Gladstein, chief administrative officer at Soros Fund Management, "is in seeing the trend long before anyone else does. George realized what was going to happen practically from the moment the Berlin Wall came down. Because he thinks in such broad terms, he saw that German reunification was going to be a lot more expensive than [Chancellor Helmut] Kohl was predicting, than anyone was predicting. His understanding of macroeconomic reality meant we were ready. He didn't need to have one eye on the machines; in his head he had already committed."

Europe's troubles were mounting. Less than a year after the Maastricht Treaty was signed, a number of European countries were hardly moving in concert.

While the British were deciding how to strengthen their economy, Soros and the other speculators shared a growing conviction that the British could not keep their interest rates high, not with their economy in such trouble. The only plausible solution seemed to be for the British to lower their rates—but that would weaken their currency. And this would force the British out of the ERM, something the British insisted they would never do. In the meantime, it was becoming clear to the financial community in London that speculators like Soros were placing bets against sterling, that they had begun to build up sizable positions over the previous few months.

Who would be right? Prime Minister John Major or the world's greatest investor, George Soros?

As 1992 moved inexorably forward, the British government was in an increasingly awkward position. It wanted German interest rates to drop. But it knew this was unlikely.

It wanted a quick fix for its economy, but this would require the kind of reversal of policy that could shake the government and perhaps even cause its collapse.

John Major had to make a decision. He decided to tough it out: Britain would stick to its policy of maintaining the value of the pound within the Exchange Rate Mechanism. At every turn, he was emphatic. So was his chancellor of the exchequer, Norman Lamont.

Nonetheless, pressure was building against the prime minister's policy of defending the pound at nearly all costs. As the prime minister spoke to the MPs, sterling fell to below 2.85 against the mark.

Early July 1992

Six leading monetarists write a letter to the *Times* of London, urging Britain to withdraw from the ERM. In doing so, they argue, the government could lower interest rates to help Britain over its economic slump.

The government, however, does not want to lower interest rates willy-nilly. That would weaken its currency, and a weakened currency would be vulnerable to speculators and currency hedgers. The British might lower their rates if the Germans cut their rates even more than they already had. The highly independent Bundesbank, however, has resisted pressure to make such a cut.

Late July 1992

The critics are getting noisier. More and more London financial experts question the government's exchange rate policy and whether Major and Lamont have the backbone to hold to that policy in the face of Britain's mounting recession.

British business leaders are demanding a realignment of sterling within the ERM to a central rate of around 2.60 marks. They want a cut in interest rates, too, of at least 3 percent. None of their pleas seem to be reaching the government.

Through the summer and early fall of 1992, Chancellor Lamont rules out devaluation. "Fool's gold" he calls such a step.

Mid-August 1992

In case someone is not listening, Lamont again says: "We are not going to devalue the pound." Answering his critics, he declares that "if, as some suggest, we cut loose from the ERM and slash interest rates, things would worsen. The pound would dive and inflation explode."

There would be no pulling out of the ERM. "I'm determined," he writes in one newspaper, "not to squander the progress we've made."

August 26, 1992, 8:26 AM

It does not seem likely that Lamont can hold firm. Just a few minutes ago, a Treasury worker was busy polishing the Treasury's brass nameplate so it would gleam for the television cameras. Then Lamont appears outside the Treasury, standing before television cameras. He clenches his fist, puts on a broad grin, as if trying to conceal a churning stomach.

The reporters there study his body language as much as his words, trying to detect the truth. The body language betrays doubts. Nodding his head constantly, usually when he mentions a particularly sensitive word, Lamont snatches breaths, and his chest rises noticeably. When he speaks, the words come out quickly, too quickly, suggesting that he is rushing to get the appearance over as soon as possible. He makes it clear he wants no interruptions. Lamont, in his sober suit, tries to convey assurance and dependability. But few seem fooled.

He rules out a devaluation of the British pound, hoping to calm financial markets, hoping to avert a rise in interest rates. And he asserts one more time that Britain will not leave the ERM. Firmly, the chancellor says that he "just wanted to make the government's position absolutely clear. There are going to be no devaluations, no leaving the ERM. We are absolutely committed to the ERM, that is our policy—it is at the center of our policy."

He repeats the words that have been heard frequently at Downing Street in recent days: "We will do whatever is necessary," suggesting that the government has no qualms about raising interest rates if necessary. He brushes aside questions. All he says as he departs is, "We are taking action."

Lamont's public statements come as the Bank of England steps in to buy pounds aggressively, about 300 million pounds. That step is meant to bring home the chancellor's message—and to try to keep speculators from driving sterling below its floor level of 2.7780 German marks.

By the end of the day the pound has closed at 2.7946. But none of these steps—Lamont's tough words, the bank's aggressive action—carry as much weight as the chancellor's highly expressive body language. "This is a man with huge doubts," says Catherine Charlton, a voice and dialect coach, one of several experts who have analyzed a videotape of Lamont's performance for the *Daily Mail*. To Charlton, the chancellor's blink rate gives away his secret. Most people, she notes, blink six to eight times a minute. But Norman Lamont gets in 64 in just 45 seconds! "Usually," she concludes, "if you're telling the truth or really speaking sincerely, your eyes are still and calm."

The body action. The blink rate. The eagerness to perform and depart. It all adds up to one thing. Speculators begin to sense that the government is weakening.

August 28, 1992

Lamont issues yet another statement, this time after a meeting of EC finance ministers.

Guess what?

He announces that the ERM will not be realigned.

The words ring hollow.

Late August 1992

George Soros has seen the writing on the wall. He has talked with Helmut Schlesinger, the Bundesbank president, and senses that the Germans have no plans to rescue the other European countries.

What Soros has learned from Schlesinger is that the Germans will do nothing to undermine their own economy. Schlesinger's unwillingness to bale out the British and others makes it even less likely that Major and Lamont can keep their country in the ERM.

Watching the recipe for disaster take shape, Soros begins to believe that a big investment play is possible. "It was almost as though we'd been preparing for an exam for six months," says an unidentified spokesman for Soros, "and now were finally taking the test."

Early September 1992

George Soros is not alone in betting against the ERM and the central banks of Europe. Mutual funds and multinational corporations that have traditionally been active currency hedgers start to sell the weaker European currencies.

Foreign exchange traders within the investment bank community quickly note the increase in volume they are handling for their customers. Clearly, the central banks in Europe are coming under tremendous pressure. Those banks will have to spend large sums to shore up their currencies. It becomes less and less likely that the Bank of England will be able to defend the pound for very much longer.

And yet Britain stands pat.

Norman Lamont is trying to buy time for his beleaguered pound.

September 3, 1992

Lamont announces that the government plans to borrow 7.5 billion pounds in foreign currencies from a group of international banks. This unprecedented step is meant to resuscitate sterling. In the City of London there is euphoria and a momentary sigh of relief as it appears that Lamont has pulled a rabbit out of the hat.

Perhaps, after all, he will manage to keep sterling strong enough to stay in the ERM. And he will stave off the need for a devaluation.

September 10, 1992

Lamont once again rules out any devaluation of the pound. That same day John Major uses tough language in a speech to the Scottish Confederation of British Industry in Glasgow. Jabbing into the air with a finger, he notes that "the soft option, the devaluers' option, the inflationary option—in my judgment that would be a betrayal of our future at this moment. And I tell you categorically that is not the government's policy."

The comment is greeted with applause.

George Soros listens to John Major and Norman Lamont, but he puts little faith in their words.

"It didn't carry much conviction," he says after the crisis, "because the realities of the situation were more pressing."

The "realities," to Soros, are that the British will be hard-pressed to keep their currency valued so high, given the stagnant economy. (A television reporter later asked Soros why he had not been convinced by Norman Lamont's words. Soros broke into a huge smile, then laughed: "All I can say is what I said before: It did not carry conviction with me.")

Soros has been eyeing the situation, waiting for the right moment. He senses that a time bomb is ticking, but he has no idea when the bomb will explode.

"I personally did not foresee a breakdown of the Exchange Rate Mechanism," he says. "I merely saw the tension between the authorities. But then it became obvious that tensions were so big, that disunity was so big, and there was one particular interview that Schlesinger, the head of the Bundesbank, gave which was published in *The Wall Street Journal,* which effectively was a clarion call to everyone to get out of sterling." Schlesinger suggested that the accord that called for the Italians to devaluate the lira in exchange for a German cut in interest rates had not gone far enough toward resolving the crisis in Europe's currency markets. And he intimated that turbulence could be avoided through devaluation. The interview becomes an invitation for speculators to sell sterling.

To Stanley Druckenmiller, Schlesinger's "clarion call" makes betting against the pound crystal clear. "The real decision was not whether to take the position we took but how deep to go. At first, I was thinking in the range of three or four billion. But that's where George's instinct, his sixth sense or whatever, the thing that makes him such a great investor, comes in. For him, it's not whether you're right or wrong, but, when you know you're right, making sure you have the maximum in play. Actually, he—we—would have bet more, but we just ran out of time."

Druckenmiller deserves no little credit for initiating the play on the pound, but Soros, as usual, provides the extreme self-confidence that encourages Druckenmiller to bet so much. "I told him to go for the jugular," Soros said. *"It's like shooting fish in a barrel.* As long as the barrel holds up you keep on shooting the fish."

When the markets explode, George Soros is right there ready to take advantage.

The game he plays is complex. It is complex because he believes that the breakdown of the ERM, now inevitable, will set in motion a sequence of developments. First, a major realignment of European currencies. Second, a sharp decrease in European interest rates. Third, a decline in European stock markets.

So he decides to short the weak European currencies. And bet on interest rates and on the securities markets. In one bold move, Soros and his associates sell short sterling on the order of some $7 billion—and they purchase $6 billion worth of German marks. To a smaller extent, they also purchase the French franc.

At the same time, Soros buys $500 million worth of British stocks, operating on the assumption that a country's equities often rise following the devaluation of its currency. In one other move, Soros goes long German and French bonds. At the same time, he shorts German and French equities. Soros's thinking is that the increased value of the German mark will hurt equities, but help bonds, since interest rates will be lower. Soros has strong credit. So he is able to maintain all of these positions with a mere $1 billion in collateral. He has borrowed $3 billion to round out the $10 billion bet.

Soros is not alone in laying these kinds of bets. Currency dealers around the world are gambling that the value of the pound cannot be maintained.

It is in New York, however, that Soros is placing the largest bet. "We had $7 billion of equity and our total position was in the $10 billion range. So it was one and a half times our entire capital," Soros observes. Against the assets of his Quantum Fund, he borrows 5 billion pounds. Then he changes the pounds into German marks at the ERM rate of 2.79 marks to the pound. He now holds strong German marks.

Then Soros waits.

Nineteen

"The One-Way Bet"

Tuesday Morning, September 15, 1992

John Major is scheduled to make a trip to Spain. He cancels it to deal with the ERM crisis.

The Bank of England remains confident it can hold off speculators like George Soros. Traders, however, begin to notice shortly before lunchtime that the lira has fallen. They begin heavier trading in sterling against the German mark.

Tuesday Afternoon

Sterling plummets to 2.80 marks to the pound. Later that afternoon word comes that the Bank of England has bought about 3 billion sterling. The pound fails to respond.

Tuesday Evening

In London the pound closes just a fifth of a pfennig above its ERM floor of 2.778 marks, its lowest value since Britain joined the ERM. Concern is growing at Whitehall that unless something drastic is done, sterling will have to be devalued for the first time since 1967.

When a nation's currency is under attack, finance officials have several options available to them in response. One is to intervene heavily in the exchange markets and buy up one's own currency. If that does not work, the next line of defense is to raise interest rates, on the assumption that high rates will attract money back to your currency and stabilize it.

The British government, however, is reluctant to raise rates—a surefire way to dampen the economy.

With the pound in the cellar and the killer bee speculators swarming, the chancellor of the exchequer undertakes an act of desperation. He is having dinner with the U.S. ambassador, but he interrupts his meal every 10 minutes to try to reach officials in the Bundesbank.

He has a big favor to ask.

Please lower your interest rates.

If Lamont can succeed in getting the Germans to comply, that will ease some of the pressure and maybe, just maybe, Great Britain will get through the next few days without a serious dislocation in its financial system. Bundesbank officials, however, refuse to budge.

After the dinner, senior Bank of England officials huddle with Norman Lamont at the Treasury in a posture of crisis. Sitting under two glittering chandeliers around a large oaken table, they plot the next day's strategy. They plan to begin the day with a large, overt intervention by the Bank of England. Held in reserve for later in the day, if needed, will be an interest rate hike.

Conscious that the British Treasury is squabbling with the German central bank, speculators predict that the British will be the first to blink. The most likely step the government will take—however disastrous it will be for the economy in the longer run—will be to raise interest rates. So goes the betting.

Tuesday Evening, 8:00 PM

The meeting at the Treasury breaks up. As the officials walk out of the gloomy session, their biggest fear is whether what they have decided to do will be enough. Events are moving quickly, however, too quickly for their plans. Five hours earlier, unbeknownst to the officials, Helmut Schlesinger has given his controversial interview. Schlesinger later suggests that he did not authorize publication of his remarks. It hardly matters. Traders attack the British pound, Italian lira, and other weak currencies with a vengeance, dumping them for marks.

Norman Lamont, hearing of Schlesinger's comments, is shocked. Publicly, he tries to play down the impact of the story. But the damage is done.

Tuesday Evening, Wednesday Morning

In a last-ditch stand, the Federal Reserve Bank of New York and the Bank of Japan support sterling.

Tuesday evening, 10:30 PM

It is 5:30 PM in New York. George Soros is sitting in his midtown Manhattan office on the 33rd floor of the skyscraper that overlooks Central Park.

His confidence is growing that the British will have to pull the pound out of the ERM. "It was an obvious bet, a one-way bet," he says later. "At worst, if I had had to repay what I had borrowed at the same rate I had borrowed at, I would have lost at most about 4 percent. So there was really very little risk involved."

He has seen it coming, felt it was inevitable, and now it is all happening and he does not have a shadow of a doubt that he will profit enormously. Later, in his Fifth Avenue apartment, Soros enjoys a simple dinner cooked by his chef. After dinner he retires to bed. Even though he has just made a $10 billion bet—perhaps the largest bet ever made in history—he is going to sleep.

He is that confident.

Wednesday, 7:30 AM

On Threadneedle Street in London, eight foreign exchange dealers have assembled in the office of the deputy governor of the Bank of England, Edie George. He is in charge of market operations for the bank. Hunched over their computer screens, they begin purchasing pounds. Their instructions are to spend $2 billion in three separate interventions.

The exercise fails horribly. Hundreds of companies with factories and offices in Britain and thousands of pension funds, insurance companies, and other investors who own sterling-denominated stocks and bonds are eager to get rid of whatever they hold in pounds.

An air of gloom hangs over Britain's financial community.

Wednesday, 8:30 AM

The Treasury crisis group has gathered in Chancellor Norman Lamont's office. Faces are somber. Lamont has just been on the phone to Ian Plenderleith, the associate director in charge of markets at the Bank of England, and to the prime minister. Hanging up the phone, Lamont orders even more intervention using the bank's foreign currency reserves.

Photographers have begun showing up outside the main entrance to the Treasury.

Wednesday, 9:00 AM

Prime Minister John Major gets into his armor-plated Jaguar and makes the two-minute drive down Whitehall to the Old Admiralty building, where he has been temporarily housed while repairs are undertaken at 10 Downing Street. At the Admiralty, he has a meeting scheduled with government officials, ironically, on the subject of the Maastricht Treaty.

When news filters into the room of the impending financial disaster, those at the meeting feel as if they have become a de facto war cabinet.

Wednesday, 10:30 AM

Norman Lamont places the phone call that everyone in the British financial community has been dreading. John Major excuses himself from the Maastricht session and moves to a secure phone where he listens as Lamont describes how the pound is continuing to sink. German interest rates are frozen in place. The Germans are not about to offer relief. Devaluation has to be avoided at all costs. At stake is nothing less than the government's credibility. Lamont asks for the prime minister's approval to raise interest rates two points to 12 percent.

Major gives the nod.

Wednesday, 11:00 AM

The announcement is made. Interest rates are being raised. Lamont says that "as the current extraordinary pressures and uncertainties abate," he hopes to bring interest rates back down. Few believe this will happen soon.

Worst of all, despite Lamont's announcement, the pound hardly moves. Finance officials know the game is over. The currency markets, viewing Lamont's ploy as an act of panic, are beginning to think the same.

John Major, meanwhile, has reversed his earlier refusal to recall Parliament from recess. He wants them back to discuss the ERM crisis and the British economy. Parliament is called into session on September 24. The step is extraordinary: Since the end of World War II, Parliament has been called back into session only 10 times.

Wednesday, 12:00 Noon

More intervention from the Bank of England. But it is too late. On that fateful day—Black Wednesday, as it came to be dubbed—the Bank of England will spend the equivalent of 15 billion pounds ($26.9 billion) of its 44 billion pounds ($78.8 billion) in foreign currency reserves to buy pounds in its ultimately futile effort to shore up its currency.

In New York it is 7:00 AM. The phone rings, waking up George Soros.

Stan Druckenmiller is on the line. He has good news.

From his own sources, he learned that Great Britain is about to throw in the towel.

"George, you've just made $958 million."

Druckenmiller is a bit premature, but it does not matter. He knows that the British are done for. And he and Soros will be big winners.

(Later Soros would learn that he made further gains because he had sided with the French authorities against speculators who had been attacking the franc.)

All in all, from the events of Black Wednesday, Soros will make close to $2 billion, $1 billion from the pound and another $1 billion out of the further chaos in the Italian and Swedish currencies and in the Tokyo stock market.

A lesser mortal might have been tempted to open a bottle of champagne, but not Soros. "It just so happens that I played the game better and bigger than other people," he said.

Early Wednesday Afternoon

The group around the chancellor is beginning to utter the awful thought.

Wednesday, 1:30 PM

It is time for the U.S. markets to open. Sterling is being sold, says one dealer, "like water running out of a tap."

Wednesday, 2:15 PM

The Bank of England tries one more time to save the day. Again it raises interest rates—the second time today. Rates are now 15 percent.

Never before in British history have rates been hiked twice in one day. The rates are now at the same level as they were when John Major, then chancellor of the exchequer, had taken Great Britain into the ERM almost two years earlier.

The speculators are not dissuaded. The pound remains below its ERM floor level of 2.778 German marks. It is becoming all too clear that the government's policy is politically unsustainable.

The markets watch British interest rates go from 10 to 12 to 15 percent in one day and understand that there is no way the country can live with such high rates for long. So the pound keeps going down, and the Bank of England keeps buying it back.

All in a futile effort to save the day. But it is becoming clear that Britain will have to leave the ERM. And sterling will have to be devalued.

Prime Minister John Major is on the phone again, this time to French prime minister Pierre Beregovoy and to German chancellor Helmut Kohl. Major's news is grim. He declares that he will have to take Britain out of the ERM. He has no other choice.

Twenty

Black Wednesday

Wednesday, September 16,1992, 4:00 PM

The afternoon of Black Wednesday grows darker and darker. The British are caving in, dropping out of the European Exchange Rate Mechanism.

The winners, like George Soros, are grinning; the losers, like John Major and Norman Lamont, are sadly admitting defeat.

Bank of England officials engage in a conference call with members of the other central banks in Europe, passing on the news that sterling is being suspended from the ERM.

The pound has fallen 2.7 percent against the mark and is trading at 2.703 marks in late New York trading, well below its former ERM floor level.

Wednesday, 5:00 PM

John Major summons his cabinet and wins its approval to take Britain out of the ERM. Italy makes clear that it will follow suit. Now the British and Italian currencies will trade freely, and their central banks will no longer have to defend them by buying them up in the open market.

Television camera crews and photographers crowd together outside the British Treasury for the expected public announcement.

Wednesday, 7:00 PM

The announcement finally comes. Norman Lamont appears before the cameras to admit defeat. His face looks worn, haggard, dismayed. *The Economist* will call him "hapless."

Placing his hands behind his back, as if he is a prisoner whose hands have been tied, Lamont forces a smile; the smile, however, lasts only a brief second. With his right hand he pushes back some hair falling over his forehead. And then he speaks.

"Today," he begins, "has been an extremely difficult and turbulent day. Massive financial flows have continued to disrupt the functioning of ERM. . . . In the meantime the government has concluded that Britain's best interests are served by suspending our membership of the Exchange Rate Mechanism."

Wednesday, 7:30 PM

Britain is permitting the pound to float. The pound closes on Black Wednesday at 2.71 marks, down only 3 percent. (By the end of September, however, the pound will drop to 2.5 German marks.)

Thursday, September 17, 1992

Britain's interest rate is back to 10 percent.

Italy follows Britain and withdraws its currency from the ERM. The pound tumbles immediately to 2.70 marks, then stabilizes at 2.65 marks, 5 percent below its previous floor level. It will eventually settle 16 percent below where it stood on Black Wednesday.

Britain is not alone in devaluing its currency. Spain's currency is devalued by 28 percent; Italy's by 22 percent.

With the news that Britain has withdrawn from the ERM, the pound is being quoted below 2.70 marks in New York trading, more than seven pfennigs below its lower ERM limit of 2.7780.

(A sad footnote to the pound crisis came the following summer when the bands were widened to a rather meaningless 15 percent. As of September 1994, the ERM was still in operation, with Germany, France, and six other countries participating.)

George Soros looked like a genius.

Others had made large profits on the devaluation of the pound, but those profits went unreported. Bruce Kovner of Caxton Corporation and Paul Tudor Jones of Jones Investments were big winners. Kovner's funds made an estimated $300 million; Jones's funds made $250 million. Leading American banks with large foreign exchange operations, particularly Citicorp, J.P. Morgan, and Chemical Banking, had profits as well. Together, in the third quarter, the banks netted over $800 million more than their normal quarterly earnings from trading currencies.

Soros's bet became public when London's *Daily Mail*, reporting on a *Forbes* piece that was soon to appear, ran a front-page story on October 24 with a huge, black, bold headline:

"I Made a Billion as the Pound Crashed."

Accompanying the *Mail's* story was a photograph of Soros, smiling and holding a drink in his hand. The lead was: "An international financier made nearly 1 billion pounds from last month's currency crisis, it was reported last night."

Anatole Kaletsky, the economics editor of the *Times* of London, was walking home with his daughter on the Saturday morning that the *Mail* story appeared. They paused for a few moments to buy some chocolate in a candy store, when Kaletsky's eye fell on the headline. Jolted by this news, Kaletsky bought the newspaper and read the article right there in the store. An hour later, by now back at home, Kaletsky's phone rang. George Soros was on the line.

"What's going on?" the *Times* man asked, hearing some commotion in the background.

"I'm here in London," Soros replied, his voice agitated. "I don't know if you saw the *Mail.*"

"Yes." Kaletsky began putting the puzzle together.

"My house is besieged by photographers and reporters. I want to go out and play tennis. I'm not sure what to do. What should I do? What's your advice?"

Before he was going to give advice, Kaletsky had to know one thing: "Is the story true?"

Soros was quick to reply. "Yes, broadly, it is true."

Kaletsky suggested that he not talk to any of the reporters at his doorstep. "If you want it on the record what you did and what you didn't do, why don't you write an article, or I'll come over and I can talk to you."

"OK, I'll think about it."

A half hour later, Soros phoned Kaletsky back to say that he thought it would be a good idea for the *Times* man to pay him a visit that afternoon. Kaletsky did, and Soros gave his first full-blown interview on how he had engineered his coup against the pound. To Kaletsky, the Soros interview in the *Times* on October 26 was the turning point in the creation of George Soros as a public figure. "From that interview came his celebrity in this country. Until then nobody had ever heard about George Soros."

Kaletsky led off his article by in effect introducing Soros to his readers: "George Soros is an intensely intellectual man who spends much of his time in eastern Europe as a political and educational philanthropist. He is also the world's biggest currency speculator. In the two weeks leading to Black Wednesday Mr. Soros engaged the British government in the highest-stakes game of poker in history."

Soros, wrote Kaletsky, acknowledged that he had made a billion dollars from the pound's collapse "with an embarrassed wince that could not entirely hide some mischievous self-satisfaction."

Explaining his moves before Black Wednesday, Soros told Kaletsky: "We did short a lot of sterling and we did make a lot of money, because our funds are so large. We must have been the biggest single factor in the market in the days before the ERM fell apart. Our total position by Black Wednesday had to be worth almost $10 billion. We planned to sell more than that. In fact, when Norman Lamont said just before the devaluation that he would borrow nearly $15 billion to defend sterling, we were amused because that was about how much we wanted to sell.

"But things moved faster than we expected and we didn't manage to build up the full position. So a billion is about right as an estimate of the profit, though dollars, not pounds."

Soros checked with his office and discovered that the running profits on his sterling positions were closer to $950 million, but his gains continued to mount as he kept his money in currencies other than sterling. Of that $950 million, Soros's personal share was one-third. Long positions on British, French, and German interest rate futures and short selling of the Italian lira had boosted his profits to an estimated $2 billion.

Kaletsky asked him why he was prepared to stake his entire wealth on the failure of a policy to which the British government had been so irrevocably committed.

Soros said he had been confident that the German Bundesbank wanted devaluations in Italy and Britain, but not in France. "I felt safe betting with the Bundesbank. The Bundesbank clearly wanted the lira and pound devalued, but it was prepared to defend the franc. In the end, the score was Bundesbank, 3–nil; speculators, 2–1. I did even better than some others by sticking to the Bundesbank's side."

Asked if Prime Minister Major might have been better off raising British interest rates earlier than Black Wednesday, Soros replied: "Absolute nonsense, poppycock. If interest rates had been raised, it would have encouraged us to speed up our sales, because the process was speeding up. In fact, we had not expected the devaluation to happen until the weekend. But when interest rates were put up on Black Wednesday we realized we could not afford to wait any longer. We had to accelerate our selling to build up our position. Time was running out."

For a brief time in the interview, Soros stopped thinking like a speculator. He took on the role of financial analyst, suggesting that speculation could be harmful, particularly in the currency markets. "But measures to stop it, such as exchange controls, usually do even more harm. Fixed exchange-rate systems are also flawed, because they eventually fall apart. In fact, any exchange-rate system is flawed and the longer it exists the greater the flaws become. The only escape is to have no exchange-rate system at all, but a single currency in Europe, as in the U.S. It would put speculators like me out of business, but I would be delighted to make the sacrifice."

How easy it seemed for Soros to make such a statement—as he was rolling up a $2 billion profit from the collapse of the pound and other currencies.

In an interview with me, Kaletsky recalled his conversation with Soros that Saturday afternoon in October and was struck most by how unemotional the investor seemed. "He always seems utterly detached and theoretical in his attitude to making money. I was certainly not conscious then . . . that it had any emotional significance to him. . . . It really does seem in his case that it's just a means of keeping score. . . . He was obviously very proud of making such a coup. That's why he decided to talk about it to me in the interview. . . . He was pleased about his acumen in having worked out what was going to happen, having defied the authorities, the Bank of England, and having won." He was pleased to use the publicity that would come his way to shine light on his philanthropic efforts in Eastern Europe.

To Soros's delight, his play against the pound fit neatly into his financial theories. The man who had been fascinated by chaos found in the ERM crisis one of the more chaotic financial episodes of the 1990s.

Armed with a theory that perceptions count for everything, and that faulty perceptions can trigger reflexive behavior in the markets, Soros had been able to identify a key misapprehension on the eve of the ERM crisis: the false expectation that the Bundesbank would support the pound under any circumstances. When the Bundesbank had demonstrated sufficiently that it was not going to bend to the wishes of the Bank of England and cut interest rates, Soros made his bet.

His theory also led him to believe that the acts of his fellow speculators would themselves become trend-following, creating the conditions for reflexive behavior in the market. As he noted: "In a freely fluctuating exchange rate system speculative transactions assume progressively greater weight and, as they do, speculation becomes more trend-following in character, leading to progressively greater swings in exchange rates until, eventually, the system collapses."

It was the turning point of George Soros's career.

If the media had exhibited only passing interest in him up to then, and if most people outside Wall Street and the City had never heard of him, that was no longer the case.

Now, everyone wanted to know who was this man who had engineered the coup against the pound. From the moment news of his coup spread, George Soros became known as "The Man Who Broke the Bank of England." Soros had not broken the bank, but he had certainly drained it of precious finances.

To most of the British citizenry, Soros acquired the status of a folk hero. "There was none of the xenophobic antagonism one might have expected," recalled Kaletsky. "On the contrary, the British public, in a typically English way, said, 'Good for him. If he made a billion dollars out of the stupidity of our government, he must be a brilliant guy.'"

George Magnus, the chief international economist at S. G. Warburg Securities in London, suggested that "some of what appeared in the media was to say, here was a financier who had a view, put his money where his mouth was . . . whereas, the Bank of England and the UK government were castigated for living in the dark ages and not being aware of what was going on. . . . In part of the media's reporting, Soros . . . was also used as an example of how unscrupulous speculators profit from governments, so it was a double-edged sword."

Soros appeared to relish the newly won publicity. Perhaps now he could turn his new status into a torch that would cast light on those parts of his life for which he sought publicity: his intellectual ideas, his philanthropy. "I am happy to have it because it gives me a platform from which I can say what I want. I had reasons to avoid it as a market operator. It can be harmful. But I am not a market operator anymore. In terms of having my voice heard on political issues, I find it very useful."

An air of humiliation and defeat hung around Prime Minister John Major and Chancellor Norman Lamont. Lamont tried to suggest that floating the pound did not amount to a devaluation. Major's Conservative Party sympathized with the prime minister, blaming instead the German Bundesbank for "talking down" the pound.

Unapologetic, Lamont defended his decision to float the pound. "What I did yesterday was simple common sense in the face of a whirlwind."

Having exploited the chaos in Western Europe, George Soros then set about analyzing just how much damage the whirlwind did.

"The net effect is a breakdown of the system, instability, and a negative effect on the economy, the size of which we don't know, but it could be very, very serious. I mean, Europe is going to go into a very severe recession. Business is practically collapsing in Germany, also very bad in France. . . . Instability is always bad. It may be bad—it may be good for a few people like me, who are instability analysts, but it's really bad for the economy."

In fact, the September 1992 pound crisis appeared to have been a plus for Great Britain and other Western European countries suffering from weak currencies. Not only did they enjoy fresh competitiveness, but their interest rates dropped sharply. And a few years later, their export sectors were prospering.

As for John Major and Norman Lamont, only Major survived, though his popularity ratings fell sharply, and by the spring of 1994 his government appeared in serious trouble.

Some of the British media were in tears over the British loss—and the Soros gain. They sought scapegoats, and George Soros was a convenient one.

One British television reporter declared: "The government's commitment to the ERM was supposed to be as safe as the Bank of England. But it didn't work out that way. The losses here were huge as the bank used up foreign reserves in its effort to defend the pound. The government won't say how much we lost, but it could run to several billion pounds. Put it a different way: It will have cost us more to defend sterling this autumn than it did to fight the Gulf War."

A former French foreign minister, Roland Dumas, said "Anglo-Saxon" speculators—this was a reference to British and American currency traders like Soros—had undermined Europe's aspirations. "You have to look at who profits from the crime," he said.

But if the British media hoped to make Soros feel guilty about his winnings, they were not succeeding. While everyone else in Britain called October 16 Black Wednesday, Soros dubbed it his White Wednesday. And he brushed off the criticism against him. "I'm sure there have been negative consequences. . . . but that does not enter my thinking at all. It can't. If I abstain from certain actions because of moral scruples, then I cease to be an effective speculator.

"I have not even a shadow of remorse for making a profit out of the devaluation of the pound. As it happens, devaluation has probably turned out to be for the good. But the point is: I didn't speculate against the pound to help England. I didn't do it to hurt England. I did it to make money."

The British media would not let up. Was not Soros's profit a loss to Great Britain? Indeed, had not Soros cost every British taxpayer 25 pounds, and every British man, woman, and child 12 and a half pounds?

He said yes, it meant a loss to Britain. "In this case, there's no question because I know who the counterpart is. In any transaction, somebody wins, and somebody loses. But in the normal course of events you don't know who your counterpart is. And you don't know whether he has a loss or profit. In this case it's clear that the counterpart is the Bank of England. And I have absolutely no sense of guilt, I can assure you, because had I not taken the position, somebody else would have taken the position."

Moreover, Soros believed that he was performing a salutary act in giving away a good portion of the money, especially because no one in the West had been willing to help the East.

He also reminded everyone that he could have lost money, "though nothing like the money we made and of course this was a bet—what is called [he smiled, and gestured with both hands] a one-way bet because a loss would have been very small. And the profit was very large."

In fairness to George Soros, he did not act alone in making the bet against the pound. One currency trader at a major British securities house noted that "the amount of money George Soros had invested was significant, but to put it into context, the daily turnover in foreign exchange markets can be as high as a trillion dollars. That's an awful lot of money. It makes George Soros's $10 billion position relatively small. In a concerted bid against a single currency, it can have an effect. But it wasn't just George Soros . . . who broke the Bank of England. It was the market speculating against sterling that did it. George Soros was just a large part of that."

Thanks to the coup against the pound, 1992 was a very good year for George Soros and the Quantum Fund.

Adding to his luster, Soros was named the highest-paid man on Wall Street. In 1992, he earned *$650 million,* over five times what he had earned in 1991. No longer could Michael Milken, the convicted stock trader, claim the record for the $550 million he had earned in 1987.

According to *Financial World,* which compiled the list of highest earners on Wall Street, Soros derived some $400 million of his income from the realized profits of the funds; management fees produced another $250 million. Four places behind Soros on the list was Stanley Druckenmiller, his 39-year-old chief trader, earning $110 million in 1992.

At the end of the year the Quantum Fund was the leading offshore fund, with total assets of $3.7 billion, up 68.6 percent. Someone who had invested $10,000 in Quantum when it was founded in

1969 and had reinvested all dividends would by the end of 1992 have had a sum of $12,982,827.62.

Remarkably, four of the six best performers were Soros funds: Quantum Emerging was third, up 57 percent; Quasar International was fourth, up 56 percent; and Quota was sixth, up 37 percent. Soros was running more than $6 billion in four offshore funds.

How did Soros do it?

Apart from his winnings in the ERM crisis in September, he had also made a great deal of money in international equities, particularly in the Japanese stock market in the early part of the year. He had also profited in U.S. equities indexes.

Writing in the Quantum Fund's Twentieth Annual Report, covering 1992, Soros noted that "the exceptional performance of 1992 can be primarily attributed to certain nonrecurring events connected with the breakdown of the Exchange Rate Mechanism in Europe. Our short position in sterling prior to its leaving the Exchange Rate Mechanism has received a tremendous amount of public attention. I should like to point out, however, that the profits on the sterling position accounted for only 40 percent of the total profits for the year and even without that position the results for the year would have been more than our average historical rate of return. . . .

"One note of caution to Quantum's stockholders. My reputation and that of Soros Fund Management have become immensely inflated in recent months. Almost on a daily basis, there are rumors of Soros Fund Management's trading in various markets and, frequently, markets tend to move based on these rumors. Often these rumors have no foundation in fact and stockholders should be skeptical of these rumors. Whenever we engage in a position that requires disclosure, we make the required filings and official announcement."

The year 1992 had been a bright one for Soros. Not only had he a dazzling amount of wealth under his command, he was now recognized as something of a miracle worker. One evening toward the end of the year, at a dinner party for intellectuals in Prague, the conversation kept returning to all the money Soros had just made. Soros, seated at a table with the people he liked best, said that he would be glad if his higher profile helped him in the East, even if it hurt him in the West. Now a celebrity, Soros was busy handing out autographs to the crowd, signing his name on five-pound British notes.

But Soros was searching for something that was still elusive: respect.

He had suddenly become a public figure. People wanted his autograph. The media wanted to dig into his career and life and describe what made him tick. That was fine for them. It was not enough for Soros. Even giving money away would not provide enough satisfaction for him.

He wanted more. He had always wanted people to respect his mind. He wanted it now more than ever.

His goal, never spelled out in public, infrequently voiced in private, was to wield power in Washington, not by winning elective office nor even by being appointed to an important cabinet post. It would have been sufficient for Soros to win the ear of the president and other prominent politicians in the nation's capital.

Soros was a Democrat, and in November 1992, Bill Clinton, a fellow Democrat, had been elected president of the United States. Soros knew that it would not be easy to gain the new president's attention. Many others who had accumulated wealth believed they had a right to be heard in Washington. What made Soros think he had more of a right than these others? How was he going to differentiate himself so that he would be heard? "I've got to change the way people look at me," he told associates, "because I don't want to be just another rich guy. I have something to say and I want to be heard."

Twenty-one

King of the Hedge Funds

I n the early 1990s, hedge funds, the largest and least regulated sector of the financial markets, dominated high finance. They had become the darling of investors, largely because of the staggering amounts of money won by the most famous of the hedge-fund managers. Leading the pack was George Soros and his Quantum Fund. But others had done well too, including Michael Steinhardt of Steinhardt Partners, Julian Robertson of Tiger Fund, and Leon Cooperman of Omega Advisers, Inc.

No wonder *The Wall Street Journal* dubbed them "Wall Street's newest great casino."

Those who run the funds have become the most powerful, best-compensated businesspeople in the country, rivaling the trading power of Wall Street's most important firms. They are, in the words of *Business Week*, the "gunslingers of the investment world—unregulated, freewheeling and often far better as investors than their conventional counterparts."

As much as $500 billion was being invested each year by the nearly 1,000 hedge funds. (Soros weighed in with $12 billion of that.) That was a hefty portion of the $3.5 trillion of investment capital spent in the market each year. Each day these hedge funds traded an estimated $75 billion, more than eight times the value of the shares traded on the New York Stock Exchange.

From 1987 to 1990, the median hedge fund rose 75.1 percent a year, compared to just 35.1 percent for the median mutual fund and 56.2 percent for the S&P 500. In 1992 alone, average hedge-fund returns were about three times those of the S&P 500. The best-known hedge funds racked up returns of between 25 and 68 percent in 1992, well beyond the 7 to 8 percent an investor would have made in U.S. stock-index funds. While Soros's fund was up 68.6 percent in 1992, Steinhardt's was up about 50 percent, Robertson's, 27.7 percent.

The best evidence of how well the hedge funds were doing came from gazing at *Financial World's* list of the top money earners for 1993. Roughly half of those on the list either ran or worked for hedge funds. Hedge-fund managers occupied the first five positions—George Soros headed the list with an income of $1.1 billion, the first American to earn over $1 billion in a year. These managers held 8 of the top 10 slots and accounted for 46 of the 100 people on the list. Number four was Stanley Druckenmiller, with $210 million. Of the 100 people on the list, 9 worked for the Soros Fund.

In 1994, Soros's fund managed more than $11 billion, Robertson, $6 billion, and Steinhardt, more than $4 billion. The latter two were each earning a 1 percent fee for managing those assets plus 20 percent of the portfolio's appreciation. Soros took 15 percent.

To rack up those profits, the hedge-fund kings exploited the global interest rate trends by betting correctly on how certain currencies would react to the sliding rates. They also bought foreign bonds, especially in Europe and Japan, often in the futures market. Many invested in the boom in third-world markets.

Wall Street has always been captivated by people who could make things happen, who seemed to have a better grasp than most of how high finance worked. At one time it might have been a Morgan or a Stanley, a Gould or a Baruch. In the early 1990s, it was George Soros and the other hedge-fund champions.

According to James Grant, editor of *Grant's Interest Rate Observer* in New York, these Wall Street titans often had far less financial clout than was ascribed to them, yet the Street seemed more comfortable believing that someone or some institution could control things, could make things happen.

"I look on Soros as one of these figures, partly mythical, partly real," he observed. "People have to project their anxieties and resentments and envy on something animate. They want to think that somebody is making markets happen. They can't believe that supply and demand are actually doing that, that markets personally discount future events. They want to believe there is a Soros.

". . . In a bear market that person could be the fall guy, but in any case I think people do like to believe that somebody has succeeded, somebody is responsible, somebody can be reached on the phone, somebody can be subpoenaed.

"I think hedge funds today are 'them.' The 'they' that people have always talked about are today the hedge funds. They move massive amounts of money at the speed of light. They do so with audacity—until recently with brilliant success. George Soros, Julian Robertson, Leon Cooperman, and Paul Tudor Jones, that ilk, together they constitute 'them.'"

How easy is it to become one of "them"? To join a hedge fund?

Not easy at all. Nor, for many investors, would it be very wise, for hedge funds carry a good deal of risk and require access to a good deal of money.

On the assumption that only the rich could or would want to carry that risk, the Securities and Exchange Commission obligates investors in U.S. hedge funds to have either a net worth of $1 million or an annual income of at least $200,000 for two consecutive years, $300,000 for a married couple. Soros's Quantum Fund has had no minimum to join, but buyers have had to pay a hefty premium to participate.

A myth has grown up that hedge funds are totally unregulated; that myth is not true. The SEC Act of 1934 requires investment managers of funds over $100 million to file information with the regulatory body. And all hedge-fund managers have been subject to antifraud legislation. A hedge fund can avoid registering as an investment firm, however, by limiting the number of investors to under 100 and by offering its products as private placements.

One big difference between Soros's offshore fund and U.S. hedge funds has to do with taxes. The shareholders in offshore funds have not had to pay taxes on capital gains as long as a majority of the fund's shareholders are not Americans. In some cases Americans can invest in offshore funds, but they do not qualify for favorable tax treatment. However, because hedge funds carry such high risks, most offshore funds ban—or, at least discourage—American investors.

As for George Soros, he worked it out so that he, an American citizen since 1961, was an exception to that practice. Despite being a U.S. citizen, he was able to qualify for his own offshore fund. Most of the Soros fund's investors are European.

For all their risk, hedge funds offer a number of allurements. One, of course, is the panache of being a member of an exclusive club. But the greatest appeal is the prospect of large profits. Because most hedge fund investors have been required to leave their money in the funds for a long period, they usually reinvest their gains. And so, their profits pile up.

Conventional money managers—those who run mutual and pension funds—try to be as conservative as possible. They use only a limited array of financial techniques, hoping for a modest but steady return. Hedge-fund managers, unconstrained by such conservatism, employ other, more risk-laden techniques, the most dazzling of which is leveraging, or investing with borrowed money. One of Wall Street's leading hedge-fund managers, who requested anonymity, described the brutalities of being heavily leveraged:

"It's gut-wrenching. Very intense. You have to have a special ability to deal with the leverage that George Soros or Michael Steinhardt do. . . . It takes a certain kind of mentality, a certain confidence in one's ability to see the play, because small fluctuations against you can have a very magnifying impact. The dollar-yen moved 4 to 5 percent in a day [in February 1994]. It cost Soros $600 million. We live in a world where 4 to 5 percent moves are not that unusual. The Federal Reserve raises its interest rates by a quarter of a point, the Dow drops 97 points. It takes . . . a certain appetite for risk. It has to be done intelligently.

". . . George Soros is a leveraged player. You figure that takes a certain intestinal fortitude, a certain degree of conviction in the bet, a basic set of financial controls. You have to make sure you're on top of the leverage."

Hedge funds rely on other techniques as well. Another scary one is shorting, or selling a security (or currency) they do not own, hoping that its price goes down so that later, when that security has to be delivered to the buyer, it can be acquired at a lower price. Soros relied on this technique in September 1992, when he shorted sterling prior to Black Wednesday.

Mutual funds used to be prohibited from shorting by the Internal Revenue Service's rule which stated that corporate mutual funds could not receive more than 30 percent of their gross income from selling short-term investments, that is, those held for less than three months. Short sales were considered short-term trades under this rule. More recently, a few conventional funds have won SEC approval to short.

The same hedge-fund manager who requested anonymity put leveraging and short sales in perspective. He noted that Benjamin Graham, the founding father of securities analysis, argued that stocks have "intrinsic value." In effect, intrinsic value is what a security is worth under given circumstances, weighing in interest rates, the state of the economy, and the company's profits. "The job of the analyst or the money manager is to identify the security that is above the intrinsic value. So a conventional investor would sell that security whereas a hedge fund might short it, and when the stock is below its intrinsic value, when it's undervalued, the investor would buy it. The difference between a conventional investor and a hedge-fund investor is that the former might buy it for cash and the latter might buy it at leverage and have more than 100 percent invested."

And the list of techniques goes on. Hedge funds are not only more likely to go both long and short, but also more likely to play options, futures, and other derivatives—whatever the markets dictate. They take more heavily concentrated positions. They trade more frequently than conventional funds; in 1988, Soros turned his portfolio over 18 times, 8 times in 1992. And they offer an investor the chance to take positions in any of the financial markets around the world—in contrast to conventional fund managers, who rely on their expertise in a single field or single market.

Hedge fund managers have great incentive to use these tools to push for profits. No matter how their assets perform, conventional managers receive a fee of about 1 percent of assets. They have, therefore, no compelling, personal incentive to act aggressively. Hedge-fund managers, in contrast, typically receive 20 percent of the fund's profits. They have every reason in the world to bring in earnings.

By 1994, hedge funds had grown so powerful that politicians began talking about the need for new regulation. Fear had mounted that the hedge-fund operators had the power to affect financial markets adversely because of the large amounts of money they put into the system. When the bond market suffered a setback in early 1994, the conviction grew among politicians that hedge funds were behind it. This belief was disputed by hedge-fund managers, who argued that their investment positions were far smaller than those of investment and commercial banks.

As for George Soros, his own position on regulation was paradoxical.

He had every reason to oppose regulation. After all, in the absence of regulation he had made a fortune. Soros liked to call himself a specialist on instability, someone who lived off of the chaotic state of financial markets. Why would he want regulation? Yet he favored a centralized banking system for the international financial community.

Therein lay the paradox. "I don't hesitate to speculate in currency markets—even though I say that currency markets ought to be stabilized," he noted. "We have to distinguish between the participant and the citizen. As a participant, you play by the rules. As a citizen, you have a responsibility to try to change the system if it's wrong."

For the time being, it appeared that the hedge funds would continue to go relatively unregulated. In 1992, the SEC had produced a huge 500-page report on offshore funds. This was around the time that suspicion arose that three major hedge funds, including Quantum, had made large purchases of U.S. Treasury bonds at auctions in which Salomon Brothers of New York stood accused of trying to execute a market squeeze. Government investigators gave all three funds a clean bill of health. The SEC report concluded that the hedge funds did not need tighter regulation.

Twenty-two

G eorge Soros had taken on a new luster as a result of the coup against the pound in September 1992.

He seemed so prescient, so endowed with investment skills, that a myth arose about him: He could, by virtue of the investment positions he chose to take, move markets up or down.

In effect, he seemed to have the powers of a guru.

If and when he spoke publicly about a currency or a stock or a company, the market for it might shift. It seemed so easy. All you had to do was wait for a Soros pronouncement, then rush out and buy whatever the guru had suggested.

The trouble was: The guru didn't speak that often.

How then to ferret out what he was up to? Just how did other investors find out what Soros was buying?

They looked for what market specialists call "footprints," clues indicating the direction or emphasis of an investment. The search for footprints was a must, for investors like Soros, even when making public statements, did not advertise when they were taking a position or how much they were investing.

Those footprints were very hard to find. One way was to notice a steady trend in the same direction in a class of securities that typically had little volatility.

Bill Dodge, senior vice president of equity research and chief investment strategist at Dean Witter Reynolds, explained: "If the Dow is down 50 points, and the traders say they don't see a lot of trading, and I start to look around and it's all in the Dow stocks and the dollar is weak against deutsch marks, I might conclude correctly that you had a foreign seller of American stocks either from Germany or shifting to German financial assets. The behavior of unrelated markets, or correlated markets, that is unusual is the kind of thing I'm talking about."

With so much interest in George Soros, it was easy to get tricked into believing that he was behind the movement of a stock—when in fact he was not. "The way to get somebody fooled quickly today," noted Dodge, "is to see something moving quickly and say George is buying. If the market comes to believe that it's George, it may do things. Just saying somebody is doing something can have an effect."

Soros's traders kept tight lips about what they were doing. Still, other traders sometimes could detect when Soros was active on the market. As Bill Dodge explained, a group of traders might begin to notice that each time they sell a stock for someone, the stock does not drop. This makes them wonder why. The traders listen carefully to what their colleagues are saying in off-handed conversations to one another. One might say that he sold a lot of oil and the price didn't drop. Another could respond that he noticed the same thing.

But none of the traders has sources within the Soros organization, at least not current ones. Nonetheless, they might still be able to deduce what George was up to.

Again, Dodge offered help: "I may call you up and say I want to buy—you make a market for me. I go all around the hub and there's 25 guys and you told me three months ago over beers you were doing a lot of business with George. You don't tell me what kind of business. I call you and say I want to buy from you and you say no. We'd be in competition. You're the only one out of 25 who won't sell and all the other 25 people keep selling. And you seem to have a relationship with George. Then the market would deduce that you are buying for Soros."

Imbued with his status as a guru, George Soros seemed to have the kind of touch that could turn almost anything into precious gold.

Real estate was a good example.

Until early in 1993, Soros had stayed away from investments in real estate. For some time, however, that area had been financially depressed; the slump had begun back in the 1980s, when developers had overbuilt. Now there was a crisis, but it did not scare off Soros, who suddenly acquired a taste for it. He saw the crisis as simply another buying opportunity. Still, it seemed strange for Soros to be entering the field, stranger still that he would choose Paul Reichmann as his partner.

Soros announced on February 8, 1993, that he was establishing a $225 million real estate fund that Reichmann would manage. The new fund, to be called Quantum Realty Fund, represented Soros's gamble that the depressed real estate market would turn around in the near future.

The Reichmann brothers—Paul, Albert, and Ralph—had been knocked for a loop when the real estate market collapsed. Before that the family's real estate holdings in Canada, New York, and London had been worth billions of dollars. Major portions of the Reichmann holdings, however, had entered bankruptcy proceedings when their firm, Olympia & York, suffered heavy losses due to the development of the London financial center known as Canary Wharf. Paul Reichmann had been the controlling shareholder of Olympia & York.

None of this seemed to matter to George Soros. He told the *New York Times:* "They [the Reichmanns] were the most successful real estate developers in the world. I am basically looking to invest my own money and I want to go with the best." Soros and Reichmann pledged between $75 million and $100 million to the new fund; most of the capital would come from existing Quantum Fund shareholders.

The following September, the new Soros-Reichmann fund made its first purchase: a $634 million package of foreclosed real estate and troubled mortgage loans from Travelers Corporation, the huge insurance firm. The purchase represented one of the largest bulk sales of real estate assets in history. Then, in November, Soros and Reichmann announced plans to build three real estate projects in Mexico City that could cost as much as $1.5 billion.

George Soros could sway markets once it became known that he was trading in a certain stock or currency or commodity. In effect, he could become the catalyst for trend-following behavior in the markets.

It happened in April 1993. This time it really was gold that he seemed to be targeting.

Inflation had remained low in recent months, but in Soros's view, it was poised to rise again. That would make gold, although it paid no dividends, a better store of real value than stocks, real estate, or bonds.

Accordingly, the Quantum Fund purchased between 2 and 3 million ounces of gold at $345 an ounce. Soros also invested nearly

$400 million in Newmont Mining, purchasing 10 million shares at $39.50 a share from Jacob Rothschild and takeover artist Sir James Goldsmith. With a 13 percent ownership, Soros was the firm's second biggest shareholder. Goldsmith remained first with a 30 percent share. Rothschild had just under 5 percent.

Soros, Goldsmith, and Lord Rothschild were all close acquaintances. One link between Soros and the Rothschild firm was Nils Taube, Rothschild's chief investment officer, a nonexecutive director of the Quantum Fund, and a close Soros associate for many years.

Sure enough, when traders spotted the footprints of the investor as those of George Soros, the price of the metal soared. Once word got out, there was massive speculative gold purchasing on the busiest trading day in gold in recent history. An ounce of gold rose nearly $5 to over $350 in London, the first time since October 1992 that it had passed that mark.

A footnote to Soros's venture into gold: By the end of the summer of 1993, Soros apparently had taken his winnings and gotten out. The *Sunday Times* of London reported on August 15 that Soros had sold his entire holdings in gold bullion at between $385 and $395 an ounce. Soros appeared to be cutting his losses: The price of gold had soared to over $400 an ounce in London two weeks earlier, but then plunged sharply.

The early part of 1993 went well for Quantum. In the first four months the fund was up 18 percent, in part due to a successful bet on the Nikkei when it was around 16,000 points. By May 11, 1993, the Nikkei had risen to 20,000 points.

In case anyone had any doubt about George Soros's market powers, he attempted to set the record straight. Interviewed on CNN's "Business Day" program by Deborah Marchini on April 26, 1993, Soros disputed her contention that the late rise in gold prices had been the result of good news from Russia, where Boris Yeltsin and his economic reforms had won a recent vote of confidence in a national referendum.

The news from Russia had nothing to do with the rise in gold prices, Soros argued. The hike had been due to his purchase of shares in Newmont Mining.

Apart from this bold claim on CNN, Soros seemed eager not to exploit his new position, even after all the headlines touting him a marketing messiah. "I'm amused by my guru status," he told *Business Week* that summer. "I acknowledge it. How can I deny it? I think it is a passing phase. I hope that actually, to the extent that I have an impact on people's thinking, it is that they'll learn how important it is to look for the flaws and to think critically."

The Reichmann and the Newmont experiences, however, appeared to offer solid evidence that a move by Soros in a market, once the word spread to other traders, would trigger further market activity. That fresh market activity, mimicking his own behavior, was almost sure to increase the value of Soros's investment position. It was a new and powerful position to be in. The *Daily Mail* asked in a headline on April 30, 1993: "Why are we so bewitched by this modern Midas?"

The answer was clear. George Soros seemed to be a modern Midas. It was easy to be bewitched by him. Following his example made people wealthier. What could be wrong with that?

In Soros's view, he could not do much about his newfound status even if he wanted to. "It is my business to trade, it is my role, it is my professional activity. I could not carry on managing a fund if I did not take positions in stocks, bonds and currencies. So I took a position in Newmont mines and look what happened."

Other financial players were duly impressed with Soros's special status. "Institutional investors who control much more money than Soros have enormous faith in his judgment," observed Peter Rona, a former investment banker who, like Soros, was a Hungarian émigré. "That's where Soros's clout comes from."

Others, however, were not so impressed. Some loved to debunk Soros, contending that he did not move markets. One was Arthea B. Nolan, the associate editor for news of the *Hedge Mar* newsletter, who argued that "while it is true that managers handling large chunks of money may move markets in the short-term, they can't impact the underlying markets because supply and demand factors determine prices in the long-term."

Others denied that Soros possessed some magical intuitive sense; rather, they insisted, he was engaging in something more nefarious. The man had friends. Not exactly a crime, they were quick to admit. But those friends were in high places. Again, they were quick to concede, not exactly an act that could send someone to jail. Still, something sinister appeared to lurk behind those old-boy network ties.

The Observer, for example, referred to Soros's close ties with Jimmy Goldsmith and Nils O. Taube: "These kinds of connections, this impression of an insiders' gang, are what make more mainstream investors occasionally raise an eyebrow where Soros is concerned. His associates may talk about a sixth sense, but even some of their comments contribute to the impression that Soros has created for himself a comprehensive network for gathering information."

And yet, what was really wrong with having friends—in the right places?

Gary Gladstein, business manager for Soros Fund Management, was pleased to explain guru Soros's ability to pick up on macroeconomic trends anywhere in the world by pointing to the man's wide constellation of friends. "George has friends who are intellectuals, a vast network of contacts all over the world. He will come into the office and say, 'I'm interested in country A, call X. . . .' And he has relied on independent advisers all over the world throughout his career. You should see his address book."

By June of 1993, Soros was again investing in real estate, this time in Great Britain. Four months after he set up the fund with Reichmann in the United States, he formed an even larger one as a vehicle for investing in British property. Soros's Quantum Fund joined with a London-based real estate developer named British Land Co., PLC, and this time Soros planned to invest $775 million in property. He also took a 4.8 percent stake in British Land.

If Soros was buying into British real estate, that had to mean that the real estate market in Great Britain had bottomed out. That, at any rate, was how British investors read the Soros investment. The effect on the stock market values of property firms was earth-shattering: They rose by 667 million pounds, giving Soros an instant profit of 5.2 million pounds on his 5 percent stake in British Land. The shares of British Land itself rose from 298 pence to 434 pence.

Clearly, the Soros magic was still working. As *The Guardian* cooed: "Last month it was gold. Yesterday, it was property. The world investment community has decided that if George Soros thinks something is worth buying then they should think the same."

Buoyed by the obvious power he commanded, Soros went one step further. He made a public declaration that, whether he intended it to or not, had the effect of influencing a market. In this case, a currency market.

It did not surprise anyone when in June 1993 Soros took the remarkable step of publicly stating that the German mark was bound to fall. This was the ultimate act of a man who had concluded that he had extraordinary powers he could exploit.

In a letter to the *Times* of London on June 9, Soros responded to one written on May 20 by Anatole Kaletsky, the newspaper's economics editor, urging Soros to attack the French franc. Soros, in his answer, said that he disagreed with Kaletsky, that it was not the French currency and bonds that needed to be sold, but the German ones. As for Germany's short-term interest rates, they had to come down even more, Soros wrote, no matter what the Bundesbank wanted. "I expect the mark to fall against all major currencies, including even sterling. I also expect German bonds to fall vis-à-vis French ones in the months to come, although German bond prices should rise in absolute terms when the Bundesbank reserves reverse course and sharply reduce short-term interest rates. (For the sake of full disclosure, I am talking my book.)

"The Bundesbank has kept interest rates too high, too long. It could have lowered short-term rates gradually without endangering its reputation, but it missed the boat. Germany is now in a worse recession than France."

To Soros, Germany would sooner or later have to bend, if only because its recession had grown so serious. "Short-term interest rates will have to be lowered, whether the Bundesbank likes it or not." Soros added that German bond prices would then rise in marks, but fall in value once exchange rates were factored in.

It was a remarkable revelation. This was not simply a case of George Soros, the expert financier, giving some advice based on his experience and intuition. This was George Soros, the speculator, openly admitting that his advice, if followed, would directly benefit his own investment position.

This was the third time in recent months that Soros's timely revelation of his investments had helped increase their value. "It's a new way of making money," according to David C. Roche, a London-based strategist for Morgan Stanley, "a combination of judicious investment at the bottom of a market and a publicity coup."

Concluding the letter, Soros sought to make clear that his two professions—investor and philanthropist—were separate and distinct. He had not gotten into philanthropy to benefit his investments. "I want to clarify my own role. In your letter you mentioned in one breath my activities in the currency markets and in Eastern Europe. There is a sharp distinction. In Eastern Europe I seek to promote open societies. In the financial markets, I am pursuing profit for my shareholders and myself. My access in the financial market enables me to finance my foundations in Eastern Europe. I do not seek profits in Eastern Europe and I do not act as a philanthropic institution in the financial markets. I try to avoid speculative activities that could prove wantonly destructive, but I see no reason to abstain from moves that would happen even without my participation. Of course, in making such judgments, I am no more infallible than the central banks."

Well, maybe not, but Soros's guru status was enhanced when the markets responded positively to his statements regarding the mark. The mark, which had been at 61 cents on June 11, two days after Soros's letter, dropped to 59 cents on June 25. The Quantum Fund climbed 10 percent, some $400 million, due, it was believed, to Soros's currency trading.

On June 23, Soros said that the mark was certain to be devalued: The dollar would soon equal 2 marks against the current 1.70 marks. Once again he attacked the Bundesbank for not taking steps that would aid other European countries. "The Bundesbank's current position is harmful to the German economy and the European economy, and very harmful to the political unity of Europe. Previously, the dollar was worth up to four marks," he added. "I am convinced it is too cheap as long as it is less than two marks."

Twenty-three

A Common Virus Known as Hubris

I t was all very ironic. For so long, George Soros had wanted the politicians to stand up and take notice of him. Now they were doing just that. He, of course, had wanted their respect, not their suspicion. He got the latter.

Soros's dazzling moves in early 1993, coupled with the news that he had earned $650 million in 1992, gave the politicians pause. They remembered all too well the 1980s and the way Michael Milken, Ivan Boesky, and the other stars of the takeover era had raked in millions of dollars.

Indelibly stuck in the politicians' minds was the unraveling of the takeover era, when it was revealed that in fact Milken, Boesky, and a host of lesser lights had been capitalizing on inside information. Everyone—at first—had been amazed at how clever these fellows seemed to be. As it turned out, the business stars of the 1980s had not been nearly as clever as they had appeared.

And now the politicians believed they should train their sights on George Soros and the whole hedge-fund phenomenon. They had no reason to believe he had behaved as Milken and Boesky had. Soros's sin, as they perceived it, was making so much money. An uneasy feeling persisted in Washington.

For here were these financiers, making huge amounts of money, and no one outside of Wall Street, and sometimes even within, appeared to know what the money men were doing, how in fact they had made their fortunes. The view was gradually taking hold in Washington that Soros and the other hedge-fund managers should be asked some probing questions. They should be called to account.

And so Henry Gonzales, the chairman of the powerful House Banking Committee, announced in June 1993 that he planned to ask the Federal Reserve Board and the Securities and Exchange Commission to take a close look at the foreign exchange dealings of George

Soros's Quantum Fund. Speaking from the floor of the House, Gonzales said he was curious to know how Soros could make such large profits. He hoped to find out how much of Soros's capital came from bank loans and just how exposed American banks were to the Soros Fund. "In the near future," promised the legislator, "I will ask the Federal Reserve and the SEC to review Mr. Soros's impact on the foreign exchange market to determine if it is possible for an individual actor such as Mr. Soros to manipulate the foreign exchange market."

Manipulate.

That was a strong word.

This was not going to be a walk in the park for Mr. Soros.

Gonzales added that "it is in the best interest of the Federal Reserve and other central banks to fully understand Mr. Soros's methodology for manipulating the FX [the foreign exchange] market. After all, they are competing head-on with him in an effort to manipulate the value of various currencies."

The hearings would not take place for nearly another year. Yet the effect of Gonzales's announcement was to cast a pall over the whole hedge-fund game. As they watched and waited, Soros and the rest of the hedge-fund community had to wonder what was in store for them.

And yet, by the summer of 1993, Soros was feeling pretty good about himself. He seemed at ease. He took all the talk about being a market guru with a certain equanimity. He seemed a happier man than he had been a decade earlier. Edgar Astaire, his London partner, found him to be much more satisfied with himself than in early years, when "he was very dour, a cold fish. All that talk now about how he can move markets, that he's a guru, it has affected him. He's more expansive. He enjoys life. I've seen him chuckle more."

Soros seemed to like all the attention, but he sensed it was a passing phenomenon. "I do not manipulate the markets but I cannot deny that for the moment I have a certain mystique around me as a market operator. Right now people pay a lot of attention to what I do. And the fact that gold went up $15 [in mid-May 1993] after the purchase of this stake in Newmont had something to do with my buying. It does happen. But after I make a few false moves, people calm down."

He did some clever manipulating of the media.

Having attracted their interest, Soros knew that he had to resist the flood of journalists' questions about what he was doing in the markets. He wanted the focus to be on his aid programs, and he succeeded magnificently in that. Indeed, by 1993 and 1994, most of the articles being written about Soros focused on his philanthropy. Reporters felt compelled to mention the investment side of his life, but given little hard information, they treated the subject superficially.

Detecting the benefits that publicity could bring to the aid program, Soros warmed up to the media. He sat down for more interviews after the September 1992 coup and accordingly received a good deal of positive press, particularly in Britain. For instance, *The Observer* headlined its January 10, 1993, story on him "Man who broke the Bank"; on March 14, the *London Standard* headlined its story, "Master of the Universe."

Television crews from England and the United States requested his cooperation for short documentaries on his career. For the first time, he gave them permission to film in his investment offices in New York and in the Budapest cellars where he had hid from the Nazis.

For Soros, it was certainly worthwhile. In an ABC-TV documentary that aired on December 13, 1993, he said: "[My fund] has become so enormous that it doesn't make sense unless I have a use for the money. . . . It seems to be easier [to make money than to spend it]. I seem to have a greater facility in making it than in making the right decisions in giving it away."

No more identity crises overtook him. Soros seemed a most satisfied individual. Still, he yearned for more from life, as he made clear in a remarkable interview he gave to *Leadership* magazine in July 1993.

The reporter asked him how he saw himself at this point?

Soros: "I am a work in progress and I am rather satisfied with the curve that events have taken. I like myself a great deal better than I did when I was purely on the moneymaking side. Now I feel more complete. . . . If I could just progress towards a better understanding of how it all hangs together it would give me great satisfaction."

In short, he still wanted answers to all those existential questions that had teased him as a student in London in the early 1950s.

The reporter asked him if he had a cutoff point, presumably meaning retirement.

Soros answered in the negative: "I think that would be a kind of a defeat. But I would like to keep things within certain bounds so that I don't come to that stage. There is clearly a moment when it could become too much and I wouldn't be able to cope with it."

Did he ever feel used? All people with large amounts of money felt that way at one time or another. Did Soros?

"No. I feel that I am reasonably good at identifying this risk and avoiding it. I accept it as part of the game."

Reporter: "You talk about the responsibility of having so much money, and dealing with it in such a way that you are not seen as a gross self-seeker. Is that a difficult thing?"

Soros: "I don't really care about that. I am sure that story will be written, if it has not been done already. I don't think I have anything to defend. I think the problem is elsewhere. Am I a slave of my success, or am I in charge of my destiny?

"There is such a thing as being too successful and having too much to do to be successful. I need to achieve the right balance and not be swept away by my own success. *I must not be sucked into something that is beyond me. That is the real game of my life,* because that is the risk-taking part."

Then, a very good question: If Soros were not making all that money and not giving chunks of it away, what might he be doing?

He confessed that he had given thought to that question himself. He first asked it of himself in the early 1960s, when he returned to Hungary for the first time. "I came to the conclusion that I would be driving a taxi with tourists in order to earn some foreign currency."

He could have pictured himself as a reasonably well-off middle-class businessman. Was he suggesting that had events taken a different turn, he could have been a plain old taxi driver, hustling to eke out a living?

Meanwhile, by the summer of 1993, Soros was proving an even larger enigma to the financial community. Until now, nine months after the September 1992 pound coup, Soros had been thought of in near mythic terms, his every utterance a signal to the markets to follow.

And yet, during this summer of troubles for the European Community, Soros-watchers found it increasingly hard to fathom what was in the Master's mind, to gauge what aspect of the financial markets he liked. He seemed to be a man on a seesaw, one minute going up, the next going down. The experience was often dizzying for those trying to follow his moves.

And everyone was trying to figure out what those moves would be as the Exchange Rate Mechanism appeared to be disintegrating. Once before Soros had taken on the ERM, and won. Now there was renewed fear that he would try again.

The French franc had been coming under increasing pressure. High German interest rates were attracting capital to German marks and away from francs, forcing the French currency down to the minimum level allowed under the ERM. Speculators were selling off the franc. The French, however, had no desire to devalue it.

On Monday, July 26, Soros told the French newspaper *Le Figaro* that he was not speculating against the franc. His reason: He did not want anyone to accuse him of destroying the ERM. In essence, Soros was giving a vote of confidence to the franc, suggesting that it would survive the current turbulence without France having to excise it from the ERM.

Soros appeared to be staying out of the fray. But when the Bundesbank met and voted against changing its key discount rate, Soros was angry and sounded as if he felt betrayed. "I think the system is going to be broken," he predicted.

On Friday, July 30, he then faxed a press release to Reuters in London in which he declared: "After the decision of the Bundesbank not to lower the discount rate, I feel no longer bound by the declaration I made in *Le Figaro*. It is futile to attempt to protect the European Monetary System by abstaining from trading in currencies when the anchor of the system, the Bundesbank, acts without regard to the interests of other members."

He compared the French franc to a battered wife who, despite the beatings, remained with her husband—in this case, the ERM. "I do not expect the present arrangement to be operative Monday morning." He declared that he now felt free to resume trading in the French franc.

Confusion reigned within the financial community over what George Soros was doing—and what he was trying to communicate. As European ministers frantically tried to rescue the ERM in Brussels, Soros remained aloof, seeking to give the distinct impression that he was above the fray, indifferent this time to another ERM crisis.

A reporter for the *New York Times* caught him by phone while he was lounging by his swimming pool at his home in Southampton, sounding, the *Times* reporter suggested, more like an elder statesman than a currency trader. "Exactly because I don't want to drive the markets crazy, I am not going to say what I am doing," he told the reporter. Soros gave away no secrets. All he would say was that he had not been speculating in European currencies prior to Friday noon. That sounded very much like he had begun to trade in the franc after that.

Was that true?

Soros wouldn't say. Eager to disabuse others of the notion that he was a mere speculator, he continued to act like an elder statesman. "I am a great believer in Europe and in having the system, and participants ought to care about preserving the system and not just making a profit for themselves."

He no longer, however, felt above the fray.

On August 4, he made a public pronouncement about the mark. He believed that the Bundesbank's policies were driving Germany farther into recession, and accordingly he was selling his marks. "I myself am speculating against the mark, selling marks and getting into dollars and yen," Soros said on German television. "In the long term this is the position one should have toward the mark." He added that the high-interest-rate policy of the German bank was self-defeating and that it should cut rates to help revive European economies.

At first Soros appeared to have it right. In June, when Soros made his first prediction, the mark was at 1.625 to the dollar. In late July it reached a low of 1.75. But by mid-September, the German currency strengthened noticeably against the dollar, trading at 1.61.

Up to this juncture, few questioned Soros's right to make public statements about his trades. Gurus did that. Yet the conviction was growing that Soros might have gone too far in giving advice to the statesmen of the world.

On August 1, for example, he appeared on a British television program to make the case for Western military intervention in the Balkans. He argued that tolerating the doctrine of the "ethnically cleansed" state marked the end of civilization.

Who had appointed him, anyway?

The *Daily Telegraph,* in an August 5, 1993, editorial, nicely summed up the ambivalent feelings many had toward Soros that summer: "Ever since he wagered $10 billion that the pound would fall out of the Exchange Rate Mechanism, his every utterance has been hailed as oracular, and his letters and articles in newspapers as holy writ. . . .

"Nor should anyone wish Mr. Soros ill. Those Continental politicians and central bankers who in recent days have blamed speculators such as he for the collapse of the ERM should curb their wrath: The fault is entirely theirs for attempting to maintain unsustainable exchange and interest rates. . . .

"But there is also scope for caution. There is a sense of hubris about Mr. Soros's increasingly grandiloquent communications to the media. . . .

"When we read this week that Mr. Soros favors air attacks to raise the siege of Sarajevo we begin to think he needs a holiday. He may have come to believe that with a nod or a wink he can determine not only foreign exchanges but foreign policies. . . . But the willingness of the world to hang on Mr. Soros's every utterance should not fool him into believing them all himself."

Two days later, on August 7, *The Economist* went even further in a piece entitled "Talkative."

"Has George Soros gone bonkers? Newspapers and broadcasts are increasingly filled with weighty pronouncements by the New York–based Hungarian-born investor on everything from banking to Bosnia. In recent days, as Europe's exchange-rate mechanism lay on its sickbed, Mr. Soros's views have attracted at least as much attention as those of the head of the Bundesbank. That the press should be interested in Mr. Soros makes sense; he, after all, is the Man Who Broke the Bank of England. . . . Yet investors with anything like his clout tend to be preternaturally silent. Why isn't he?"

The magazine asked why Soros was tipping his hand publicly so much?

"The first [reason] must be that Mr. Soros is not averse to being seen as the outstanding investment guru of his age. He deserves to be.

"Another motive may be that Soros is no longer content to remain a rich green eye-shade but wants to influence public policy on the big issues of his time. An admirable ambition, though perhaps better fulfilled through the sort of philanthropy that he is practicing in Eastern Europe.

"A final reason behind Mr. Soros's apparent desire for publicity may be that he is less concerned than he was in the day-to-day management of Quantum."

The media barrage continued as *Barron's* weighed in on August 16.

"In the old days, George was the taciturn type. He was a witty and valued member of our Roundtable for a bunch of years, but other than that he preferred to let his performance talk for him, and gosh knows, it spoke volumes.

"Lately, though, George has broken his vow of silence with a vengeance. You can hardly turn on the telly in London some weeks without his visage filling the screen. He dashes off letters to newspapers, pens op-ed pieces, grants audiences to journalists, scolds the Bundesbank publicly—in short, he has become a Public Person as well as a Legendary Investor.

". . . That George would feel an urge to howl a bit about his philanthropic exertions, or play worldly philosopher the way rich people are wont to do when making money becomes a bit of a bore, doesn't surprise us. It's his musings aloud on less cosmic matters, like whether the deutsch mark will go up or down or whether one should short the franc, that we find a bit of a puzzle. If we didn't know him better, we'd suspect a touch of the common virus known as hubris."

A *Business Week* reporter had the chance that summer to ask Soros why he had become so "talkative."

"I generally don't want to have a public presence unless I have something to say," Soros began. ". . . And to the extent that it is possible, I prefer to say it in my own words. Because that is one definite policy that I'm developing—I find that if I give an interview, I will be quoted out of context. Even though they are my own words, the slant is different than what I intended.

"I don't have a love-hate relationship [with the media]. If anything, I [keep] a really wide distance. If you now write a devastating critique and find some flaws or something in me . . . it won't hurt me. So you are at liberty to do it."

Soros appeared to be saying that he did not really care about the media, yet that was clearly not the case. Without the benefit of a large and sophisticated public relations machine, Soros had become rather adroit as his own best spokesman. Shrewdly, he understood that he had a better chance of getting *all* his views across if, instead of granting an interview to a newspaper, he sent a fax or wrote a letter to the editor. Time and again, the technique worked. The newspaper receiving a Soros fax or letter wound up printing it in full. He had also learned that there was a time to comment to the press, and a time to keep quiet. When he took the bold step that year of hiring an outside public relations firm—the prestigious Kekst & Co. of New York—Soros was determined that the Kekst publicity machine would say as little as possible about him.

To some, Soros, in making public statements about investment positions, was being a bit too clever. One of Wall Street's leading money managers, insisting upon anonymity, was clearly troubled by Soros's behavior: "I don't understand the reason for all these public pronouncements, particularly when they're actively trading the markets." Making such statements, the manager asserted, was "inappropriate. . . . In Soros's case, it may not be a legal issue, just an ethical issue."

But toward the end of August, Soros, still talking, pulled off another media coup, this time getting his face on the cover of *Business Week,* an achievement that in the past he might have considered the kiss of death. Some of his aides went apoplectic.

Just how apoplectic could be gleaned from the opening paragraphs of the cover story.

The *Business Week* reporter noted that Soros was about to give an interview to the magazine. Gerard Manolovici, described as a veteran Soros portfolio manager, was disturbed.

"Gary,"—he is talking to Gary Gladstein, Soros's chief administrator—"you've got to stop it. I'm serious. You've got to stop this story."

Gladstein, turning to the reporter, smiled apologetically and observed: "We don't like publicity around here. We like to keep a low profile."

One knowledgeable Wall Street observer noted that for someone like Soros to attract publicity, "Not only is it considered imprudent, but it's also considered very unlucky. Wall Street is a kind of philistine business and place. In George Soros's investment operation he is surrounded by people who care nothing except about making some money. They do not care about their place in history. Soros may, but they do not. There is a pretty soundly based body of lore on Wall Street that says once you have become conspicuous you are history. Once you land on the cover of *Business Week,* you can kiss it good-bye. And Soros has just been on the cover."

Soros came under increasing pressure from his own aides, including Stanley Druckenmiller, to control his tongue. The feeling within Soros Fund Management was that Soros's public pronouncements had given the fund less mobility. As one former associate noted, "He may have thought he was being God's gift to the average investor, but there was a phenomenon where his positions got so large that he needed big follow-on buying to make it a reality. He became the market in some sense. He became so large in currencies, so large in fixed income, that the fund lost its flexibility in the market."

So following the talkative summer of 1993, Soros adopted a new tack. He refused, when asked by reporters, to say what stock or currency he liked or did not like. He seemed to sense that his every word was being monitored. If he had the power that was imputed to him, it could be turned against him. He knew that. And so he became less talkative.

Soros earned little applause from the very European politicians he was trying to cultivate. They were angry at him for continuing to "meddle" in European monetary affairs.

In late September 1993, Belgian foreign minister Willy Claes, at that time president of the European Community's Council of Ministers as well, accused Soros indirectly of attempting to subvert the cause of European unity. In an interview with the French weekly magazine *Le Point,* Claes said: "There is a kind of plot. In the Anglo-Saxon world, there exist organizations and personalities who prefer a divided Europe, condemned to a secondary economic role, rather than a strong Europe with its own monetary and foreign policy."

Soros spokesman David Kronfeld brushed aside Claes's comments, noting that "we're not going to respond to this nonsense about Anglo-Saxon plots." Soros, he reemphasized, favored an effective European Monetary System but was convinced that the system had ceased to function positively for European nations before its recent collapse.

All in all, 1993 had been a very good year for the Quantum Fund, up 61.5 percent. A mere $10,000 invested in Quantum back in 1969 would now be worth $21 million. The same $10,000 put into Standard & Poor's 500 index stocks over the same period would have been worth a paltry $122,000.

Each of the Soros funds had done incredibly well. The best was Quantum Emerging Growth, up 109 percent before fees, followed by Quantum and Quota, each up over 72 percent. Since 1969, Soros had produced a compounded annual growth rate of about 35 percent. The yearly growth for the S&P 500 had been only 10.5 percent.

Soros's major purchase in the final quarter of 1993 had been Paramount Communications; his second- and third-largest purchases were both in the computer networking field: Newbridge Networks and DSC Communications. His top sale was Medco Containment Services, although other large sales suggested that he was trying to extricate himself from financial services; of his 10 largest sales, 5 had been in that area.

The following chart shows Soros's largest stock holdings; roughly half of his assets are in stocks.

LARGEST STOCK HOLDINGS

Company	Holding value (millions)	Shares owned, 12/31/93
Newmont Mining	$488	8,461,000
Paramount Communications	225	2,894,000
Deere & Co.	116	1,569,000
Perkin-Elmer	78	2,036,000
Home Depot	66	1,665,000
Newbridge Networks	56	1,019,000
Motorola	47	507,000
Tektronix	44	1,869,000
Kemper	42	1,144,000

TOP FOURTH-QUARTER STOCK PURCHASES RANKED BY DOLLAR VALUE

Company	Shares bought, 4th Q 1993	Shares owned, 12/31/93
Paramount Communications	1,674,000	2,894,000
Newbridge Networks	569,000	1,019,000
DSC Communications	439,000	651,000
Philip Morris	424,000	436,000
Motorola	253,000	507,000
Host Marriott	2,500,000	3,750,000
WMX Technologies	714,000	714,000
Raytheon	238,000	250,000
American Home Products	208,000	208,000
LIN Broadcasting	116,000	119,000

TOP FOURTH-QUARTER SALES RANKED BY DOLLAR VALUE

Company	Shares bought, 4th Q 1993	Shares owned, 12/31/93
Medco Containment Services	4,086,000	—0—
Newmont Mining	365,000	8,461,000
Chase Manhattan	561,000	150,000
Shoney's	790,000	—0—
Transamerica	275,000	—0—
American Express	519,000	550,000
Marriott International	529,000	720,000
Federal National Mortgage	185,000	145,000
General Re Corporation	134,000	205,000
Burlington Resources	305,000	592,000

Source: *Federal Filings* (quoted in *USA Today,* March 12, 1994).

Twenty-four

I'm a Hungarian Jew

I t was ironic that the man who, as a child, thought he was God treated his religion largely as an irrelevancy.

Neither his parents nor his own experiences drew George Soros closer to Judaism. Even the Holocaust, a sharp reminder of his religious background, had no lasting effect on his religious feeling. Hiding from the Nazis in 1944 had provided him with a great adventure and a set of survival skills, but it did not make him more Jewish.

If he derived any lesson from the Holocaust, it was that minorities—as the Jews were in Europe—had to be protected in the future and the best way to assure that was by building pluralistic societies where minorities were given their rights.

"I went to England in 1947 and then to the United States in 1956," he wrote. "But I never quite became an American. I had left Hungary behind, and my Jewishness did not express itself in a sense of tribal loyalty that would have led me to support Israel. On the contrary, I took pride in being in the minority, an outsider who was capable of seeing the other point of view. Only the ability to think critically and to rise above a particular point of view could make up for the dangers and indignities that being a Hungarian Jew had inflicted on me."

Judaism was a burden to him. It offered no special advantage, only the "dangers and indignities" that had been "inflicted" upon him for being born a Hungarian Jew. Accordingly, during the postwar years he played down his religion. None of his intellectual ideas sprang from Jewish sources.

His longtime friend and business associate Byron Wien noted that "George has never thought of himself as anything but Jewish. He never tried to suggest that he wasn't Jewish. He never backed away from his identity, but I think at the same time he did not want that to be the central fact of his identity.

217

"When he was growing up it was the central fact of his identity. The fact that he was Jewish meant that he had to run away. He had to escape, to hide. When he came to the United States, being Jewish did categorize you, and George wanted to be free of all categories. He wanted to be accepted for what he was, for his intellect and for his accomplishments. . . . He didn't identify with Jewish causes, but on the other hand he didn't back away from [being Jewish]. He assumed that everybody knew he was Jewish, but he didn't wear a sign saying, in case you were wondering, I'm Jewish."

In early October 1992, Soros invited an Israeli entrepreneur named Benny Landa to have dinner with him at his New York apartment. The evening turned out to be one of the most remarkable either man had ever spent.

In 1977, Landa had founded a high-tech company called Indigo in the Israeli town of Rehovot, not far from Tel Aviv. Indigo was fast becoming the world's leader in high-quality digital color-printing products.

In June, Landa had asked First Boston, the American investment-banking firm, to do some strategic planning for Indigo. First Boston had recommended starting with a private placement, followed some years later with a public offering. As First Boston neared completion of the private-placement memo that would be circulated to potential investors, Soros got word of the company's intentions. After further inquiries, he asked Indigo to put off issuing the private-placement memo and said if he was interested, he would assume the entire amount, $50 million, as an investment.

"It was a pleasant shock to us because we had anticipated having at least half a dozen investors," recalled Landa, sitting in his fourth-floor office in Rehovot in August 1994. Terms were negotiated, but Soros told Landa that he had a personal interest in the deal and wanted to meet the entrepreneur before they finalized anything. He invited him to come to New York for dinner.

And so Soros and Landa met. They were joined by two others, P. C. Chatterjee, a Soros associate, and Robert Conrads, managing director at First Boston. What was remarkable about the evening was the nature of the discussion. One would expect that four businessmen, getting together for a working dinner, would talk mainly, if not exclusively, about work. But Chatterjee and Conrads said virtually nothing the entire evening. Later, Landa explained that he believed the two men, hearing Soros and him discourse the entire evening on nonbusiness subjects, were too stunned and shocked to speak.

In describing the evening nearly two years later, Landa recalled the details as if he had dined with Soros the day before. The evening began at 7:30 PM and was to last four hours. After sitting down to the elegant dinner, Soros asked Landa to talk about himself and his company. That took maybe 20 to 30 minutes. Landa then asked Soros whether it was his turn to ask the investor about himself.

"Sure," Soros replied, assuming he would be asked some questions about his investment ventures.

"Well," Landa started, "I'm not very interested in your economic and political philosophy that I've read about." If Soros winced at hearing this, Landa did not notice. "What I am interested in is"—Landa reminded himself not to sound too blunt—"how you feel about being Jewish. Whether doing a deal with an Israeli-based company has any significance."

Landa had known something of Soros's indifference toward Judaism, yet he had known also that the investor was Jewish, a Holocaust survivor. Somehow it was difficult for Landa to reconcile Soros's survival of the Holocaust and his neutrality toward his Jewishness. Hence, the question.

Soros seemed surprised at the question, though not uncomfortable.

"It means nothing whatsoever to me. It's not because you're an Israeli-based company that we have an interest. It seems like a great opportunity." For the next three and a half hours, Soros then spoke about his Jewishness, about his childhood experiences, and especially about hiding from the Nazis during World War II. "It was one of the most exciting things in my life," he told Landa. "Hiding like that was like playing cops and robbers. *It was a great thrill.*" They also talked about Jewish nationalism and Jewish self-hatred. At times the evening took on the atmosphere of a debate—always friendly, yet always sticking to what Landa later described as "these intimate, thorny issues."

As he and Soros talked, Landa wondered what had caused the investor to deny his Jewish roots. Listening to Soros talk about his war experiences, Landa found a possible explanation. He noticed that Soros always portrayed his experiences in World War II as an exciting game. Yet in reality, he had to have gone through inconceivable terror, and only because he was a Jew. He concluded that being Jewish must have become a burden, never a joy, to Soros. At one stage in the evening, Soros disclosed that only in the early 1980s did he feel comfortable admitting in public to being Jewish. Before that, he simply avoided the issue. "Perhaps being a success in business finally gave me enough confidence to acknowledge my Jewishness," Soros suggested.

The subject of nationalism arose. Landa suggested that nationalism had some constructive, positive elements, and that Zionism in particular was a very positive force and a worthy cause. "I would like to draw you nearer to it," he told Soros.

Soros had experienced too much of the Nazis to think highly of nationalism. "It only causes evil and destruction and chauvinism and war," he responded. "I am against nationalism of any kind. If it were possible to have the constructive facets of nationalism without its negative characteristics and the resulting political and social damage that it causes, then you would be right. But it isn't possible."

Even as they spoke, Soros was under assault by the nationalist regimes in Eastern Europe. "It's so ironic," Soros said. "They are trying to tie me to a world Zionist plot, with the Elders of Zion. It's just terribly ironic." Ironic, because Soros barely identified himself as a Jew.

As the hour neared 11:30, both Soros and Landa were emotionally weary from the experience.

Landa turned to Soros with an air of finality and declared, "I feel it is one of my missions to bring you back after all to the same kind of identification with Israel that you have with your other political causes. To bring you back to the Jewish world."

"This will be interesting," Soros replied vaguely.

In the elevator, Chatterjee turned to Landa and said, "I'm shocked. I've never seen anything like this in my life. I never knew any of this about George." Landa, too, was surprised. The evening had been a deeply personal experience for both Landa and Soros.

A few months later, in January 1993, Landa met Soros in the investor's New York office for a handshake and a signing. Soros must have remembered the evening they had spent in October, and he may have felt that he had left the impression that he was reluctant to do a deal with an Israeli company, that it somehow might overexpose his Jewishness. He sought to dispel any such notion with Landa.

Shaking his hand, Soros said, "You know, I'm glad this company is in Israel." Landa took that to mean that the deal did have some personal meaning for Soros after all. Landa took the opportunity to invite Soros to come to Israel, and Soros agreed.

The encounter with Benny Landa was symptomatic of a deeper change in George Soros. In the early 1990s, his friends and associates began noticing a change in his attitude toward his religion, a new interest in his past. He began asking some acquaintances, among them Daniel Doron, to supply him with some books, including the Talmud. "He became interested in Jewish civilization," said Doron. "Suddenly he realized that he didn't spring out of a vacuum." Awakening occurred in other ways as well. At the official opening of the Soros Foundation in Bucharest, Soros stood up in front of the crowd and proclaimed, "I'm George Soros and I'm a Hungarian Jew." Sandra Pralong was there, and she remembered the crowd being stunned. Romanians were not used to hearing someone say publicly he was proud to be Jewish.

It was an incredible transformation, especially by a man who until his early fifties had not been willing to identify himself as a Jew, who had thought his Jewishness was a burden. Now, however, in the early 1990s, all that seemed to be changing.

What caused George Soros's Jewish awakening? First and foremost, it was the attacks on him and on his Jewishness from right-wing nationalists in Eastern Europe. Next, it was his growing ease with his Jewishness. He had become a huge success in the business world, and therefore he was in a sense attack-proof. He no longer needed to be concerned that his Jewishness would penalize him.

Finally, the suffering he had witnessed in Eastern Europe, particularly in the Bosnian war in the early 1990s, had reminded him of how much his own Jewish brethren had gone through earlier in the century. After he had funded the reconstruction of Sarajevo's water supply and natural gas lines, a reporter asked him why a Jew like himself would sympathize with a Muslim country. In a rare comment on his Jewishness, Soros noted that "it has a particular resonance if you have experienced one type of Holocaust and you see another. I have a particular concern for the Holocaust in the former Yugoslavia."

It was, however, the visit he would pay to Israel in January 1994—his first public visit there—that became the most visible sign of his fresh warmth toward Judaism. For years, his Jewish associates had been trying to get him to pay more attention to the Jewish state, but to no avail. They were annoyed at his indifference toward Judaism, annoyed that he seemed to be ashamed to be Jewish. But they understood that however persuasive they might be, Soros himself would have to undergo some sort of change in order to make such a visit.

He had always said that he stayed away from Israel because of Israeli treatment of the Arabs. Another reason was his view that the socialist Israeli economy was too rigid, too inhospitable to investors. With the thrust of his aid efforts aimed at opening up closed societies in Eastern Europe and later in the former Soviet Union, Soros had no good reason to seek a foothold in democratic Israel. He did not think Israel needed "opening up."

That did not stop others from trying to woo Soros and to lure him to Israel.

In the fall of 1993, when Israel announced that it had been secretly negotiating with the Palestine Liberation Organization aiming toward an agreement with the Palestinians, Israeli economics professor Gur Ofer thought it a good time to write Soros asking him to think anew about visiting Israel.

"You remember that we talked and you refused to come to Israel?" Ofer wrote. "Well, Israel has been undergoing a very serious economic reform for the past few years. And we are going to have peace. It's time to reconsider your relations with Israel." Ofer never got an answer to his letter. The answer came indirectly when Soros announced that he would visit Israel in January 1994.

Soros may have decided to visit Israel not out of new interest in the Jewish state but rather to show the world that he was not intimidated by the attacks from right-wing nationalists in Eastern Europe. Having been accused of working for Israeli intelligence, Soros may have wanted to demonstrate that such assaults could not keep him away.

Though Israelis were eager for a man of Soros's stature to visit Israel, some Israelis greeted the news cautiously. The caution had less to do with Soros than with an international financier named Robert Maxwell. A few years earlier the Israelis had laid out the red carpet for Maxwell, who, like Soros, had rediscovered his Jewish roots only late in life. After Maxwell's visit, the Israelis discovered to their great chagrin that Maxwell was at best a shady individual, and at worst a crook. So some Israelis feared that Soros was another Maxwell, with his billions of dollars and mysterious financial activities.

While most Israelis had never heard of George Soros, important members of the Israel government had, and they made sure that the investor received four-star treatment. It was important to them that Soros come away from his visit with a positive impression of Israel, for a good word from him in the international financial community could bolster Israel's attractiveness to outside investors. Indeed, the very fact that he had paid a visit to Israel for business purposes could be used by Israel's public relations machinery to indicate that its economy was moving in the right direction.

So, Soros was granted meetings with most of Israel's key political and economic officials, from Prime Minister Yitzhak Rabin to Jacob Frankel, the governor of the Bank of Israel with whom Soros had worked in the past. Rabin told Soros that Israel was trying to step up efforts to privatize some of its state-sponsored firms and welcomed the investor to take part. Soros has two small investments in Israel and he visited those facilities. One was Geotek, which operated specialized mobile radio and wireless communications; the other was Indigo. Soros had a 17 percent stake in that latter firm, worth $70 million in 1993, twice that in 1994.

One evening a dinner was arranged for Soros at the Accadia Hotel in Herzylia, north of Tel Aviv along Israel's Mediterranean coast. Some 250 leading members of the country's financial community were in the audience. Soros was due to speak to the group. Early in the evening, Soros asked Benny Landa what he should talk about. Landa said that the audience would appreciate hearing not only about the business side of his life but how as a Jew he felt being in Israel today. "Tell them what you told me that evening we had dinner." Soros agreed.

Soros spoke for 20 minutes. Normally Soros is a capable public speaker, but this time, speaking extemporaneously, he faltered. Landa remembered that Soros "became very awkward, he stammered, stuttered, and rambled." This was perhaps the first time that

Soros had stood before a public audience and tried to talk in a personal way about his Jewishness. Had he been a proud Jew all of his life, the words might have come out smoothly. In trying to be honest about his longtime concealment of his Jewishness, however, Soros must have sensed that everyone in this audience was proud to be Jewish and that no small number of them had probably lost friends and relatives in the Holocaust. He must have understood that he would have trouble sounding convincing or appealing with his tales of Jewish self-hatred and denial.

In those 20 minutes, Soros repeated much of what he had said to Benny Landa nearly a year and a half earlier. He spoke of what a thrill it had been for him as a child to be called a gentile by his friends; of how he had never been able to come to terms with being Jewish; of how he had kept silent about Israel all these years, believing that, since he felt negatively toward the Jewish state, it was better to say nothing. And he talked about how, because Israel now seemed to be abandoning its chauvinism and was taking steps toward peace with its Arab neighbors, he now felt comfortable enough to pay this visit. He spoke about his philosophy of philanthropy, explaining that Israel had always been a country with its hand out but that, in his view, it should not be doing this, that it was a place for investors, not for philanthropists. He had no intention to spread his philanthropy to Israel, but he had two investments thus far, and he was considering more.

The response to Soros's visit was not entirely positive. Many Israelis simply did not know what to make of him, and when they heard him speak at the Accadia Hotel that evening, they were dismayed. "It was a shocking evening for those people in the audience," recalled Benny Landa. "The level of disappointment with his noncommitment was great.

"Many Israelis were upset by the speech, very upset by it, because, while everyone understood that he was candid, and intimate, and that it was a very difficult disclosure for George to make, some wondered why he was making all the fuss. They said, 'We were in concentration camps, we lost our families, we didn't become anti-Semites. Did we abandon Israel? Did we abandon Judaism? What's the big deal? Why should we understand his distancing himself from Israel?'"

True, Soros had high expectations to overcome. Some Israelis had expected, or at least hoped, that Soros would surprise everyone and announce that he planned to invest a billion dollars in the Jewish state. But at least he convinced Israelis that he was an upright, serious financier. Even as they found his lack of Zionism disturbing, Israelis were quick to admit that they found Soros modest and unassuming, with none of the bombast or shadiness they had come to associate with Maxwell. They stopped making the comparisons.

Soros now thought of himself as something of an expert on the Jewish state. Shortly after his trip, he appeared on CNN's "Larry King Live" on January 11, 1994. Former UN ambassador Jeanne Kirkpatrick, also a guest on the program, had expressed doubt that Israel and Syria would make peace soon. Soros disagreed, noting that he had just been in the Jewish state. "I was really impressed, because there's a real change of heart. And I think there's a real commitment to it. I think there will be peace."

Twenty-five

The St. Valentine's Day Massacre

A t the start of 1994, Soros had a huge investment shorting the German mark. Some reports suggested that he was short as much as $30 billion, using his funds' capital and leveraging the rest. While Soros had believed the year before that German interest rates would fall, they did not; But high interest rates were harming Germany's economy immeasurably, so Soros was betting that it would lower interest rates, dragging the German mark down with them. The Germans were not pleased. They did not like George Soros betting against them.

While the year seemed to start well, the horizon was slowly clouding. Cynics pointed to a bad omen in January—a cover story on Soros in the *New Republic*.

Basically a sympathetic piece written by Michael Lewis, the best-selling author of *Liar's Poker*, it focused on George Soros the philanthropist. Soros had taken Lewis on one of his "aid journeys" for two weeks the previous November, and Lewis had been let in on a whole set of experiences designed to show how influential George Soros was in Eastern Europe.

Less than a month later the roof fell in.

What was so incredible about the harm that came George Soros's way in February 1994 was not that he lost money. He had done that before. Not even that the sum was large, very large, *$600 million* this time.

What was remarkable was that Soros treated the setback with a matter-of-factness that seemed to belie the size of the disaster. The setback occurred on February 14, 1994. Employees inside the Quantum Fund called it the "St. Valentine's Day Massacre."

For some time Soros had been betting that the yen would keep falling against the dollar. The U.S. government had been encouraging a stronger yen. This was a tactic to pressure the Japanese during trade negotiations; if the yen rose, Japanese exports would become more expensive and more difficult to sell around the world. Soros believed that President Clinton and Japan's prime minister Morihiro Hosokawa would settle their trade dispute; that settlement would then cause the U.S. government to let the yen fall.

Soros bet wrong. The talks between Clinton and Hosokawa collapsed on Friday, February 11. When the markets reopened three days later, the yen, which until then had been falling, suddenly shot up. Traders had concluded that the United States would try to push up the yen in order to narrow the trade deficit with Japan. A strong Japanese yen would make imports from Japan more expensive in the United States.

The Japanese currency closed in New York that Monday at 102.20 yen to the dollar, a change of nearly 5 percent from its close the previous Friday of 107.18. To his chagrin, Soros had not taken into account that the collapse of the trade talks would cause the yen to move so sharply and so quickly.

In one of his rare references to the February 14 loss, Soros noted that "the yen dropped by 5 percent in one day. We dropped by 5 percent on the same day, of which maybe half was due to our exposure to yen. I don't know what is more unsound—our position or the position of the governments, which go to fight with each other and create that kind of movement."

What was astonishing about Soros's $600 million setback was the relatively small impact it had on his reputation. Hardly a murmur of dissent, hardly a comment to suggest that the Soros money machine had self-destructed overnight. No one voiced an opinion that the world-class investor had buried himself, or that he would not be heard of again.

Soros not only survived, he flourished. He managed this trick through a very, very clever stroke of genius.

At the time of the October 1987 crash, Soros tried to convince the media that his losses had amounted to only $300 million—not the rumored $850 million. He had not succeeded.

Now, in February 1994, rumors were floated again, rumors that suggested that Soros had lost far more than a mere $600 million. This time, Soros knew that he had to move quickly to quash those rumors.

He turned to his right-hand man, Stanley Druckenmiller, and asked him to go before the press. For Druckenmiller to talk to the press would have taken an earthquake. On February 14, 1994, the earthquake had already happened, and George Soros needed someone who could dig his fund out from under the rubble.

Meeting the press, Druckenmiller cleverly pointed out first how much had been lost: $600 million. Not a penny more, not a penny less.

Confirming that the Soros Fund's main losses were due to its incorrect expectation of a fall in the yen against the dollar, he noted that its short position in the yen was much smaller than rumored, only about $8 billion—not $25 billion, as some market reports had indicated.

Druckenmiller next indicated that the fund did have a larger yen position at one point—he did not say how much—but had cut it back by February 14.

Reconstructing the Soros Investment That Went Astray, Druckenmiller explained that some time before he had concluded that during 1994 the Japanese economy would grow stronger and that higher output would reduce Japan's trade surplus. All this would drive down the yen. Accordingly, the Soros Fund took a large short position in the yen, purchased a large number of Japanese shares, and sold Japanese bonds. From the summer of 1993 to the latter part of that year, the yen-dollar play had worked well for Soros.

But by year's end, Soros's position on the yen was "incredibly oversubscribed." It hardly mattered now, but Druckenmiller acknowledged that he and his colleagues should have reassessed their yen position then.

It was time to put some perspective on the Soros loss.

The $600 million, Druckenmiller pointed out, represented only 5 percent of Soros's total assets. It may have seemed that the bottom had dropped out of the Soros magic machine. No way, insisted Soros's number two; there was still that other 95 percent. Oh, and by the way, Druckenmiller slipped in, Soros's assets these days happened to total $12 billion.

So, some simple arithmetic showed: The man whose reserves had just been depleted by hundreds of millions of dollars still had assets of $11.4 billion. Moreover, Quantum had already recovered some of its losses from the disastrous February 14 setback, Druckenmiller reported. The fund was, as of February 23, down only 2.7 percent.

That would still be enough money to pay the staff at Soros Fund Management in the skyscraper overlooking Central Park; there would still be plenty of money to distribute to all those foundations in Eastern Europe and the former Soviet Union.

The work of the foundations continued full steam ahead. Soros could lose $600 million overnight and not raise the slightest ripple of doubt about his ability to keep his money machine going. That's how much confidence he was generating in the early months of 1994.

To be sure, the $600 million loss had a serious effect on Soros's money management picture. But the key point was that the public perception of Soros as a financial magician had not changed, not in the slightest.

Twenty-six

Mr. Soros Goes to Washington

Despite the Soros Fund's February fiasco, when it came time in April for George Soros to appear before the House Banking Committee in Washington, D.C., Soros remained the guru, the world-class investor. His stature still warranted him front-page coverage in the *New York Times*.

The front-page coverage was the result in part to a nagging sense in the financial community, shared by the media, that Soros and the hedge funds were a source of growing concern. That concern stemmed from the tumultuous events in the financial markets in early 1994. Yet Soros felt no need to apologize: "I still consider myself selfish and greedy. I am not putting myself forward as any kind of saint. I have very healthy appetites and I put myself first."

Soros had not been alone in betting against the yen. Other hedge funds had joined in and taken heavy losses as well. Compounding the problem, some of these hedge funds needed to raise cash, forcing them to sell part of their holdings, such as Japanese securities and some of their European positions. A chain reaction developed around the world in the wake of these forced sell-offs by dealers who had been caught holding lots of yen.

Even hedge-fund dealers who had not been involved in the bet against the yen got caught in the tumult. These fund managers believed that high unemployment would force European governments to stimulate their economies by lowering interest rates. So they took large positions on European bonds; their view was that as European interest rates fell, the value of their bonds would rise.

Then the hedge funds dropped all that money because of the yen, so the other hedge funds started to sell some of their European bonds. That drove the price of bonds down and forced bond issuers in Europe to raise their interest rates to attract purchasers. European bond markets were in turmoil, and some hedge-fund dealers took major losses.

George Soros might have preferred to adopt a low profile to give himself time to recoup his losses—to make sure that the St. Valentine's Massacre was a "nonrecurring" event. That was not going to happen. He had become too much of a public figure. Europe's central banks were meeting in March in Basel. Congressional hearings were scheduled for April. The pressure grew on Soros and the hedge funds as both institutions were threatening to take action against them.

In response, Soros became a kind of spokesman for hedge funds that spring. He decided to be as conciliatory as possible. In Bonn on March 2, he declared that it would be legitimate for central banks to regulate the giant hedge funds. "I feel that there is an innate instability in unregulated markets," Soros told reporters. "I think that it behooves the regulators to regulate.

"I do believe that markets without regulation are subject to crashing and therefore it is a very legitimate issue for [central banks] to investigate. We are ready to cooperate with them on it. I just hope that whatever regulations they introduce do not do more harm than good."

Asked for his response to charges that hedge funds increased market volatility and instability, Soros said: "I would say that markets have a tendency to overshoot and so I don't believe in the perfect market at all. Therefore, I don't think that hedge funds are perfect either; otherwise, they wouldn't lose 5 percent in a day."

When the Basel meetings were over, central bank governors from the Group of 10 industrialized nations had come up with no good reason to write new regulations for hedge funds or for banks that used their own capital to trade on the international markets. The markets had corrected themselves following the turmoil earlier in the year, and no reason existed to anticipate further trouble. Nonetheless, some observers had a distinct feeling that hedge funds had been getting away with all sorts of chicanery and needed more regulation.

William E. Dodge, senior vice president for equity research and chief investment strategist at Dean Witter Reynolds, put the case this way: "If you said, give me $50 today and you can own a hundred ounces of gold, and you can come get it whenever you want as long as you pay me the difference between the current price and the $50 whenever you come to get it, [I'd be] selling you an option to own a hundred ounces of gold. Now when I came into the business, if I entered into an agreement like that with a large number of people, that would be classified as dealing in unregistered securities.

"Today it's a mystery to me how derivative products have proliferated without being registered. Because things aren't registered, they aren't required to trade in a certain place. If they don't trade in a certain place, the records and transactions are not available; the dimensions of markets, the terms of trade, the dimensions of individual transactions are not known or understood. . . .

> "**M**arkets have a tendency to overshoot."

"The dimensions of investing in hedge funds have become so big that . . . if they were to fail, [they] would create a systemic risk to the banking system and therefore endanger the financial structure of the society."

The tumult early in the year set the stage for the Gonzales hearings in Congress. Those hearings, scheduled to investigate hedge funds in general, now had a specific case before them, suggesting that hedge funds were the number one villain in the financial markets. Congressman Henry Gonzales had been targeting Soros and the hedge funds for a year. It did not seem to matter to Gonzales that Soros had suffered one of the worst setbacks of his career. With the stock and bond markets so volatile earlier in the year, he had enough reason to go after Soros.

And so Mr. Soros went to Washington.

The purpose of the hearings—and Gonzales made no secret of it—was to find out whether the hedge-fund operators were as Machiavellian as they had been painted, whether they were actually influencing the financial markets by their actions, whether they needed more regulating. Gonzales's legislative manifesto, issued the day before the hearings, threatened to make "improper management" in this field "a direct violation of the law" and indicated a desire to "enhance congressional oversight of derivative activities."

That was fine. But before the committee could get around to proposing new regulations, it had to come to terms with a more fundamental problem. Though the committee's province was finance, few committee members knew how a hedge fund worked. Few had any understanding of the esoteric financial instruments they used.

To get some answers—indeed, to get a lesson that could have been called Hedge Funds 101—they invited the Master to appear on April 13, 1994. As the hearing room began to fill, it was clear that the George Soros show was the best one in town that day.

The hearing room was packed, and eventually it was standing room only. Hedge Funds 101 was about to start. The "teacher" opened the "seminar" by reading a statement, putting on the table parts of his financial theories to explain why the legislators were barking up the wrong tree. He turned to his theories to explain why.

He began with the assertion that financial markets could not possibly discount the future correctly, but that they could affect an economy's fundamentals. When they do, markets behave far differently than the theory of efficient markets considers normal. Though they do not occur that often, these boom/bust sequences can be disruptive, precisely because they influence an economy's fundamentals.

> "Lopsided trend-following behavior is necessary to produce a violent market crash."

Soros went on to note that a boom/bust sequence can develop only if the market is dominated by trend-following behavior. "By trend-following behavior, I mean people buying in response to a rise in prices and selling in response to a fall in prices in a self-reinforcing manner. Lopsided trend-following behavior is necessary to produce a violent market crash, but it is not sufficient to bring it about.

"The key question you need to ask then is, what generates trend-following behavior? Hedge funds may be a factor and you are justified in taking a look at them, although, as far as my hedge funds are concerned, you are looking in the wrong place."

More to the point, it was Soros's view that mutual funds and institutional managers—not hedge funds—had destabilized the market, for both tended to be trend followers. "When money is pouring in, they tend to maintain less-than-normal cash balances because they anticipate further inflows. When money is pouring out, they need to raise cash to take care of redemptions." As a result, "They created part of the financial bubble."

Briefly, Soros then talked about the current market situation: "I should like to emphasize that I see no imminent danger of a market crash or meltdown. We have just punctured a bit of a bubble that has developed in asset prices. As a result, market conditions are much healthier now than they were at the end of last year, and I do not think that investors should be unduly fearful at this time." In other words: It was OK to buy U.S. stocks or S&P futures.

Soros assailed the Clinton administration for the hard line it was taking with the Japanese on trade and for trying to talk the dollar down. "That's quite harmful for the stability of the dollar and the stability of the markets.

> "**Free-floating currencies are flawed because the markets always overshoot to excess.**"

Dollar bashing as a method of dealing with trade policy with the Japanese is a dangerous instrument that we ought not to use." Cynics read a not-so-subtle market message from the Master: Go long the yen and short the dollar until trade negotiations stabilize.

Continuing to try to prevent hedge funds from becoming the focus of the hearings, Soros noted that hedge funds were not that large a segment of the investment world. Even though Soros Fund Management's daily currency trades averaged $500 million, this level of currency trading, Soros told the committee, should not affect the markets, since hedge funds controlled at most .005 percent of the daily foreign exchange markets.

Soros's solution to currency crises and turbulence was not fixed exchange rates. "Too rigid," he said. Not floating exchange rates either. "Free-floating currencies are flawed because the markets always overshoot to excess." His solution: "The monetary people in the G-7 group of seven industrialized nations need to coordinate their monetary and fiscal policies so there are no great disparities where the markets are fundamentally unstable."

It became clear from committee members' questions to Soros that they were still stumped about what exactly a hedge fund did. "Just what is a hedge fund?" they asked over and over again. Soros tried to enlighten them, but he had to admit that the label had become a catch-all for a great many things that were originally not within its province. "The term is applied so indiscriminately that it covers a wide range of activities. The only thing they have in common is that the managers are compensated on the basis of performance and not as a fixed percentage of assets under management." That seemed an odd way to describe a hedge fund—especially by the King of the Hedge Funds. Soros was not, however interested in conducting a seminar on how to define hedge funds. He wanted to get a message across: that hedge funds—no villains—actually performed good deeds in the financial markets.

Hedge funds, Soros argued, because they were rewarded on absolute performance, provided "a healthy antidote to the trend-following behavior of institutional investors." His own fund, as an example, had a benign effect on volatile markets by moving against—not with—buying or selling trends. "We tend to stabilize rather than destabilize the market. We are not doing this as a public service. It is our style of making money."

In his bluntest comment in defense of hedge funds, Soros said to his listeners: "Frankly, I don't think hedge funds are a matter of concern to you or the regulators." Hedge funds should not be blamed, he argued, for the plummeting prices in stocks and bonds earlier in the year. "I reject any assertion or implication that our activities are harmful or destabilizing."

Soros was asked if it was possible for a private investor like himself to amass enough capital to manipulate the value of a currency such as the Italian lira or British pound.

"No," he replied. ". . . I do not believe any market participant can, other than for a short time, successfully influence currency markets for major currencies contrary to market fundamentals. . . . hedge funds are relatively small players given the size of the global currency markets. The lack of liquidity in markets for smaller currencies also acts to prevent any investor from successfully influencing prices for a minor currency. Any investor trying to influence prices by acquiring a large position in that currency will, because of the lack of liquidity, face disastrous results when the position is sold."

Soros sought to distance himself as much as possible from derivatives, those financial contracts derived from stocks, debt, or commodities. The committee had been intensely curious about these financial instruments. Soros sounded as if even he, the consummate investor, had a hard time trying to figure out what to make of them. Moreover, he pointed out that hedge funds "do not act as issuers or writers of derivative instruments. They are more likely to be customers. Therefore, they constitute less of a risk to the system than

> "**I**nvestors trying to influence prices by acquiring a large position in a currency will face disastrous results when the position is sold."

the dynamic hedgers at the derivatives desks of financial intermediaries. Please do not confuse dynamic hedging with hedge funds. They have nothing in common except the word 'hedge.'"

Why the confusion over derivatives?

According to Soros: "There are so many of them, and some of them are so esoteric that the risk involved may not be properly understood even by the most sophisticated investor, and I'm supposed to be one. Some of these instruments appear to be specifically designed to enable institutional investors to take gambles which they would not otherwise be permitted to take.

"We use options and more exotic derivatives sparingly. Our activities are trend-bucking rather than trend-following. We try to catch new trends early, and in later stages we try to catch trend reversals."

Soros left the distinct impression that he would not mind if Congress decided to regulate derivatives. "If you look at the instruments that came unglued recently, or instruments where you separate the interest from the principal . . . I am not quite sure that they are really necessary."

(Writing in *The Wall Street Journal,* Tim W. Ferguson observed that Soros had been a bit unfair here; just because some others had suffered losses recently, "that doesn't behoove an investment luminary to cast aspersions before Congress on a technique for which he has no use.")

Soros felt guilty endorsing regulation, and he admitted that others in his firm had tried to convince him to speak out against it. "You know," he told Rep. Bruce Vento, a Minnesota Democrat who had asked him about recent volatility in financial markets, "as we were preparing for my appearance here we talked about this a little bit. I said that frankly it may be the issuing of derivative instruments [that] ought to be regulated. And then my partner . . . pointed out that unfortunately regulation has an unintended consequence, because the regulators are interested only in the downside; they are not interested in the upside. In other words, they want to avoid a catastrophe.

"So . . . if you imposed an obligation [to register derivatives with a commission, like stocks] . . . it would really create a bureaucratic resistance because of this asymmetry between the interests of the regulators and the interests of the market. And so he dissuaded me from making that recommendation."

Soros was not the only one at the hearings to testify against the need for further regulation. Regulators testified, downplaying the risk that hedge funds and derivatives posed to the banking system and to investors. The comptroller of the currency, Eugene Ludwig, noted that eight national banking firms had no more than an average 0.2 percent of assets at risk in derivatives. Arthur Levitte, Jr., chairman of the SEC, assured the hearing that nearly all hedge-fund activities were already highly regulated under current banking and securities laws, so no new regulation was required. The three regulators who testified all thought more information was required. "We're not in favor of regulation," stated John P. LeWare, a Federal Reserve Board governor, "but we have a strong tilt toward more disclosure."

What was the committee's reaction to the Soros presentation?

Thomas Friedman, writing the next day in the *New York Times,* summed up their feelings well: "Members of the House Banking Committee seemed to alternate between awe at being schooled by the man with the Midas touch and immense curiosity about the secretive world of hedge funds—the partnerships of wealthy investors that scour the globe for often-exotic investments in currencies, bonds and stocks. The mystique of the funds seemed to have been burnished—rather than tarnished—by tales of the wide swings they experience, including Mr. Soros's loss of $600 million in one recent currency deal. . . ."

Soros left no stone unturned in making his point that day in Washington. It was not enough to take on Congress. He sought to convert the media as well. Assigned to that task was Robert Johnson, a Soros Fund managing director who accompanied his boss to Washington.

In posthearing remarks to the press, Johnson indicated that more work needed to be done to educate Congress and the public about what George Soros the investor did. "The biggest problem is the mythology of hedge funds. There will be more interaction with the press."

In an apparent effort to show more candor, Johnson revealed how Soros allocated his assets and how he used leverage.

- 60 percent of Soros's capital was usually in individual stocks; Soros rarely traded on margin in this category.
- 20 percent was devoted to macro trading—bets on currencies and global indexes; in this sector, he had sometimes leveraged as much as 12 times his capital.
- The other 20 percent was in what Johnson called "precautionary reserves" such as T-bills and bank deposits. This 20 percent cushion, he said, was to be used "to buy time in adverse circumstances to cushion the portfolio." In other words, to meet margin calls.

George Soros had gotten through the hearing, and from all indications, he had acquitted himself well.

Two months later, Byron Wien had dinner with a member of the SEC. The hearings and Soros's appearance came up. Wien reported later that the SEC member "said that he thought George did such a great job that the SEC stopped worrying—and Congress stopped worrying about hedge funds." All in all, Soros could be immensely satisfied.

Twenty-seven

Richer Than 42 Countries

eorge Soros the intellectual never gave up hope of trying to win respect. It had been seven years since *The Alchemy of Finance* had been published, and while Soros had been pleased to see his views in book form, he knew all too well that few of his readers bought the book out of intellectual curiosity. "The trouble is," he told Anatole Kaletsky, the economics editor of the *Times* of London, "that everybody bought the book in order to find the secret of how to make money. I suppose I should have foreseen that." In May 1994, the book appeared in paperback for the first time, and once again Soros hoped that readers would take the time to study his ideas and theories, not just look for clues to making a buck.

Meanwhile, Soros and Druckenmiller were struggling to emerge from 1994 with a credible investment year despite the huge loss suffered in February. Not helping matters, according to *USA Today,* was a minor, but significant, error of judgment in the spring, when Quantum went short on Genentech, a leading biotech firm. The loss was only about $10 million, pocket change for Soros, but the error proved costly to other investors and led journalist Dan Dorfman to write: "There's a lesson for investors: It's dumb to get involved in a stock just because Soros is a rumored player in it." Because of the fund's losses, however, its premium was down to just 14 percent for those buying in at the end of April. It rose to 21 percent when the fund's investments rallied. (Late in 1993, the premium had hit a record high of 34 percent.)

As of June 22, 1994, the Quantum Fund had fallen by only 1 percent since the start of the year. This, of course, was not good news, for it left open the possibility that Soros might suffer his second down year in his fund's history. But compared to the other leading hedge funds, he was having a stellar year: Tiger's Jaguar Fund had fallen by 11.5 percent during the same period; the Omega fund run by Leon Cooperman was down 23 percent; and Michael Steinhardt's fund was down 30 percent.

Reflecting some of the pressure Soros felt was his disclosure in June that he had reversed himself on one of his sacred principles. For a decade, he had not permitted any of his funds to invest in regions where he had philanthropic foundations—Eastern Europe and the former Soviet Union. As late as January 1993, a *Financial Times* reporter asked him if the ban meant that he would not buy bus factories in Eastern Europe. Soros snapped: "Not at all—no investments. In fact, I consider it a conflict of interest."

No longer.

During 1994, Soros let the managers of his investment funds know that they were now free to invest in Eastern Europe and the former Soviet Union. According to a Soros spokesman in June, $139 million had already been committed in the past six months to projects in Hungary, Poland, the Czech Republic, and Russia. The search for further investments would continue, the spokesman said, as part of "the normal course of our business activity."

These recent Soros investments included a "quite significant" slice of a $45 million capital increase based on a rights issue and private placement of shares in the First Hungary Fund, an equity fund based in Budapest and supported mostly by British and American institutional investors. The fund had invested in food-processing, pharmaceutical, and T-shirt firms. Soros had been on the board of the First Hungary Fund briefly when it was organized in 1991, but he resigned soon after, believing it to be a conflict of interest with the work of his Budapest philanthropic foundation.

In explaining his turnabout, Soros said in a *Wall Street Journal* interview that he felt his foundations were strong enough and independent enough to withstand whatever pressures might arise from his investments in the region. Besides, he said, the region presented investment opportunities and his funds should exploit them. "I used to have a clear and simple rule that we don't invest in countries where there are [philanthropic] foundations because I didn't want them held hostage to my financial interests, or vice versa. But this has been modified due to the fact that markets are really developing in the region and I have no rhyme or reason or right to deny my funds, or my shareholders, the possibility of investing there, or to deny those countries the chance to get hold of some of these funds." He did note that while Quantum was now free to invest in these regions, he himself would still not invest there from his own account.

Perhaps the philanthropist was trying to set in motion some "trend-following" behavior with himself as the Pied Piper. Asked if the Soros Fund's foray might induce other investors to turn to Eastern Europe—as his previous statements in gold, real estate, and currency movements had done—Soros said that would be all right with him.

In late June came the news that Soros ranked as the number one money earner on Wall Street for 1993, according to *Financial World*. Soros, according to the magazine, had earned $1.1 billion in 1993, the first time anyone had earned that much in a single year, and twice as much as the second-highest earner, Julian Robertson.

There was Soros once again on the cover of the magazine, this time sitting next to a chessboard, looking like he was having a rough time deciding where to move. Inside the magazine were photos of him in different poses—on the phone, lounging on a couch with comfortable shoes and no socks and a red sport shirt, reading an art book.

Having a little fun, *Financial World* tried to put Soros's $1.1 billion salary for 1993 into perspective: "If Soros were a corporation, he would have ranked 37th in profitability, between Banc One and McDonald's. His compensation exceeded the gross domestic product of at least 42 member nations of the UN and was roughly equal to that of nations such as Chad, Guadeloupe, and Burundi. Put another way, he could buy 5,790 Rolls Royces at $190,000 a pop. Or pay the annual tuition for every student attending Harvard, Princeton, Yale, and Columbia combined for more than three years. Not a bad idea, some parents might say."

The magazine also noted that in 1993, Soros had earned as much on his own as McDonald's had with 169,600 employees. Each of Soros's funds turned in great years: Quantum Emerging Growth was up 109 percent before fees; Quantum and Quota were each up over 72 percent.

What was perhaps the most amazing fact of all: Of the 100 people on the magazine's list, 9 were members of Soros's operation.

Commenting on Soros's $1.1 billion, *The Guardian* noted that "we are used to billionaires, but they have always been people who owned, and may well have built up or inherited, wealth-making assets, oil wells, tankers, that sort of thing, possessions that none of us could ever have possessed. That was their luck and our excuse. Yet here is a man who gets this amount as a salary. So now we all have to fantasize about being as rich as Soros this year. . . ."

The irony, of course, is that once again, the minute Soros showed up on a magazine cover, he and his funds were struggling.

That fall, Soros was busier than ever with his main work, the foundations. He was still not sure if they would outlast him, not with all the controversy and turmoil in their midst. Though he had tried to leave much of the decision making in the hands of local staffs, it was obvious that Soros and his money were the dynamic forces that kept the foundations going, that gave them direction and motivation. He was more confident that his investment funds would carry on indefinitely. He had institutionalized them sufficiently, he believed, with good people, good organization, and he knew they were being run very well.

All throughout 1994, the pressure on George Soros to remain at the top was mounting. Investors galore were tracking his every step in the financial markets, hoping that some of his wizardry would rub off on them, hoping as well to become another Soros. A story was making the rounds of Wall Street in the fall of 1994 that on a mountain opposite Mount Rushmore were places for four heads; two of the heads, those of George Soros and Warren Buffett, had already been chiseled into the mountain. Said one senior investment manager, who related the story, "There are a lot of guys down at the bottom who are waiting to be chiseled."

Adding to Soros's burden: the media. Having discovered Soros, they would not let him go. If two and a half years earlier he was a virtual unknown, now he was being dissected, analyzed, measured, judged. In 1992 he had been a rising star. Now just two years later, segments of the financial media, watching his lackluster performance in 1994, declared him dead in the water. The shovels were out, ready to dig the graves of Soros and the other hedge-fund managers even though the hedge-fund era seemed to be only in its swaddling clothes.

In earlier years, Soros would not have been bothered by all the attention, all the interest in his career. Now he was. He had risen so far, so fast, and he wanted to savor the pleasure of being on top of the financial world. Had 1994 gone better for him, he would have sat back and tended his philanthropic foundations, distancing himself from his investment operation. Because of his setbacks in 1994, though, Soros felt he had to keep a hand on the tiller of the investment operation. His associates argue that all Soros did was proffer advice to Stanley Druckenmiller. But the fact was that Soros still found it impossible to just walk away—not quite yet, not while he was being watched and analyzed with such frequency. Throughout 1994, Soros searched and searched for the Big Score. He could not believe that his September 1992 coup against the pound had been a fluke, a one-time thing. He had done it once, he could do it again. He simply had to do his homework.

Over the past few years, Soros had believed that British real estate might produce large numbers, and he had not been far wrong. His profits were decent, but not spectacular: a 17 percent from the land deal since its establishment. That, however, was not good enough. He was reported to have told John Ritblatt, British Land's chairman and chief executive, that he needed gains of 40 to 50 percent. Decent was no longer good enough for Soros; he wanted spectacular.

Thus, in the third week of November 1994, Soros announced that he was pulling out of the languishing British property market. Only 18 months earlier, he had promised to join with British Land in investing $775 million in that market. But now Soros announced that Quantum was selling its half of the new British Realty Fund to British Land, which, as the original accord stipulated, had first refusal rights.

Soros, when he was feeling modest, would boast that he too made investment mistakes. The real secret of his success, he would insist, was in spotting his mistakes earlier than most. Was that what he was doing by pulling out of the British real estate market?

Throughout the year, George Soros clung to an unwavering faith in the dollar. Although that faith had cost him dearly earlier in the year, he nonetheless believed that the U.S. economy was getting stronger, and he was convinced that the government would continue to take measures to keep the dollar from deteriorating. He also had faith that the United States and Japan would resolve their trade dispute sooner rather than later, and that would boost the dollar against the yen. Yet the dollar seemed immune to help, including several attempts at intervention by the Federal Reserve and the efforts of central banks around the world.

Even Soros's own public relations efforts failed. In an August 2 interview on WNET's Charlie Rose-PBS television show, Soros defended the dollar, asserting that it should not be permitted to depreciate a great deal because that would destabilize the U.S. economy. "If you allow the currency to depreciate too much, that . . . can be very destabilizing because of its inflationary implications and its implications for the bond market," he told Rose. When Rose asked if he was buying dollars, Soros was evasive. "I don't choose to tell you, and I may be buying or selling at this very minute, without me knowing."

Soros's 1994 setbacks had not kept traders from following his every step, from hanging on his every word. And so traders were all ears on October 4, when, in an interview with Reuters, Soros said he saw potential for a large retreat by the yen against the dollar. "I would say there is a potential for a 15 to 20 percent correction," Soros asserted, predicting that this correction could take the yen from 99.55 to around 115 to 120 per dollar.

Two days later, at a dinner gathering of large institutional money managers at a client's home in New York, the major subject of conversation was Soros's large dollar bet. The guests were frustrated that evening. They wanted to believe that Soros knew what he was talking about. He had been right so often; when he played guru and issued a public pronouncement, his views seemed to be self-fulfilling. And yet—Soros had been wrong before on the dollar. Was he making the same mistake again?

Soros's public comments at the time betrayed the frustration he was feeling about currency speculation in 1994. In an interview with *Business Week* in its October 3 edition, Soros was asked what his Japanese losses had taught him about the currency market. "That this is a time which is not particularly rewarding for currency speculation. The tensions that were there for the past two or three years, the large imbalances that lead to large currency movements, are not currently there. The biggest unresolved problem is in Japan—the war of words [with the United States] over the balance-of-payments surplus. We think it will be resolved, because it makes a lot of sense to resolve it. That is where we have erred since the beginning of the year. We thought it would be resolved sooner, rather than later. Funnily enough, we still think exactly the same thing."

But clinging to the hope that the dollar would strengthen appeared an increasingly flawed strategy. By early November 1994, the dollar had fallen to a postwar low.

No matter how upbeat Soros and Druckenmiller tried to sound about 1994, the financial media—*Financial World, The Wall Street Journal,* and others—sang a different tune.

"Soros Took Hit on Yen Again, Traders Say" was the headline in *The Wall Street Journal* on November 10. According to the newspaper, Soros Fund Management had lost $400 to $600 million betting that the dollar would rise against the yen, the same bet it had made—and lost—the previous February.

If the Soros machine had exhibited a certain blasé attitude toward the February loss, this time—in November 1994—it took a more defensive, angrier, vaguer tone. Once again, Druckenmiller was paraded before the press, but now he was much less specific. He told *The Wall Street Journal:* "Normally, we don't comment. But these rumors are absolutely ludicrous." Noting that the net asset value of the Quantum Fund was "flat on the year," he added that "we were happy to disclose our losses earlier this year. But an additional loss of any magnitude in currencies is ludicrous and totally unfounded." The funds' currency positions were "marginally profitable," he indicated, but Druckenmiller would not comment in any specifics about the funds' dollar-yen position.

It mattered little to the outside world that Soros was faring far better than his fellow hedge-fund managers. While in 1994 the Quantum Fund suffered its second-worst year in its history, with a mere 2.9 percent increase over the previous year, others were down 20 to 30 percent—and they were losing clients; other hedge funds had to leave the business entirely. None of this seemed to matter, as the financial media focused largely on Soros. It continued to find him mysterious, fascinating, and it continued to try to penetrate the inner sanctum of his investment empire. At times, the results were most unpleasant for him.

For example, *Financial World,* which in July 1994 had ranked Soros as the top U.S. money earner for 1993, dismissed his 1994 efforts with the November 8 cover title "Porous Soros: The Alchemist Loses His Touch." A cover photograph of Soros showed him looking weary, his forehead resting on his right hand. He seemed to be saying: "How did I get into this mess?"

Financial World challenged the Soros claim that those who had invested in 1993 in the Quantum Fund, then holding $5 billion in assets, had made a 63 percent profit. Wrong, said the magazine, it was only 50 percent. It challenged another Soros claim that in the first six months of 1994, the Quantum Fund was up 1.6 percent; in fact, there had been a loss, the magazine insisted, of 9 percent.

The magazine also suggested another way in which Soros could be getting himself into trouble: By the end of 1993, according to *Financial World,* Quantum owed Soros $1,549,570,239 in accrued and deferred advisory and performance fees—or 25 percent of the fund's net assets. This "debt" represented no real problem as long as the fund performed well and Soros did not try to cut his own losses by calling the debt.

The media assault against Soros persisted. In late November, newspaper reports suggested that while the Quantum Fund had a gain in net asset value of just over 1 percent for 1994, it was trading at far less than in the past. The net asset value of the shares had dropped from $22,107.66 on December 31, 1993, to $17,178.82 in early November 1994; the drop was due almost entirely to a payout in April 1994 of $4,900 a share. The crucial indicator, however, of the market value of the share was the premium above asset value. That premium had been 36 percent at the start of 1994 but had plummeted to only 16 percent by early November. The meaning was clear: Investors were no longer prepared to pay as much extra to be a part of the Soros money machine.

Soros defenders tried to put the drop in premiums into perspective: Hedge funds in general had come under enormous pressure in 1994; Soros, even in these dire circumstances, was doing better than the rest of the hedge-funds managers; the Quantum Fund premiums had been inflated artificially because of all the media hype surrounding George Soros.

By the end of 1994, fewer and fewer people were asking: Is George Soros too powerful? The Soros Fund Management's performance, far less glittering than in previous years, appeared to answer that question all too bluntly. And yet, even 1994 did not tarnish his reputation as King of the Hedge Funds. Because of his year-in, year-out investment record, his larger-than-life image as a Superinvestor, and his unquestionable leadership in the hedge-fund field, Soros still was regarded as the king.

The fact was that despite 1994, Soros's influence remained large. Long after Soros had declared that he was no longer handling the day-to-day affairs of Soros Fund Management, years after he had turned to philanthropy in Eastern Europe and the former Soviet Union nearly full-time, he was still seen as the most powerful force on Wall Street and in the City in London. Ask any money manager in New York or London whether Soros was still worth tracking, and the answer was always yes.

And yet there was still a lingering sense that Soros—as well as the other major hedge-funds managers—was getting too big, too powerful. That their sheer size and their collective actions, however uncoordinated, had an effect on the behavior of the financial markets. In the fall of 1994, for example, the collective dollar positions of the hedge funds were so large, and their wish to jump ship so intense, that Soros and the other hedge funds were, in the minds of traders, actually adding to the dollar's weakness. By selling dollars nearly every time the dollar started to rally, the hedge-fund managers were weakening the dollar, they argued.

If some on Wall Street believed that Soros was too powerful, that view was of far less interest to him than the perception of him in Washington. He truly believed that his expertise in certain regions of the world should be of interest to the capital's decision makers. It shocked him to find out that they were not all that interested in George Soros the Foreign Policy Expert.

Having won the praise of many for his performance before a congressional committee earlier in 1994, Soros was beginning to convince himself that perhaps the right people were finally starting to listen to him—and to take him seriously. What Soros failed to understand was that at the head of some of the world's most vaunted financial institutions were people who didn't want to be told what to do, certainly not by a George Soros. There was a sense that Soros, in taking on such institutions as the Bundesbank of Germany, or the Bank of England, was overstepping himself. "Say you're the senior person at the Bank of England, you make the equivalent of $45,000 a year, you have three degrees and have written learned monographs, and you've been reading for the last year and a half that Mr. George Soros has been saying what a moron you are," observed James Grant, editor of *Grant's Interest Rate Observer* in New York. "Mr. Soros has inflamed the animosity of the global regulatory community against him."

Soros understood that he still had not gained the full respect of his peers. "He has a problem influencing policy," Byron Wien acknowledged. "He makes the speeches and he feels that 'they're still not listening to me. They're not doing what I'm telling them to do. Other people get in the way. There's a "not-invented-here" problem.'"

Soros knew enough to refrain from expressing opinions in those areas where he had little or no expertise. But where he had personal, hands-on experience, and where he had sat with the political and economic leaders, he felt he deserved to be listened to. He believed that the West was not taking a strong enough interest in opening up the closed societies in the East. While Western countries had understood and responded to earlier threats to liberty posed by fascism and communism, Soros argued that in the absence of such threats in the 1990s, the West was dithering. "We don't even recognize the need for a new world order to replace the Cold War," he said in July 1994, "or that without it we will have world disorder." Soros made it sound as if it had fallen to him to take up the slack. "I find myself in the strange situation where an individual is doing more for an open society than most governments."

He noted that when he had said that the German central bank's high interest rate policy was not wise, the markets pushed the German mark down. "But when I inveighed against European policy on Bosnia, I was either ignored or told to stick to the field of my expertise." At times he came close to the bastions of power—but not close enough. In July 1994, he was in Washington for an international conference. But there was no meeting with the president, no meeting with congressional leaders.

Those kinds of meetings were what Soros wanted. Instead, he spoke to reporters. To them, he urged the major nations of the world to agree on a new system of economic coordination that would help stabilize currency rates. "We are in a very serious situation not only in the monetary field, but politically also," he said. With the collapse of the Soviet Union, he suggested, Western nations had less reason to stick together. "We have now no system [of coordinating policies and stabilizing exchange rates]." He thought little of the idea of major nations announcing currency target zones. "All exchange-rate systems are flawed. They work for a while, and then they break down. So you have to be constantly flexible and adjust the system."

Put simply, what Soros wanted was power. He had already tasted it and liked the experience. "Power is intoxicating, " he said, "and I have gained more power than I ever thought possible—even if it is only the power to spend hard currency in situations where it is in extremely short supply."

But that kind of power, the power to distribute large sums of money, was not enough for Soros. He wanted more. "I wish people would listen to me more. I have access, and yet beyond the things I have done myself through my foundations I've had very little impact on Western policy towards the old Soviet Union." He once said, "It's remarkable how the White House doesn't use one of the few resources it's got, which is me."

To Soros's close friend Byron Wien, it was clear that the investor wanted to breathe the heady atmosphere of the White House. "George would probably like to be Bernard Baruch. Bernard Baruch was a successful, sagacious person, and President Roosevelt would bounce ideas off of him. George would like to think that Clinton would bounce ideas off him. Or that Warren Christopher would bounce ideas off him, or that Strobe Talbott would bounce ideas off him."

An event occurred on September 27, 1994, that seemed to sum up the frustration Soros felt as he neared his 65th birthday. On that day, Hungary presented Soros with the Medium Cross of Hungary's

Republican Order with Stars, the second highest decoration Hungary awards. It was given to him for his contribution to Hungary's modernization. The highest decoration, the Large Cross, was given to statesmen; the decoration given to Soros was for "ordinary mortals."

An ordinary mortal.

That was something to which George Soros, who as a child believed he might be God, did not aspire.

How must he have felt as the country of his birth treated him in this manner? Pride, certainly. For he had fled the country in 1947, seeking a better life; he had found that better life. And he had given some of it back to his native land. Now he was being shown respect. But it was not the respect he had been searching for. He had no desire to be treated like any ordinary mortal. Not George Soros.

George Soros. The Man Who Broke the Bank of England. The Man Who Beat the Pound. The World's Greatest Investor. The Man Who Moves Markets.

What are we to make of these catchy phrases?

Many people have held him in great awe, and that is only natural. He has outgunned all of his peers, using the basic tools of his trade—his brainpower, his computer, his gift of analysis. And yet a certain cynicism has abided, a cynicism that often attaches to those who *only* make money, who are not builders or toilers. Some people are suspicious, mistrustful, doubtful of anyone who could amass such a fortune by sifting through company reports, talking to other investors, reading the newspapers, and making educated guesses.

"How did Soros do it? How did Soros make so much money?"

The questions come to mind quickly, easily, because it seems so unthinkable that anyone could make that much money without having to tread the same bumpy paths that all of us have had to take. To George Soros, however, the accumulation of all that wealth was no simple, easy task, certainly not in the early years. Hence, there was no reason for others to mistrust him, or to be suspicious of him.

Yet, Soros himself, however unwittingly, contributed to our suspicions, by telling us, as he did repeatedly, that he has had an easier time making money than spending it, by being secretive, by offering us a bookful of explanations about his investment secrets, yet being obtuse about it, by declaring that he had come up with a theory to explain the financial markets, then suggesting that it was not really a theory at all, for it didn't work in every instance. At times it appeared that Soros offered glimpses into his inner financial soul so that we would be appeased and leave him alone. At other times, Soros sounded as if he genuinely wanted us to understand what had made him so successful. However secretive, mysterious, obscure George Soros has been, one way or the other he has allowed the public to see his Geiger counter at work, to marvel at the Soros successes. Watching Soros perform, people try to put their suspicions aside. They want to believe that Soros is no fluke, that he can be imitated, that they too can become money-making machines. Causing others to dream of reaching his heights, that, when all is said and done, is Soros's ultimate power.

Afterword

I n 1997, George Soros was devoting most of his time and energies to his philanthropy work, looking forward to the day that he could turn the running of his foundations over to others just as he had done nearly a decade earlier with his business ventures. He still hoped to be recognized as a great philosopher, a designation, he claimed, that would give him more satisfaction than being called a great money-maker. "I should like to change the world by improving our understanding of the world," he told an audience at his alma mater, the London School of Economics on September 21, 1995.

As of February 1997, Soros's money-making activities continued to do quite well indeed. The flagship Quantum Fund (with $4.93 billion) plus the other Quantum Group funds, now totaled $15 billion in investments. The Quantum Fund had a good year in 1995, with an increase of 39 percent; but in 1996, it had a much less remarkable one: In the first half of that year it rose just 5.7 percent and wound up 1996 up only 1.5 percent. Soros proudly boasted that the Quantum Fund was still generally recognized as having the best performance record of any investment fund in the world in its 27 year history.

Forbes magazine early in 1997 put Soros's worth at $2.5 billion.

At the age of 66, Soros was giving away more than $350 million a year toward his goal of building open societies in Eastern Europe, the former Soviet Union, and other parts of the world. He was funding a network of foundations that operated in 25 countries in Eastern Europe, the former Soviet Union as well as South Africa, and Haiti.

In the mid-1990s, he decided to expand his philanthropy to include the United States. He had become frustrated at what he called America's failure to help Eastern Europe move toward open societies. His annoyance at that failure, he said, caused him to reflect on the social and economic problems of the United States: "I have started to pay more attention to my adopted country, the United States, because I feel that the relatively open society we enjoy here is in danger," he wrote in an article in *The Washington Post* on February 2, 1997.

He admitted his American-oriented philanthropic efforts would be less visible than his Eastern European ones. "I felt that I had a greater contribution to make in former Communist countries because I was in a unique position," he noted in *The Chronicle of Philanthropy* in its September 5, 1996 issue. "In the United States, I'm not in a unique position. I'm just one of the many players, and I think our activities will be less unique. In Eastern Europe we were blazing the trail. Here we are joining the pack."

Soros provided $1 million to a number of programs aimed at helping prisoners rehabilitate themselves. One program aided former women prisoners in finding housing; another helped first-time, non-violent offenders locate work once out of jail. In one of his more controversial activities, he advocated what he called a "saner" American drug policy, suggesting that heroin and certain other illicit drugs be made available on prescription to registered drug addicts. He wrote in *The Post* article, "Criminalizing drug abuse does more harm than good, blocking effective treatment and incarcerating far too many people." For proposing such radical changes in American drug policy, Soros was assailed both by Washington politicians and media columnists. But he was not deterred: "...I look forward to the day," he wrote in *The Post*, "when the nation's drug control policies better reflect the ideals of an open society."

Soros, in *The Chronicle of Philanthropy* article, predicted that his foundations would last only another decade after his death. He hoped soon to extricate himself from his day-to-day monitoring of the foundations. "I am off the line of the actual decision making in my business and I want to get off the line of the decision making in the foundation as well. I want to create an organization that can function without me. In the business I have achieved that. In the foundation I am on my way."

Also in February 1997, Soros unleashed an attack against Western capitalist societies, charging them with not sharing their riches with poorer nations.

Interviewed on CNN cable television, Soros argued that the West, ruled as it was by the stock market, always left poor people, such as those in Eastern Europe, behind. "The belief that the markets are perfect," he told CNN, "is dangerous, because in fact they are very unstable. And they don't lead to the best allocation of resources because they tend to make the rich richer."

More attacks on the West came from Soros that same February 1997 in an article he published in *The Atlantic Monthly* in which he suggested that "the main enemy of the open society, I believe, is no longer the Communist but the capitalist threat." He charged that open societies, having removed the threat of the Communist menace, were now facing a new, internal threat—what he dubbed "excessive individualism."

Critics of Soros's assertions called him hypocritical for attacking those countries from whom he had benefited by making billions of dollars playing Western financial markets. Yet, Soros brushed aside the criticism. "It's easy to say that here's a guy who got rich," Soros commented to CNN, "and he shouldn't be taken seriously. The fact that I made so much money is proof that the markets are not perfect. I recognized it and exploited it and this is how I got rich."

Notes

Chapter One

4   "Soros thought differently . . . ," *The Observer,* January 16, 1994.

5   "That dependence upon Germany . . . ," Thames Television documentary, "The Man Who Broke the Pound," December 3, 1992.

5   "Just as Soros had predicted . . . ," *The Observer,* January 16, 1994.

5   "He understood how dire . . . ," "The Man Who Broke the Pound."

6   "As September 15 wore on . . . ," ibid.

7   "Currently, the influence I have . . . ," ABC-TV documentary, *Day One,* December 13, 1993.

9   "I am a critic . . . ," *Financial Times,* January 2, 1993.

11   ". . . an intense, squarely built . . . ," John Train, *New Money Masters* (New York: HarperPerenniel, 1990), p. 69.

11   "He doesn't look particularly . . . ," *The Guardian,* December 19, 1992.

11   "He is a slightly built . . . ," *The Observer,* January 10, 1993.

11   "He is no glitzy . . . ," *Independent,* June 25, 1993.

Chapter Two

15   "If truth be known . . . George Soros . . . ," *Underwriting Democracy* (New York: The Free Press, 1991), p. 3.

16   "It will come as no surprise . . . ," George Soros, *The Alchemy of Finance* (New York: Simon & Schuster, 1987); paperback version: (New York: John Wiley & Sons, 1994), pp. 362–63.

16   "Why? I'm the Pope's . . . ," *The Guardian,* January 6, 1993.

18   "He was never seriously . . . ," Ferenc Nagel, interview, March 6, 1994.

18   "What side of the revolution . . . ," *The Guardian,* December 19, 1992.

18   "My father does not work . . . ," *The New Republic,* "Mr. Soros's Planet," January 10–17, 1994, pp. 19–29.

18   "When he heard that . . . ," Ferenc Nagel, interview, March 6, 1994.

19   "Part of what I learned . . . ," *Business Week,* "The Man Who Moves Markets," August 23, 1993, pp. 50–60.

20   ". . . a very pretty little boy . . . ," ibid.

20   ". . . not easy . . . ," Yehuditte Simo, interview, March 5, 1994.

20   "I grew up . . . ," Benny Landa, interview, August 12, 1994.

21   "When he believed . . . ," Ferenc Nagel, interview, March 6, 1994.

21   "George was a very audacious . . . ," Miklos Horn, interview, March 8, 1994.

22   "Underneath you could feel . . . ," ibid.

22   "George was not an exceptionally . . . ," ibid.

22   "George was very sarcastic . . . ," Pal Tetenyi, interview, March 6, 1994.

Chapter Three

27   "This is a lawless . . . ," Adam Smith television program, April 15, 1993.

28   "Had I been caught . . . ," "The Man Who Broke the Pound."

29   "I'm very concerned with . . . ," ibid.

30   "The discipline in the class . . . ," Pal Tetenyi, interview, March 6, 1994.

31   "Here I am . . . ," *Day One.*

31   "I carried certain fears . . . ," ibid.

Chapter Four

33   ". . . though I didn't get . . . ," *Physics Today*, "Soros Fund Launches 'Noah's Ark' with $100 Million for Science in Former Soviet Union," pp. 63–65.

34   "He came into my office . . . ," Karl Popper, interview, March 10, 1994. Popper died on September 15, 1994.

35   "This is the occasion . . . ," George Soros, *Underwriting Democracy*, p. 4.

36   "best summer," *New York Times*, April 3, 1994.

36   ". . . like Freud or Einstein," *The Observer*, January 16, 1994.

36   "Unfortunately, Soros's grades . . . ," Daniel Doron, interview, March 28, 1994.

36   "I came to the conclusion . . . ," Adam Smith television program.

37   ". . . could not make head or tail . . . ," George Soros, *Opening the Soviet System* (London: Weidenfeld and Nicolson, 1990), p. 4.

38   "He was never . . . ," Edgar Astaire, interview, March 11, 1994.

Chapter Five

40   "The things George was . . . ," *The Observer*, January 16, 1993.

40   "Nobody knew anything . . . ," *The Wall Street Journal*, May 28, 1975.

42   ". . . wanting . . . ," George Soros, *Opening the Soviet System*, p. 4.

42   "I always hope . . . ," *Institutional Investor*, "The World's Greatest Money Manager," June 1981, pp. 39–45.

43   "You saw that he was . . . ," Edgar Astaire, interview, March 11, 1994.

43   ". . . the worldwide situation . . . ," Arthur Lerner, interview, April 11, 1994.

Chapter Six

45   "The more you're able . . . ," Byron Wien, interview, June 29, 1994.

45   "Ever since I became . . . ," George Soros, *The Alchemy of Finance*, paperback version, p. 11.

46   "What one thinks . . . ," ibid., p. 11.

46   ". . . that basically all our views . . . ," Adam Smith television program.

47   "The major insight I bring . . . ," *Sunday Times*, March 14, 1993.

47   ". . . fascinated by chaos . . . ," ibid.

47   "any idea of what . . . ," *The Observer*, January 16, 1994.

48   "But distortion works . . . ," ibid., p. 14.

49   "When events have thinking . . . ," George Soros, *The Alchemy of Finance*, paperback version, p. 12.

50   ". . . processes which are . . . ," Adam Smith television program.

52   "The reason reflexive processes. . . . ," *The Wall Street Journal*, George Soros, "Brady Commission Should've Stressed Market Stability," January 14, 1988.

52   "His idea is that . . . ," Byron Wien, interview, June 29, 1994.

53   "When people lose confidence . . . ," "Brady Commission Should've Stressed Market Stability."

53   "Loans are based . . . ," George Soros, *The Alchemy of Finance*, paperback version, p. 17.

55   "I believed that . . . ," ibid., p. 16.

55   "What I have is an . . . ," ibid., p. 21.

56   "What George is pointing . . . ," William Dodge, interview, April 8, 1994.

56   "In *The Alchemy of Finance* . . . ," George Soros, *The Alchemy of Finance*, paperback version, pp. 6–9.

Chapter Seven

59   "We pretend [at being] . . . ," *The Wall Street Journal*, July 7, 1987.

59   "No. It's not his . . . ," Robert Miller, interview, April 11, 1994.

60   "He liked to say . . . ," *New York Times Magazine*, "World-Class Performers," May 3, 1987.

60   "I sat in his office . . . ," Daniel Doron, interview, March 28, 1994.

61   The Watergate incident is cited in *New York Times Magazine*, "George Soros," April 3, 1994, pp. 26–29.

61   "You can count them . . . ," Allan Raphael, interview, June 28, 1994.

62   "Basically, the way I . . . ," *The Wall Street Journal*, July 7, 1987.

62   "George's genius is that . . . ," Byron Wien, interview, June 29, 1994.

62   "His greatest key . . . ," Edgar Astaire, interview, March 11, 1994.

63 "You see, I have one. . . . ,"
"Mr. Soros's Planet."

64 "Soros does have an understanding . . . ," George Magnus,
interview, March 16, 1994.

64 "He wasn't a person . . . ," James
Marquez, interview, April 11, 1994.

65 ". . . to be successful," "The World's
Greatest Money Manager."

65 "He feels that he should . . . ," Byron
Wien, interview, June 19, 1994.

66 "If you liked something . . . ," Allan
Raphael, interview, April 11, 1994.

66 "When I was an adolescent . . . ,"
George Soros, *The Alchemy of
Finance*, paperback version, p. 12–13.

66 "Using leverage can produce . . . ,"
ibid., p. 15.

67 "George always used . . . ," *Futures,*
"The Futures Interview: James
Marquez: Runs Counter to the Market,"
February 1994, pp. 30–32.

68 "People are basically . . . ," "The Man
Who Moves Markets."

Chapter Eight

71 "George was one of the early . . . ,"
Arthur Lerner, interview, April 11,
1994.

73 "I was putting my money . . . ,"
George Soros, *The Alchemy of
Finance*, p. 13.

73 "Since Act III was at least . . . ," "The
World's Greatest Money Manager."

75 "Usually if we disagreed . . . ," Jack D.
Schwager, *Market Wizards: Interviews
with Top Traders* (New York: Harper
Business, 1990), pp. 283–320.

76 "We aren't as much interested . . . ,"
John Train, *The New Money Masters,*
p. 10.

Chapter Nine

81 "He worked hard . . . ," Allan Raphael,
interview, April 11, 1994.

82 "George has never . . . ," Byron Wien,
interview, June 29, 1994.

82 "Money management is about . . . ,"
The Wall Street Journal, May 28, 1975.

83 "Look at the bank trusts . . . ," *The
Wall Street Journal,* May 28, 1975.

83 ". . . had a knack for . . . ," Robert
Miller, interview, April 11, 1994.

84 ". . . malicious pleasure . . . ," George
Soros, *The Alchemy of Finance,*
paperback version, p. 15.

84 "In the case of Avon . . . ," *The Wall
Street Journal,* September 2, 1982.

84 "It was just a case . . . ," *The Wall
Street Journal,* September 27, 1982.

85 "Remember you had Jimmy . . . ," "The
World's Greatest Money Manager."

86 Soros's response to the SEC charges is
found in "The World's Greatest Money
Manager."

85–86 Details about the stock manipu-
lation case appear in *The Wall Street
Journal,* May 22, 1979, and *New York
Times Sunday Magazine,* "George
Soros," pp. 26–29.

87 "These people didn't need . . . ," *The
Wall Street Journal,* September 27,
1982.

Chapter Ten

89 "Totally wrapped up . . . ," *Sunday
Times,* March 14, 1993.

90 "He made life extremely difficult . . . ,"
"The World's Greatest Money
Manager."

90 The author held a brief phone
conversation with Jimmy Rogers, April
13, 1994.

90 ". . . in fact, somewhat burned . . . ,"
"The World's Greatest Money
Manager."

90 "Eventually, in 1980 . . . ," George
Soros, *Underwriting Democracy,*
p. 140.

91 "If you are getting . . . ," The *Wall
Street Journal,* September 27, 1982.

92 "In a dozen years . . . ," "The World's
Greatest Money Manager."

93 "adding to the mystery . . . ," ibid.

94 ". . . flighty European . . . ," John
Train, *New Money Masters,* p. 57.

Chapter Eleven

95 ". . . a benign circle at the center . . . ,"
George Soros, *The Alchemy of
Finance*, paperback version, p. 19.

95 ". . . you had a self-reinforcing . . . ,"
Adam Smith television program.

96   "George is a good . . . ," James
     Marquez, interview, April 11, 1994.

100 Details of the wedding incident appear
     in the *Sunday Times,* "Master of the
     Universe," March 14, 1993; and *The
     New Yorker,* by Conny Bruck, "The
     World According to Soros," January 23,
     1995, pp. 54–78.

100 "All this pressure was . . . ," James
     Marquez, interview, April 11, 1994.

101 "I was his first . . . ," Allan Raphael,
     ibid.

Chapter Twelve

105 "What we thought in . . . ," Allan
     Raphael, interview, April 11, 1994.

106 "Back in the 60s . . . ," Anthony
     Sampson, *The Midas Touch,* (London:
     Hodder and Stoughton Ltd., 1989);
     (paperback edition, London: Coronet,
     1990), pp. 97–98.

108 "The positions obviously to take . . . ,"
     Allan Raphael, interview, April 11,
     1994.

109 "the killing of a lifetime . . . ," George
     Soros, *The Alchemy of Finance,*
     paperback version, p. 158.

109 "Supposedly, George came bolting . . . ,"
     Jack D. Schwager, *New Market
     Wizards* (New York: HarperBusiness,
     1992) (paperback edition: New York:
     HarperBusiness, 1994), p. 208.

110 "The reason I am nevertheless . . . ,"
     George Soros, *The Alchemy of
     Finance,* paperback version, p. 165.

110 "I have about as firm . . . ," ibid.,
     p. 173.

111 Figures quoted in *New York Magazine,*
     "The Iceman Cometh," February 3,
     1986, pp. 12–14.

111 "I'm not particularly . . . ," ibid.

112 Figures cited in *Financial World,* "The
     Financial World One Hundred: The
     Highest Paid People on Wall Street,
     July 22, 1986, p. 14.

Chapter Thirteen

113 "If he made another . . . ," Byron
     Wien, interview, June 29, 1994.

113 "The rich no longer . . . ," Anthony
     Sampson, *The Midas Touch,*
     pp. 52–55.

114 "I would really like . . . ," *New York
     Times,* October 15, 1990.

114 "I don't spend much . . . ," *New York
     Magazine,* February 3, 1986.

114 "For many years I refused . . . ," "The
     World's Greatest Money Manager."

115 "My ego was really . . . ," George Soros,
     Underwriting Democracy, p. 140.

115 ". . . I have to accept . . . ," *Leadership,*
     "South Africa Finds a Friend in The
     World's Greatest Speculator," July
     1993, pp. 14–19.

115 "He likes the theater . . . ," Edgar
     Astaire, interview, March 11, 1994.

115 "I used to collect . . . ," *Financial
     Times,* January 2, 1993.

116 "How can I reach . . . ," Tibor Vamos,
     interview, March 4, 1994.

116 "If you have a plane . . . ," Byron
     Wien, interview, June 29, 1994.

116 "He likes to live . . . ," ibid.

117 "good in crowds . . . ," ibid.

117 "The only thing that could . . . ,"
     George Soros, *The Alchemy of
     Finance,* paperback version, p. 363.

118 "It's basically a . . . ," "The Iceman
     Cometh."

118 ". . . just as genetic . . . ," George
     Soros, *The Alchemy of Finance,*
     paperback version, p. 16.

118 "I think that I really . . . ," "George
     Soros."

118 "I had a very low . . . ," George Soros,
     The Alchemy of Finance, paperback
     version, p. 15.

118 "He was imbued with . . . ,"
     James Marquez, interview, June 27,
     1994.

Chapter Fourteen

119 "Goes against the grain . . . ," "South
     Africa Finds a Friend in The World's
     Greatest Speculator."

121 "If you expose . . . ," *Financial Times,*
     January 2, 1993.

121 "George Soros is seen . . . ," Jeffrey
     Sachs, interview, May 6, 1994.

122 "It was a cheap . . . ," Neil MacKinnon,
     interview, March 17, 1994.

122 "South Africa was a vale . . . ," "South
     Africa Finds a Friend in The World's
     Greatest Speculator."

122 "It was heroic . . . ," *The Independent,*
June 25, 1993.
125 "These people are actually . . . ," "The
Man Who Broke the Pound."
125 "The notion of debate . . . ," Laszlo
Kados, interview, March 3, 1994.
125 "Instead of going . . . ," "Capitalist
Who Cracked the Iron Curtain."
126 "There is a Confucian . . . ," "South
Africa Finds a Friend in The World's
Greatest Speculator."
129 "When I first met . . . ," Alin
Teodoresco, interview, March 1, 1994.
130 "I'm completely infused . . . ," Anca
Haracim, interview, March 1, 1994.
131 "This was a way . . . ," Anca Haracim,
ibid.
131 ". . . quintessential closed . . . ," *Day
One.*
132 "We were actually . . . ," Alex
Goldfarb, interview, April 18, 1994.
132 "As the economies of . . . ," Herta
Seidman, interview, April 21, 1994.
133 "It's not at all . . . ," Alin Teodoresco,
interview, March 1, 1994.
135 "When I wonder aloud . . . ," "Mr.
Soros's Planet."
135 "Let's fly to London . . . ," ibid.
135 ". . . little stock-exchange brain . . . ,"
Tibor Vamos, interview, March 4,
1994.
136 ". . . the last instance . . . ," Adam
Smith television program.
136 "George Soros . . . operates in a . . . ,"
interview, Jeffrey Sachs, May 6,
1994.
136 "I feel that I have . . . ," Adam Smith
television program.

Chapter Fifteen

137 ". . . like mushrooms, fortunes . . . ,"
James Grant, interview, April 7,
1994.
138 "For all his personal . . . ," "The
World's Greatest Money Manager."
139 "To George . . . ," James Marquez,
interview, April 11, 1994.
139 "We were known as . . . ," Allan
Raphael, interview, April 11, 1994.
140 "There is a point . . . ," George Soros,
The Alchemy of Finance, paperback
version, p. 363.

141 "They are not understood . . . ,"
"South Africa Finds a Friend in The
World's Greatest Speculator."
141 "He gave me a number . . . ," James
Marquez, interview, June 27, 1994.
141 "I tried to read . . . ," James Grant,
interview, April 7, 1994.
141 "The book is meant for . . . ," Allan
Raphael, interview, April 11, 1994.
142 "It was such a . . . ," Byron Wien,
interview, June 29, 1994.
142 ". . . experiences in the financial
market . . . ," George Soros, *The
Alchemy of Finance,* paperback
version, pp. 22–23.
144 " . . . an impenetrably dense . . . ,"
Esquire, "The Master Money Manager,"
December 1987, pp. 67–68.

Chapter Sixteen

145 "That stocks have moved . . . ,"
Fortune, "Are Stocks Too High?",
September 18, 1987, pp. 28–40.
147 "Considering the scale . . . ," Anatole
Kaletsky, interview, August 9, 1994.
147 "The other pit traders . . . ," *Barron's,*
"A Wall Street Star Loses $840 Million,"
November 2, 1987.
148 "I made a very . . . ," Adam Smith
television program.
148 "This could be the second . . . ," *New
York Times,* October 28, 1987.
148 "Soros had lost . . . ," "A Wall Street
Star Loses $840 Million."
148 "It's very unfortunate . . . ," Allan
Raphael, interview, April 11, 1994.
149 "A week after the crash . . . ,"
according to Lipper Analytical Services
Inc., which follows mutual-fund
performance; quoted in *The Wall
Street Journal,* October 27, 1987.
149 "It was also reported . . . ," figures are
cited in *The Wall Street Journal,*
October 27, 1987.
149 "He was perfectly . . . ," *Washington
Post,* January 9, 1994.
150 "A lot of people . . . ," "The Master
Money Manager."
150 "Reflexive connections do not . . . ,"
The Wall Street Journal, January 14,
1988.
151 Survey mentioned in *The Wall Street
Journal,* June 6, 1988.

Chapter Seventeen

154 "He seemed to be . . . ," Jack D.
Schwager, *New Market Wizards,*
p. 202.

154 "my successor," ibid., p. 202.

155 "You just can't have . . . ," ibid., p. 202.

155 "At the beginning, he found . . . ,"
George Soros, *The Alchemy of
Finance,* paperback edition, p. 4.

156 "With George off . . . ," Jack D.
Schwager, *The New Market Wizards,*
p. 203.

156 "In the summer of . . . ," George Soros,
The Alchemy of Finance, paperback
version, p. 4.

157 "Profitably, because you can . . . ,"
James Grant, interview, April 7, 1994.

158 "We had a lucky . . . ," *The Wall Street
Journal,* December 2, 1991.

158 "top American income earner," quoted
in *Financial World,* July 21, 1992.

158 ". . . through preservation of capital . .
. ," Jack D. Schwager, *New Market
Wizards,* p. 207.

159 ". . . that it's not whether . . . ," ibid.,
p. 207.

159 "How big a position . . . ," ibid.,
pp. 207–8.

160 These details of the butler and cook
incident are from the *Sunday
Telegraph,* October 2, 1992.

160 "Tempers soon flared . . . ," *New York
Post,* June 6, 1991.

161 "It didn't have the ring . . . ," Anatole
Kaletsky, interview, August 9, 1994.

Chapter Eighteen

165 "George's genius is in . . . ,"
The Observer, January 16, 1994.

169 "It was almost as . . . ," *Daily Mail,*
October 24, 1992.

170 "It didn't carry much . . . ," "The Man
Who Broke the Pound."

171 "I personally did not . . . ," *Forbes,*
"How the Market Overwhelmed the
Central Banks," November 9, 1992,
pp. 40–42.

171 "The real decision was not . . . ," *The
Observer,* January 16, 1994.

171 "I told him to go . . . ," "Mr. Soros's
Planet."

Chapter Nineteen

175 "It was an obvious . . . ," *The Observer,*
January 16, 1994.

178 ". . . like water running . . . ,"
Financial Times, "Sterling Was Being
Sold Like Water Running out of a Tap,"
September 19, 1992.

Chapter Twenty

179 ". . . hapless . . . ," *Economist,*
"Mayhem," September 19, 1992,
pp. 15–16.

181 "What's going on? . . . ," Anatole
Kaletsky, interview, August 9, 1994.

182 "George Soros is an intensely . . . ,"
Times of London, October 26, 1993.

184 ". . . in a freely fluctuating . . . ,"
George Soros, *Opening the Soviet
System,* p. 60.

184 "There was none of the . . . ," Anatole
Kaletsky, interview, August 9, 1994.

184 "Some of what appeared . . . ," George
Magnus, interview, March 16, 1994.

185 "I am happy to have . . . ," "South
Africa Finds a Friend in The World's
Greatest Speculator."

185 "What I did yesterday . . . ," *Daily
Telegraph,* September 18, 1992.

185 "The net effect is . . . ," Adam Smith
television program, October 15, 1992.

186 "Anglo-Saxon speculators . . . ," *New
York Times,* August 8, 1993.

186 "I'm sure there have been . . . ," *The
Guardian,* December 19, 1992.

187 ". . . though nothing like the
money . . . ," "The Man Who Broke
the Pound."

Chapter Twenty-one

191 ". . . gunslingers of the investment . . . ,"
"The Man Who Moves Markets."

192 "I look on Soros as . . . ," James Grant,
interview, April 7, 1994.

196 "I don't hesitate to speculate . . . ,"
"The Master Money Manager."

Chapter Twenty-two

197 "If the Dow is down . . . ," William
Dodge, interview, April 8, 1994.

199 "They [the Reichmanns] were the most . . . ," *New York Times,* February 9, 1993.

201 "I'm amused by my . . . ," "The Man Who Moves Markets."

201 "It is my business . . . ," *New York Times,* August 2, 1993.

201 "Institutional investors who control . . . ," *Newsweek,* "Rothschild and Carnegie," June 21, 1993, pp. 36–38.

201 "While it is true," *Hedge Mar* newsletter, Arthea B. Nolan, "Myths and Realities about Hedge Funds, March–April 1994, pp.1–2.

202 "These kinds of connections . . . ," *The Observer,* January 16, 1994.

202 "George has friends who . . . ," *The Observer,* January 16, 1994.

202 "Last month it was . . . ," *The Guardian,* June 3, 1993.

203 "It's a new way . . . ," *New York Times,* June 10, 1993.

204 ". . . I want to clarify my . . . ," *Times* of London, "Down with the Mark: Soros Now Targets the Bundesbank" (an open letter from George Soros), June 9, 1993.

204 "The Bundesbank's current . . . ," *Daily Telegraph,* June 24, 1993.

Chapter Twenty-three

206 ". . . he was very dour . . . ," Edgar Astaire, interview, March 11, 1994.

206 "I do not manipulate the . . . ," "South Africa Finds a Friend in The World's Greatest Speculator."

207 "I am a work in progress . . . ," "South Africa Finds a Friend in The World's Greatest Speculator."

210 "I am a great believer . . . ," *New York Times,* August 2, 1993.

211 ". . . ethnically cleansed . . . ," opinion program produced by Open Media for Channel 4 in London.

212 "I generally don't want . . . ," "The Man Who Moves Markets."

213 "We don't like publicity . . . ," ibid.

214 "We're not going to . . . ," *New York Times,* September 23, 1993.

Chapter Twenty-four

217 "I went to England . . . ," George Soros, *Underwriting Democracy,* p. 3.

217 "George has never thought . . . ," Byron Wien, interview, June 29, 1994.

218 "In early October . . ."; the source for the Landa-Soros meeting was Benny Landa, interview, August 12, 1994.

218 "It was a pleasant . . . ," Benny Landa, interview, August 12, 1994.

221 "He became interested . . . ," Daniel Doron, interview, March 28, 1994.

221 "It has a particular . . . ," "South Africa Finds a Friend in The World's Greatest Speculator."

224 "He spoke of what a thrill . . . ," Benny Landa, interview, August 12, 1994.

224 "It was a shocking evening . . . ," ibid.

Chapter Twenty-five

228 "The yen dropped by . . . ," *The Wall Street Journal,* March 3, 1994.

Chapter Twenty-six

231 "I still consider . . . ," *The Independent,* March 6, 1994.

232 "If you said . . . ," William Dodge, interview, April 8, 1994.

237 ". . . that doesn't behoove . . . ," *The Wall Street Journal,* April 19, 1994.

239 ". . . said that he thought . . . ," Byron Wien, interview, June 29, 1994.

Chapter Twenty-seven

241 "The trouble is . . . ," Anatole Kaletsky, interview, August 9, 1994.

241 ". . . There's a lesson . . . ," *USA Today,* June 20, 1994.

242 "Not at all . . . ," *Financial Times,* January 2, 1993.

242 "I used to have . . . ," *The Wall Street Journal,* June 1, 1994.

243 ". . . if Soros were a corporation . . . ," *Financial World,* July 5, 1994.

243 "We are used to . . . ," *The Guardian,* June 19, 1994.

246 "If you allow the currency . . . ,"
Charlie Rose-PBS Show, WNET,
quoted by Reuters, August 23, 1994.

246 "I would say there is . . . ," Soros
interview with Reuters, October 4,
1994.

246 "That this is a time . . . ," *Business
Week,* "For Once, We're All in
Sync . . . ," October 3, 1994.

247 "Normally, we don't . . . ," *The Wall
Street Journal,* November 10, 1994.

248 "For example, *Financial World . . .*";
the material cited here is from
Financial World, "Porous Soros:
The Alchemist Loses His Touch,"
November 8, 1994.

250 "Say you're the senior . . . ," *Los
Angeles Times,* March 7, 1994.

250 "He has a problem . . . ," Byron Wien,
interview, June 29, 1994.

250 "We don't even recognize . . . ," *Daily
Telegraph,* July 11, 1994.

251 "But when I inveighed . . . ," George
Soros, *The Alchemy of Finance,*
paperback version, p. 5.

251 "Power is intoxicating . . . ," *Sunday
Times,* "Master of the Universe," March
16, 1993.

251 "I wish people would . . . ," ibid.

251 "George would probably . . . ," Byron
Wien, interview, November 10, 1994.

Index

Other books of interest to you from McGraw Hill . . .

BOGLE ON MUTUAL FUNDS
New Perspectives for the Intelligent Investor
John C. Bogle

Explains the basic principles of mutual fund investing and reveals the unique nuances and subtleties of this alluring field. Gain the expert knowledge needed to customize a fund portfolio to match needs, while avoiding excessive fees, high taxes, and other investing risks.
1-55623-860-6   320 pages

STOCKS FOR THE LONG RUN
A Guide to Selecting Markets for Long-Term Growth
Jeremy J. Siegel

Offers solid strategies for long-term investment success, showing investors how to understand and interpret the movement of the market over time. Includes a detailed description of market performance since 1802 and an examination of the economic, political, and fiscal changes that affect the stock market.
1-55623-804-5   250 pages

THE MUTUAL FUND MASTERS
A Revealing Look into the Minds & Strategies
of Wall Street's Best & Brightest
Bill Griffeth

In a series of revealing interviews, Bill Griffeth elicits the philosophies, strategies, and formative experiences of 20 of today's most successful and most popular fund managers.
1-55738-582-3   368 pages

Available at fine bookstores and libraries everywhere.